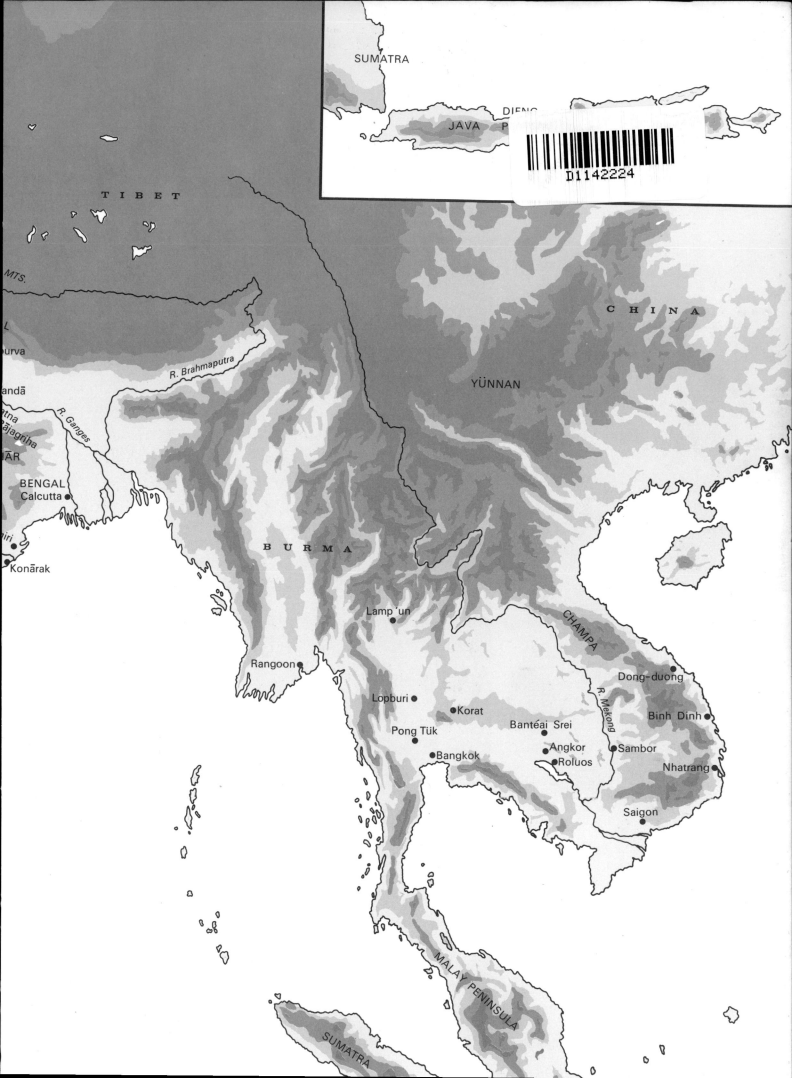

TIBET

R. Brahmaputra

R. Ganges

MTS.

ourva

andā

tna
ājagriha

ĀR

BENGAL
Calcutta

iri

Konārak

BURMA

CHINA

YÜNNAN

Lamp'un

CHAMPA

Rangoon

Lopburi

Korat

Bantéai Srei

R. Mekong

Dong-duong

Binh Dinh

Pong Tük

Angkor

Sambor

Bangkok

Roluos

Nhatrang

Saigon

MALAY PENINSULA

SUMATRA

SUMATRA

JAVA

DIENG

P

The Oriental World

THE ORIENTAL WORLD

India and South-East Asia

JEANNINE AUBOYER

Chief Curator, Musée Guimet, Paris

China, Korea and Japan

ROGER GOEPPER

Director of the Museum of Far Eastern
Antiquities, Cologne

PAUL HAMLYN · LONDON

General Editors

TREWIN COPPLESTONE   BERNARD S. MYERS
London   *New York*

PREHISTORIC AND PRIMITIVE MAN
Dr Andreas Lommel, Director of the Museum of Ethnology, Munich

THE ANCIENT WORLD
Professor Giovanni Garbini, Institute of Near Eastern Studies, University of Rome

THE CLASSICAL WORLD
Dr Donald Strong, Assistant Keeper, Department of Greek and Roman Antiquities, British Museum, London

THE EARLY CHRISTIAN AND BYZANTINE WORLD
Professor Jean Lassus, Sorbonne, Paris, Institute of Art and Archaeology

THE WORLD OF ISLAM
Dr Ernst J. Grube, Curator, Islamic Department, Metropolitan Museum of Art, New York

THE ORIENTAL WORLD
Jeannine Auboyer, Chief Curator, Musée Guimet, Paris
Dr Roger Goepper, Director of the Museum of Far Eastern Art, Cologne

THE MEDIEVAL WORLD
Peter Kidson, Conway Librarian, Courtauld Institute of Art, London

MAN AND THE RENAISSANCE
Andrew Martindale, Senior Lecturer in the School of Fine Arts, University of East Anglia

THE AGE OF BAROQUE
Michael Kitson, Senior Lecturer in the History of Art, Courtauld Institute of Art, London

THE MODERN WORLD
Norbert Lynton, Head of the School of Art History and General Studies, Chelsea School of Art, London

PUBLISHED BY
PAUL HAMLYN LIMITED · DRURY HOUSE
RUSSELL STREET · LONDON · W.C.2
FIRST EDITION 1967
SECOND IMPRESSION 1967

PRINTED IN THE NETHERLANDS BY JOH. ENSCHEDÉ EN ZONEN
GRAFISCHE INRICHTING N.V.   HAARLEM

List of Contents

Colour Plates

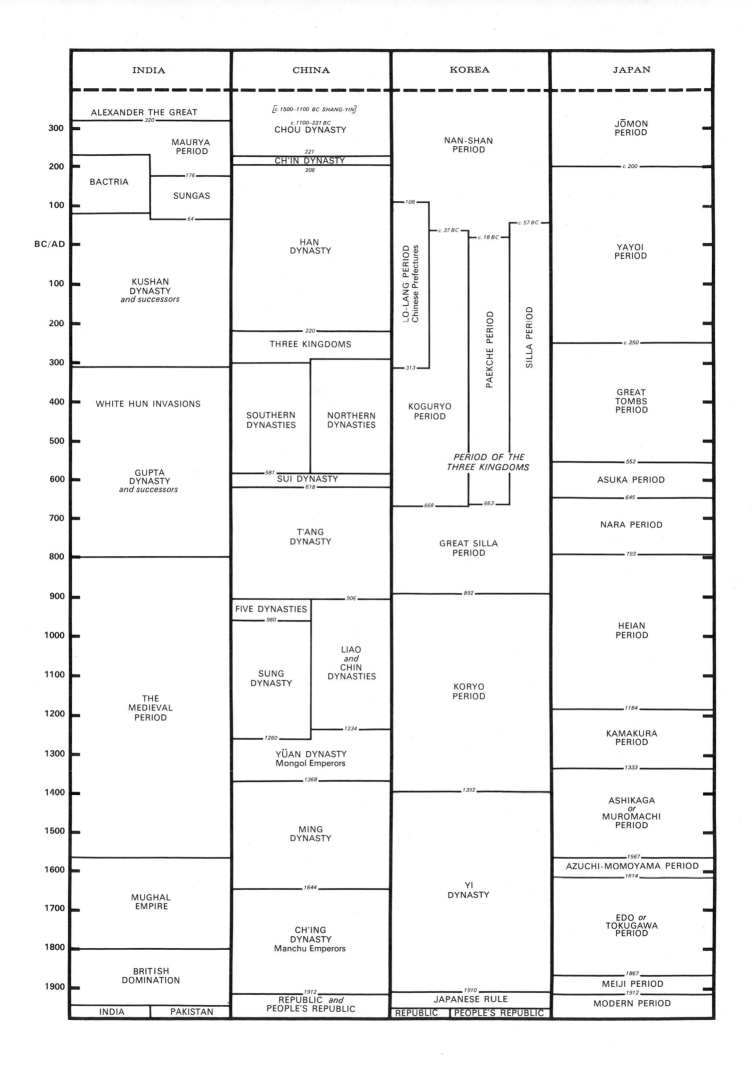

INDIA | CHINA | KOREA | JAPAN

INDIA
- ALEXANDER THE GREAT — 320
- MAURYA PERIOD
- BACTRIA
- 176 — SUNGAS
- 64
- KUSHAN DYNASTY and successors
- WHITE HUN INVASIONS
- GUPTA DYNASTY and successors
- THE MEDIEVAL PERIOD
- MUGHAL EMPIRE
- BRITISH DOMINATION
- INDIA | PAKISTAN

CHINA
- [c. 1500–1100 BC SHANG-YIN]
- c. 1100–221 BC CHOU DYNASTY
- 221 CH'IN DYNASTY
- 206
- HAN DYNASTY
- 220
- THREE KINGDOMS
- SOUTHERN DYNASTIES | NORTHERN DYNASTIES
- 581 SUI DYNASTY
- 618
- T'ANG DYNASTY
- 906
- FIVE DYNASTIES
- 960
- SUNG DYNASTY | LIAO and CHIN DYNASTIES
- 1234
- 1260
- YÜAN DYNASTY Mongol Emperors
- 1368
- MING DYNASTY
- 1644
- CH'ING DYNASTY Manchu Emperors
- 1912 REPUBLIC and PEOPLE'S REPUBLIC

KOREA
- NAN-SHAN PERIOD
- 108
- c. 37 BC
- c. 18 BC
- c. 57 BC
- LO-LANG PERIOD Chinese Prefectures
- PAEKCHE PERIOD
- SILLA PERIOD
- 313
- KOGURYO PERIOD
- PERIOD OF THE THREE KINGDOMS
- 668 | 663
- GREAT SILLA PERIOD
- 892
- KORYO PERIOD
- 1392
- YI DYNASTY
- 1910 JAPANESE RULE
- REPUBLIC | PEOPLE'S REPUBLIC

JAPAN
- JŌMON PERIOD
- c. 200
- YAYOI PERIOD
- c. 250
- GREAT TOMBS PERIOD
- 552
- ASUKA PERIOD
- 645
- NARA PERIOD
- 793
- HEIAN PERIOD
- 1184
- KAMAKURA PERIOD
- 1333
- ASHIKAGA or MUROMACHI PERIOD
- 1567
- AZUCHI-MOMOYAMA PERIOD
- 1614
- EDO or TOKUGAWA PERIOD
- 1867
- MEIJI PERIOD
- 1912
- MODERN PERIOD

Time scale (left axis): 300, 200, 100, BC/AD, 100, 200, 300, 400, 500, 600, 700, 800, 900, 1000, 1100, 1200, 1300, 1400, 1500, 1600, 1700, 1800, 1900

Introduction

By its size alone—it stretches from the 37th to the 8th parallel—India is a land of contrasts and varied climates, from the eternal snows of the Himalayas to torrid jungles, from burning heat in summer to extreme humidity in the rainy season. The mountainous region in the north includes the highest peaks in the world and feeds the great rivers, the Indus and the Ganges and their tributaries, whose irregularity brings about sudden and catastrophic floods. The vast Indo-Ganges plain, with its particularly fertile alluvial soil, was the cradle of the essentially rural Indian civilisation—and throughout history it provoked the envy of invaders. For although at first sight India may seem difficult of access, her coast often inhospitable, invaders could enter the country through the north-west frontier, where, in spite of the altitude, there were mountain passes. These invasions were sporadic and always spread out to the north-east and centre of the country, thus driving the original inhabitants to the south.

THE EARLY HISTORY OF INDIA

The first invaders, the Aryans, came from the Iranian plateau. They entered India from the north-west, settling at first in the Punjāb. It was they who destroyed, in about 1500 BC, the cities of the Indus valley—cities that provided evidence of a highly developed civilisation of the third and second millennia BC. They seem to have descended the course of the Indus to its estuary—which was then at a higher latitude than it is today—and then settled in the region between the Indus and the Ganges, gradually advancing eastwards along the fertile Ganges valley. This invasion had incalculable consequences for India, since it brought with it the Sanskrit language, the Vedic religion and the principal elements of its historical culture.

In the 6th century new invading forces reaching the north-west of India: the Achaemenians, first under Cyrus (559–29), then under Darius (521–485), conquered Bactria, Gandhāra, Arachosia and the Indus valley, turning all these regions into satrapies. For two centuries they remained provinces of the Persian empire, which explains why motifs that were typical of Achaemenian art passed into the sculptural repertoire of India.

The end of the Persian domination was brought about by yet another invasion, that of the armies of Alexander the Great in 326–5. Although short-lived, this invasion brought a wave of Greek influences into the north-western provinces from the Indo-Greek kingdoms of Sogdiana and Bactria.

TRADE AND BARTER

Invaders were not alone in using the mountain passes; they were also used for trade. From the third millennium BC merchandise had been carried in both directions between the Indus valley and the Near East. Indeed, an Elamite or Sumerian seal has been found in the ruins of Mohenjo-daro, one of the most important sites of the Indus valley civilisation, while seals from the Indus valley have also been dis-covered in Mesopotamia and fragments of teak of Indian origin in Babylonia. This international trade increased considerably towards the beginning of the Christian era and both sea and land routes became more clearly defined. Navigators made use of the monsoon periods, and by about the 1st century BC, there was regular maritime traffic between Egypt and India. Descending the Red Sea, and following the Arabian coast and the Persian Gulf, the ships would put in either at one of the ports of Gujarāt or continue towards Ceylon and the ports of the Coromandel coast. But trade did not stop there; it extended also to Indo-China and the East Indies, famous for their gold and spices. It brought into these regions an increasing number of merchants and immigrants and the influence of India was thus to increase considerably during the 4th and 5th centuries. It spread over a large area that included parts of Burma, Indo-China, the Malay peninsula, and the East Indies, finally reaching Borneo, which was the farthest point reached by the Indian fleets. Afghanistan and Chinese Turkestan formed a kind of turn-table where the land routes from the Near East, western India and central China met. Works of art were highly prized in this trade, as is demonstrated by discoveries at such places as Begrām (Afghanistan), Brahmapuri (Deccan), and Arikamedu (on the Coromandel coast). Artistic influences, legends, beliefs and ideas followed the same routes.

In about 80 BC, the provinces of the north-west passed from the domination of the Greek satrapies to that of the Sakas. The Sakas were probably Scythians from eastern Iran, whence they had been driven by a semi-nomadic people, the Yüeh-chih from Mongolia. In the 1st and 2nd centuries AD the Kushans, a Yüeh-chih dynasty, built up a powerful empire stretching from the Oxus to the Ganges plain embracing both the Hellenised states and the Aryan territories. This empire lasted for about a century, when it began to fragment under the attacks of Sassanian Iran. A new wave of Iranian influences then spread through this area, and, since the Sassanians blocked the routes between the Mediterranean world and eastern Asia, India was now cut off from the West.

In the 5th century, when India was at last unified under the national dynasty of the Gupta, the White Huns from Bactria appeared at her frontiers. Their attacks were repulsed, but did much to weaken the power of the Gupta.

Lastly, in about the year 1000, Muslim forces reached the Indus valley. They spread slowly eastwards, gradually overthrowing the Indian kingdoms they attacked.

RELIGION: THE BASIS OF SOCIETY
VEDISM AND BRAHMANISM

In ancient India, religion was closely bound up with human behaviour and the conduct of public affairs; it was the very basis of the social structure. The earliest known religious beliefs are to be found in the sacred texts known collectively as the Veda. The essential expression of the Vedic religion and its central object was sacrifice; basically, this consisted of a libation of *soma*, a liquor made from vegetable matter. The Vedic gods personified the forces and phenomena of nature: fire, the dawn, the sun and stars, water, the sky, earth, thunder, the winds, etc. Their names are close to those of the Iranian Avesta, which would indicate a common origin. Associated with the Vedic cult were certain elements deriving from local folklore—in particular the worship of trees, stones and water. The popular cult of Rudra-Siva was to have a long history in India. Demons, known as *asura*, were the enemies of both gods and men and could only be controlled by prayers and magic words. The universe was divided into three zones: the earth, the 'middle' space and the sky. We know little of any belief in the punishment for evil acts in an after-life; in any case heaven was the world of pious actions (self-denial, sacrifice, offerings, etc.) and hell was reserved for enemies and sinners.

At some period that cannot accurately be fixed in time Vedism became so obscure that explanatory commentaries were required. These commentaries—the *Brāhmana*, the *Upanishada* and the *Āranyaka*—gave rise to a new form of Vedism, Brahmanism, which is perhaps the most 'Indian' of all religions. Service now replaced sacrifice, and the concept of the individual soul (*atman*), to which Vedism had attached little importance, became central. The indentification of the individual soul with the universal Self (*brahma*) was the basis of the new religion, and the life of the individual acquired a new reality. A code of private behaviour was established and obedience to rules of the moral and ascetic life were offered as a way of escaping the cycle of the transmigration of souls (*samsāra*)—a concept that dominated the whole of Brahmanic thought and action. Although many local cults developed, the quality of universality in the Brahmanic religion was already emerging, for minor deities could be drawn into the company of the great gods. A tendency to unify was evident; certain Vedic gods were reduced to a secondary role, while others, such as Indra, the king of the gods, Vishnu and Siva rose to pre-eminence. Religious mythology became complicated but colourful anecdotes abounded.

Brahmanism was an abstract religion: its teaching was the preserve of initiates. The Brahmins guarded for themselves a monopoly of the sacred and encouraged an atmosphere of mystery about their knowledge. But Brahmanism was not only a religion; it also gave order and hierarchy to the structure of society. It preserved the divine right of the emperor and the rule of life of the different levels of society, where the caste system was an expression of a taste for rules and regulations which, with the respect for tradition, is an essential part of the Indian character.

BUDDHISM AND BRAHMANISM

In the 6th century BC, as a reaction against the inflexible Brahmins, two new religions were born. One of these, the Jain religion, was founded by Vardhamāna, who was known under the names of Mahāvīra, 'the Great Hero', or Jina, 'the Victorious One'. Jainism is based on asceticism and *ahimsā*, the theory and practice of non-violence. The other religion, Buddhism, was destined to have a future of the utmost importance. Crossing the frontiers of India it was to spread throughout the rest of Asia. Its founder, a prince of the Sākya, was born in a small kingdom between the frontiers of Nepal and Magadha. He was known generally as the Buddha, or 'Enlightened One', since he had attained spiritual enlightenment. He preached charity to all creatures, the equality of all beings and the practice of moderation in all things. He rejected the caste system, but retained the fundamental concept of the transmigration of souls. Moreover, he recognised the Brahmanic pantheon, which meant that a lay person who adopted the Buddhist rule was not obliged to renounce his personal beliefs so long as they did not contradict the practices of Buddhism. Buddhism offered the virtuous soul an improvement in the conditions of his successive rebirths until finally, through the practice of charity, it attained to a permanent state of liberation. It was essentially an ethical system, illustrated by edifying stories and imbued with a missionary and evangelical spirit.

Towards the beginning of the Christian era, Brahmanism, like Buddhism, underwent changes. Brahmanism developed an increasingly pronounced theism and a heroic tradition that reflected the military character of the India at that time. This was the period of the great epics, the *Rāmāyana* and the *Mahābhārata*, which contains a very beautiful mystical poem, the *Bhagavad Gītā*, or 'Song of the Blessed'. Buddhist teaching took a more mystical turn, and in the 2nd century there was a split—the Theravada remaining faithful to the ancient rules, and the Mahāyāna, or 'Great Vehicle', which offered the worship of the bodhisattvas, or creatures of charity. A synthesis is then apparent between Buddhism and Brahmanism, of which there were soon innumerable sects. The Brahmanic theory of *bhakti*, or 'trusting worship', makes its appearance; with asceticism (*yoga*) and spiritual knowledge (*jñāna*), it becomes one of the ways to salvation. A slow, but steady evolution leads India from polytheism to a mystical pantheism. Numerous examples can be cited to prove both the diversification of the One with its implicit contradictions and the channelling of the Many towards the One, in which all contradictions are resolved.

ART AS THE REFLECTION OF CIVILISATION

Art is a true expression of Indian civilisation, which, with its essentially conservative outlook, is unique in possessing a continuous cultural evolution from prehistory until our own times. In spite of the absence of chronological landmarks—the Indian has no sense of history—one can construct quite a coherent picture of the development of this art. It evolved not through sudden changes, but slowly, by a process of accumulation, and by the juxtaposition of old and new forms. Perhaps an explanation of this phenomenon can be found in the slow rhythm of rural life and above all in the influence of the Brahmins, whose primacy was a guarantee of conservatism. Among the fluctuations of taste and fashion, a general line of development can be distinguished which, over a period lasting more than two thousand years, dominated the styles of Indian art, leading it eventually, through too rigorous a respect for rules, towards decadence.

Although recent excavations have revealed at certain sites a continuous occupation from the fall of the Indus valley civilisation to the accession of the Maurya dynasty at the end of the 4th century BC, no example has yet been found, either in architecture or in sculpture, that reveals conscious aesthetic intentions. Art, in the true sense of the word, appeared only with the Maurya period (3rd century BC). At first, under the emperor Asoka (264–27 BC), it seems to have been more imperial than religious in character. It then became particularly associated with Buddhism, until the time came when it reflected both the complexity and the solidarity of Indian civilisation.

Indian architecture is essentially religious. It has an important place in the history of that civilisation, for it is part of India's religious, as well as aesthetic expression. Every architectural work is infused with symbolism, bound up with a conception of the universe and with hallowed traditions. The temple is conceived as a microcosm, a model of the universe, which is itself a reflection of the earthly world. In its centre is the sanctuary, the seat of the deity, the sacred mountain, the pivot of the world; around this sanctuary, a simple or more complex enclosing wall represents the mountain ranges that border the earthly world; and around the temple are pools, just as the world is surrounded on all sides by oceans. At four cardinal points there are gates, which symbolise openings in the vault of heaven, that is, the stars, and through which contact is established between god and man. These buildings range from small, rudimentary structures, surrounded by a simple wall to the vast architectural complexes of the 16th century in southeast India, which are more like fortified towns than temples, and in which the sanctuary itself is relatively small.

Among the architectural forms adopted by Buddhism, it was the *stupa* (reliquary), which was based on the Vedic funeral mound, that represented the cosmic mountain, the pivot of the world. The Buddhist architect, who had to build sanctuaries that were intended for communal prayer, was faced with a quite different problem from that of the Hindu. The Hindu tried to convey the idea of the mysterious and the divine; the sanctuary housed the sacred image, and was served by a single priest. The Buddhist sanctuary *(chaitya)*, on the other hand, was spacious, airy and sufficiently light to enable one to admire the painted and carved decoration.

Relief carving plays an important part in the architecture of the ancient period; indeed sculpture in general has an essential place in Indian art. It illustrates various aspects of everyday and religious life, as well as the legends and epics. It expresses in a visible form, and in a style that is only slightly idealised, the beauty of Indian life, its rhythm and its idiosyncracies, and imbues their images with appropriate sanctity. The sacred image was not only an object of adoration but an aid to meditation. It had to conform to the rigid canons which were laid down, but also be pleasing to the eye. This too was a perfect microcosm, in which the features and proportions of the human body were expressed in an idealised form. Once made, a special ceremony was required to give it life, to turn it into an object of devotion. Yet although the sculptor was obliged to conform with the iconographical canons, he was ultimately able to transcend these limitations and produce masterly works of art.

Although secular art must have existed, it is the enormous mass of religious statues and reliefs that give us a true knowledge of Indian aesthetics. Throughout its entire development, Indian sculpture was an expression of the artists' feeling for the beauty of the naked figure and his need to glorify it. It combined restraint in expression with great assurance in the balance of pose and gesture.

Like sculpture, painting too played a great part in the decoration of the sanctuaries—and, like sculpture, it reflected ritual. Most of the texts attribute to painting a very ancient, divine origin. Whether executed on panels, scrolls or walls, it had an important place in the social life of India from the earliest times. Not only did it form part of the education of men and women of the upper classes, but it was also a means of describing events and of teaching through pictures the different episodes in the Buddhist legends and the Brahmanic epics. Owing to the delicacy of the materials employed, only fragments of mural painting from the ancient periods have come down to us, nor have panel paintings earlier than the 11th–10th centuries survived. But despite these gaps in its development, painting is one of the finest manifestations of Indian art.

Prehistory, Protohistory and Early History

The existence of man in India in the palaeolithic period (the Son 'culture') is attested by tools of the Chelleo-Acheulean type, generally made from quarzite. They are similar in form to those that we know in Europe—from the the Acheulean axe of an elongated almond shape, to the pointed implement sharpened only along the edges and left rough at the handle. Some of the pieces are elliptical, others circular.

The neolithic culture is characterised by tools made from carved or polished silex, remarkable for their variety of form and similar in every way to those of western Asia or Europe.

In the northern regions, a new influx of populations introduced an industry based on pure copper. This is represented by a large number of objects: flat celts, spear-heads, daggers, swords, axes, arrow-tips, bracelets. A whole series of 'civilisations' flourished, particularly in Baluchistan. They seem to have provided a link between those of Iran and those of western Asia and India itself, where, in the third and second millennia, there emerged the highly developed Indus valley civilisation.

THE GREAT PROTOHISTORIC CITIES

The Indus valley civilisation is so called because the first two sites to be explored, Harappā in the Punjāb and Mohenjo-daro in Sind, are situated in the valley of the Indus. Later excavations have revealed nearly a hundred sites of the same type. Harappā and Mohenjo-daro are nonetheless typical of this period. Although separated from each other by some three hundred and seventy miles, they are similar in their stratigraphy. They mark the beginning of Indian protohistory, for a great many inscribed seals were discovered there which, unfortunately, have so far remained undeciphered. Their town planning was elaborate and seems to have been the work of experienced architects. The towns' foundations were built with unbaked bricks while baked bricks were employed for the buildings themselves. The streets intersected at right angles and were bordered by houses, most of which had a well and many a bathing pool. The wells and baths were supplied with water channelled from the nearby river; there was also an efficient drainage system.

The remains of quays seem to indicate that these towns practised river trading. They were defended by a fortified citadel and, in addition, comprised public buildings with colonnades, a bathing establishment, large residential buildings, a craftsmen's quarter, flour mills, public ovens, collective granaries and cemeteries. The articles and tools that have been found there are of a wide variety of materials: gold, silver, copper, brass, steatite, semi-precious stones, bone, ivory and shell. The pottery, which was turned on the wheel, is often painted. Some of these articles have definite aesthetic qualities: a male bust, hieratic and stylised, with Semitic features, wearing a garment decorated with trefoil motifs; stone figurines in subtle relief, which remind one of ancient Greek art; brass statuettes that are very Indian in feeling; striking silhouettes of animals. The numerous carvings which have been found also display an advanced technique in the portrayal of animals; they are shown in profile, which already anticipates the naturalism that Indian art was later to develop with such mastery.

That relations existed between this Indus valley civilisation and Mesopotamia is shown by the finds of steatite seals, identical with those of the Indus valley, at various sites in Mesopotamia, while a Sumerian seal has been found at Mohenjo-daro.

THE END OF PROTOHISTORY

In the Deccan, however, the neolithic phase lasted until about the 2nd century BC; it is characterised by a large number of megalithic tombs and by red and black pottery.

Comparison between Indus valley and later sites reveals a distinct deterioration, from the point of view of both town planning and culture generally. Most of the buildings were constructed in perishable materials. But stone was not

1. **Bust of a man from Mohenjo-daro.** 3rd millennium BC. Steatite. h. 6¾ in. (17 cm.). Museum of Central Asiatic Antiquities, New Delhi. This bust of a bearded man belongs to the Indus valley civilisation. It has undoubted aesthetic quality and recalls the art of Mesopotamia. The treatment is stylised, the features Semitic. The detail of his headdress and garment are carefully observed: a headband ornamented with a single circular jewel, and a robe decorated with a raised trefoil motif.

2a, b, c, d. **Seal impressions from Harappā.** Third to second millennia BC. Museum of Central Asiatic Antiquities, New Delhi. Finds from the Indus valley include many steatite seals like these. Most of them show animals in profile. Others suggest the existence of a pre-Sivaite cult, but since the characters cannot yet be deciphered this remains hypothetical.

entirely absent for parts of the enormous wall that defended the town of Rājagriha have been found. There is, however, no sign of any artistic activity. The art of this period is of a popular, domestic kind and consists mainly of terracotta effigies of human figures or animals, probably used in fertility cults.

EARLY HISTORY

The movement of the Aryans towards the east of the Ganges plain in about 800 BC shifted the centre of gravity of the conquered lands to the region between the Ganges and its tributary, the Jumna—a rich area which was to be a cause of dispute throughout the history of India. The establishment of Aryan kingdoms continued steadily. India was soon to look like a mosaic of states of different sizes, some of which tried to dominate others. Magadha (southern Bihār) ruled over the whole of the Ganges valley in the 6th and 5th

centuries BC and was the true political and religious cradle of ancient India. Its kings were converted to Buddhism by the Buddha himself and are known for their role in Buddhist literature.

At this time, north-western India, which had been conquered by Achaemenian Iran and turned into satrapies, was strongly marked by Persian influences, traces of which were to persist in a number of fields: administration, a metric system, writing and, above all, architecture.

THE MAURYA DYNASTY

Towards the end of the 4th century BC, the Nanda dynasty was reigning in Magadha; from them perhaps sprang the Maurya who, in about 320, succeeded in founding the founding the first pan-Indian empire. A young Magadha general, Chandragupta, known to the Greeks as Sandrakottos, revolted against his sovereign just as Alexander the

3. **Cave sanctuary in the Barabār Hills.** 3rd century BC. The caves cut into the hillside of Barabār constitute the most ancient sanctuary that has come down to us. Situated near Bodh Gayā, in Bihār, some of the caves bear inscriptions dating from the Maurya period. The plan, which combines rectangles and circles, is quite unusual.

Great of Macedonia was reaching the banks of the Indus— and, according to Plutarch (*Alex.*, LXII), solicited the help of the Greek conqueror. For various reasons, Alexander, who had had to confront the imposing army of Poros, an Indian sovereign who probably reigned in the Punjāb, was unable to accede to the request. Chandragupta was to play a very considerable role in the destiny of India. In about 313–12, he came to the throne of Magadha, overthrowing the Nanda dynasty and inaugurating that of the Maurya. His empire soon stretched from the Indus to the Ganges. The administration seems to have been efficient; it was supervised by imperial inspectors and facilitated by the good state of the roads. Seleucus, satrap and conqueror of Babylon, founder of the kingdom and dynasty of the Seleucids, sought an alliance with Chandragupta when he arrived in the Punjāb, in the footsteps of Alexander, in about 305. Seleucus left the territories beyond the Indus to Chandragupta and even gave him the hand of a Greek princess in marriage. It was then that India emerged as one of the great world powers. Megasthenes, Seleucus's ambassador at the Maurya court, left in his *Indika* a very interesting description of their capital, Pātaliputra, a large and beautiful city, situated at the confluence of the Ganges and one of its tributaries, the Son. It was over nine miles long and nearly two miles wide, and the public buildings, the palace (inspired, it is said, by that of Darius at Persepolis) and the great city walls, were made of wood. The

abundant forests, which at that time covered a far larger area than today, and the relative scarcity of quarriable stone probably explain this use of wood.

Of the reign of Bindusāra, Chandragupta's son, very little is known, but it appears that he conquered central India and a large part of the Deccan. The Maurya dynasty reached the height of its power with Bindusāra's son, the famous Emperor Asoka (*c.* 264–27 BC), who is known above all for the edicts that he had engraved in public places throughout his territory and which reveal a high moral tone and a strong personality. He seized power in about 264 BC and after his bloody conquest of Kalinga (which stretched from the delta of the Godavari to that of the Mahanadi), he experienced a spiritual crisis and was converted to Buddhism. This conversion was to have incalculable repercussions for India. In his hands, Buddhism became a powerful civilising influence; with his encouragement it spread to Kashmir, to the Hellenised territories and even as far as Ceylon. He constantly made pilgrimages to the Buddhist holy places. Yet his zeal did not prevent him from recommending religious toleration; indeed, he sometimes favoured sects other than his own. On two occasions, he gave several rock sanctuaries situated in the Barabār hills to the non-Buddhist sect of the Ājīvikas. His empire comprised the whole of north and north-west India and extended as far as the country of the Āndhras (the lower valleys of the Godavari and the Kistna). He was on

4 (left). **Capital from Rāmpurva.** Maurya period. Polished sandstone. h. 6 ft. 6 in. (2 m.). Indian Museum, Calcutta. This capital surmounted one of the columns on the shaft of which the Emperor Asoka ordained that moral codes should be inscribed. Such columns which combine imperial and cosmological symbolism recall those of Persepolis with their bell shape and polished surface.

5 (above). **Mother goddess.** Maurya period, *c.* 3rd century BC. Terracotta. h. 9 in. (23 cm.). Archaeological Museum, Mathurā. This statuette is particularly typical of the ancient period of Indian art. It belongs to a long series of examples which cover a considerable period of time. They were probably connected with fertility rites which played an important part in the early rural and agrarian life of India.

diplomatic terms with Syria, Cyrenaica, Egypt, Macedonia, Epirus and Corinth.

THE APPEARANCE OF MONUMENTAL ART

It was in the reign of Asoka that true sculpture sprang into life, using, apparently for the first time, durable materials. The impetus thus given to the production of works of art in India was to last for many centuries; moreover Maurya art contained within itself the essence of the styles that followed. Several quarries, particularly that of Chūnar, near Banāras, were developed. It was these that supplied stone
4 for the commemorative columns, sometimes 42 feet high, that were scattered throughout his empire. The shafts of these columns were crowned with bell-shaped capitals based on those of Persepolis and surmounted by one or several animals joined together: the foreparts of a bull, lions etc. The style of these sculptures is close to that of Hellenistic Iran. It seems evident that the sculptors of this period learned a great deal from Irano-Parthian and Greek artists, while retaining nevertheless a pronounced Indian feeling. Apart from monumental sculpture, small,
5 terracotta figurines have been found.

The artificial caves built as sanctuaries and as living quarters for monks were excavated mainly in the Barabār hills (Bihār). They reproduced in minute detail the rec-

tangular or circular buildings, with wooden walls and thatched roofs that must have existed at that period. The 3 walls and columns of the sanctuaries were carefully polished. This polishing seems to have been peculiar to the Maurya period, and it has been suggested that it was achieved by burnishing the stone surfaces with agate. The cave that bears the modern name of Sudāma is rectangular in plain; its interior measures about 33 feet by 18 feet wide, with a semi-circular recess at the back measuring 18 feet in diameter and 5 feet 6 inches high. The walls are scratched in imitation of real timbers, and surmounted by a hemispherical, thatch-like roof. It is a replica in stone of a double building comprising a rectangular construction (or an enclosure of that shape) and a circular hut, placed at the end of this enclosure, which served as the sanctuary.

Brick and wood were not abandoned for open-air constructions, as is confirmed by the fragments of Asoka's palace at Pātaliputra. These remains testify to a remarkable technical accomplishment—the teak platforms, for example, were thirty feet long and composed of beams that were adjusted with the greatest precision and care. An examination of the exterior walls of the temple at Bairāt, ascribed to the 3rd century BC, shows that the bricks of the period were large, about 19 inches by 12 inches, but only 2 inches thick.

Ancient Schools and Transitional Styles

HISTORY

After the death of Asoka, the Maurya empire gradually broke up; the centre of power moved westwards and was concentrated on Malwa and Magadha under the dynasty of the Sungas (*c.* 176–64 BC), then under that of the Kānvas (*c.* 75–30 BC). For about a hundred years—the duration of their supremacy—events occurred in the north-west that were to have a profound effect on the future of India. Indo-Greek kingdoms were founded in Bactria, Gandhāra and Kapisa. One of the kings of Bactria, Demetrius, undertook the conquest of India in about 189 and reached as far as Pātaliputra. His successor, Menander, celebrated in Buddhist tradition for the 'Questions' he asked the master Nāgasena, retained a kingdom in the Punjāb. It was the Sungas who drove the Indo-Greeks beyond the Indus. In about 80 BC, the Greek kingdom of Bactria fell under the attacks of semi-nomads who had been driven from central Asia by the advance of the Huns from Mongolia. The Greek influence was followed by that of the Scytho-Parthians, nomadic peoples from central Asia much influenced by Iran. Confronted by these invasions, the Sunga kings, who were already being threatened by the growing power of the Āndhras in the Deccan, were unable to maintain the unity of the India of the Ganges and it soon fell back into the political disunity from which the Maurya had saved it.

This period, so complicated in its political environment, was nevertheless one of the most fruitful in the field of sculpture. It saw the establishment of the great styles of Indian art, the creation and gradual development of the Buddhist iconography and the fusion of foreign influences with Indian elements into an artistic whole. Although the works of this period are exclusively Buddhist, they are above all typically Indian. Buddhism gives them their grace and smiling gentleness, but they are also a faithful expression of the life and temperament of the Indian peoples.

ART, ARCHITECTURE AND SCULPTURE

Both categories of Indian architecture are represented in this period: monolithic, rock-cut buildings and free-standing constructions. It seems likely that the basic principles of rock-cut architecture were laid down by Brahmanism (Barabār) and by Jainism (Udayagiri and Khandagiri in Orissā), but it was the fact that it was Buddhist that explains its magnificent development and that provided it with an artistic character quite unknown to the other two religions. The monasteries *(vihāra)* consist basically of cells and one or more fairly small chapels. The sanctuaries, such as that at Bhājā (in the Western Ghats), have a basilical ground-plan, with a central nave and two half side-

6. **Façade of the chaitya at Bhājā.** *c.* 1st century BC. This sanctuary is a faithful reproduction in stone of the wooden structures which are represented on the reliefs of the period.

The façade is broken by a large horseshoe-shaped bay, and the sanctuary is apsidal in plan.

7. **Detail of a balustrade from Bhārhut.** *c.* 2nd century BC. Sandstone. Indian Museum, Calcutta. This detail from one of the upright supports to the balustrade at Bhārhut is carved with a *Yakshinī* or female tree spirit *(salabhañjika)*. Her left arm encircles the trunk of the tree, while in her right hand she holds a branch. With her relaxed pose, she possesses a simple dignity.

naves, usually with very low ceilings. They are bordered with pillars, simple shafts quarried out of the rock, without either bases or capitals. Above a wide frieze and spanning the pillars is the curve of a barrel vault whose original wooden beams have been carefully imitated. Towards the end of the sanctuary is the *stūpa*, which is relatively small in size, and which must be honoured by making the ritual circumambulation around it. These sanctuaries are open to the façade in the form of a broad, horseshoe-shaped bay. The technique used in the hollowing out and carving of these sanctuaries is not described in contemporary texts; only an examination of the works themselves will enable us to reach some conclusions. The work must have begun at the top and proceeded downwards.

The free-standing architecture is represented by the stūpa built out of stone and brick. These sturdy constructions were designed to contain holy relics, to indicate the sacred character of the places on which they were built, or to commemorate an important event. They consisted of a hemispherical calotte, or flattened dome, placed on a low, square base and surmounted by a sort of small railed balcony *(harmika)*. The stūpa itself was enclosed by railings

pierced by from one to four openings, and with monumental gates *(torana)*. The uprights, horizontals, hand-rails, **3** pillars and lintels were assembled on a mortise and tenon principle, like pieces of wood. The most typical stūpa are those of Sāñchī (central India); of those at Bhārhut and **2, 1** Bodh Gayā, which are obviously contemporary, only fragments of the carved railings remain. The narrative reliefs **7, 8** which decorated the hand-rails, uprights and horizontals **9, 10** of the railings (Sāñchī II, Bhārhut and Bodh Gayā), and the lintels over the gateways (Bhārhut, Bodh Gayā, Sāñchī **11, 12,** I and III) were designed to teach the many pilgrims who visited the site the virtues of Buddhism. These vivacious and charming illustrations of Buddhist legend are among the jewels of Indian art. Moreover, they are very instructive for the study of Indian civilisation, for the sculptors depicted their legendary characters in the clothes of their own time. At Bhārhut the perspective is rather naive, but at Sāñchī I and III it is much more subtle. The planes are still vertically imposed but they often overlap, thus creating an impression of greater depth. The Indian artist is already displaying his gifts as a portrayer of animals that are to characterise him throughout the history of his national art. One cannot but admire the naturalism, often coupled with a profound feeling for form, the simple, spontaneous stylisation and the attentive, loving observation of nature. Following an iconographical rule that was still not very explicit, the Buddha himself was never depicted: his presence was represented by symbols.

The statues of this period are hewn from a single block **14** of stone. The earliest of these preserve a frontality that was not without distinction. Here too, every detail of dress and ornament is carefully observed. Apart from large-scale, probably official statuary, small figures of stone or terracotta were made, which were more spontaneous in style.

THE DYNASTY OF THE KUSHANS IN THE NORTH

In the 1st century AD, a new force was being built up in the north-western regions, that of Tokharian nomads, the

(Continued on page 33)

1 (opposite). **Relief from Bhārhut.** *c.* 2nd century BC. Indian Museum, Calcutta, h. 1 ft. 7¼ in. (49 cm.). Of the stūpa at Bhārhut only fragments of the carved balustrade now remain. These are important, however, for one can discern already all the essential traits of Indian art: a strong feeling for narrative, vivacity, directness, a concern to render detail precisely, and a tendency towards stylisation. This medallion depicts incidents from an earlier life of the Buddha *(Ruru Jātaka)* when he lived as a golden stag in the Ganges valley.

2 (opposite, below). **Stūpa I at Sāñchī.** 2nd century BC – 1st century AD. The Buddhist site of Sāñchī is famous for the beauty of its sculpture. There are three main stūpa, of which Stūpa I is the most typical. The decoration of the four gateways or *torana* is regarded as central for the study of ancient Indian art.

3. **North torana of Stūpa I at Sāñchī.** 2nd century BC – 1st century AD. The sculptural technique of this *torana* clearly derives from the art of the woodcarver. It is covered with reliefs and sculpture in the round, and one can see at once how far the sculptor has progressed since the Bhārhut era (see plate 1). The relief is more pronounced, the perspective more elaborate and the composition more orderly.

4. Pediment of the Gandhāra school.
c. 2nd century AD. Schist. 1 ft. 10 in. × 2 ft. 1½ in. (56 × 65 cm.). Musée Guimet, Paris. This pediment is typical of the tympana of the Gandhāra school. While the form and subject-matter are Indian, the style is still Hellenistic. Adoration scenes are depicted in each of the three registers. At the top, the object of worship is the Buddha's begging bowl, and in the lower two registers the Buddha himself receives homage.

5. **The story of Dīpankara.** Narrative
relief of the Gandhāra school. *c.* 2nd
century AD. Schist. 10⅝ × 14½ in.
(27 × 37 cm.). Musée Guimet, Paris.
This is one of many reliefs which
decorated the walls of Buddhist buildings
of the Gandhāra school. They are
devoted to scenes from the life of Buddha,
whether in his ultimate incarnation as the
Buddha Sākyamuni, or from one of his
previous lives. Here the future Buddha is
shown as a student. Megha prostrates
himself before the Buddha Dīpankara,
spreading his hair beneath his feet.

6 (opposite). **Bodhisattva of the
Gandhāra school** from Shabaz-Garhi.
c. 2nd century AD. Schist. h. 3 ft. 11 in.
(120 cm.). Musée Guimet, Paris. The
Buddhism of Mahāyāna, or the 'Great
Vehicle', appeared at the beginning of the
Christian era. In this later theistic form
of Buddhism, the person of the Buddha
was deified, and Bodhisattvas, or
ministering spirits, were created,
characterised by their charity. They also
acted as intermediaries between god and
man. In Indian iconography they are
depicted in princely costume, richly
jewelled.

7 (opposite). **Ivory plaque from Begrām.** *c.* 2nd century AD. h. 13⅜ in. (34 cm.). Musée Guimet, Paris. A series of ivories of the 2nd century have been discovered at Begrām (see also plate 8). Since there is an almost total absence of male figures among the carvings, it is assumed that they were designed for the private apartments of women. Here we see two women shown in the pose of triple flexion. They are dressed in pleated skirts or *dhotī* held at the hips by a belt of several rows of pearls fastened in front with a jewelled clasp. Their other adornments include necklaces, bracelets, anklets, and earrings, and on their heads they wear striped turbans decorated with rows of pearls and with the branches of asoka.

8. **Ivory fragment from a chair.** Begrām. *c.* 2nd century AD. h. 9 in. (23 cm.). Musée Guimet, Paris. This ivory fragment bears a carved representation of a woman riding a leogryph, a fabulous animal, part bird, part lion. It originally formed part of a chair of the type to be seen in the reliefs of Mathurā and Amarāvatī. Such chairs had rectangular backs, the horizontal member being joined to the vertical by means of arc-shaped pieces like this one.

9 (opposite). **Nāgarāja, or serpent-king.** School of Mathurā. *c.* middle of the 2nd century AD. Red sandstone. h. 3ft. 9¾ in. (116 cm.). Musée Guimet, Paris. The Nāgarāja was the king of the nāga or water spirits, protectors of cisterns and sacred waters. He is often represented in the form of a man resting against the coils of a great serpent. The serpent raises its many heads behind him to form a halo about his head and shoulders. He raises his right hand in an appeal for rain, and in his left he holds a drinking cup.

10 (above). **Chakravartin.** Amarāvatī school. *c.* 1st century BC. Veined limestone. h. 3 ft. 8 in. (112 cm.). Musée Guimet, Paris. King Chakravartin is 'he who turns the Wheel' *(Chakra)*, that is, the sovereign of the world who holds in sway the entire universe, for the wheel symbolises the sun which dominates all space. The Seven Jewels of his office are grouped about him: the Wheel, the jewel, the elephant, the horse, the woman, the ministering priest and the general.

11. (right). **The Attack of Māra.** Amarāvatī school. *c.* 2nd century. Veined limestone. h. 4 ft. 1¼ in. (125 cm.). Musée Guimet, Paris. This relief illustrates an episode in the life of the Buddha. After years of abstinence he is about to attain to the state of Enlightenment when the Buddhist devil, Māra, tries to prevent this happening. First he sends groups of devils and monsters to molest him and then tries to tempt Buddha by offering him young girls, but Buddha resists him. In this instance Buddha himself is depicted only by symbols: an empty throne is placed beneath the tree of Enlightenment *(bodhi)*, and the footstool bears the imprint of his feet.

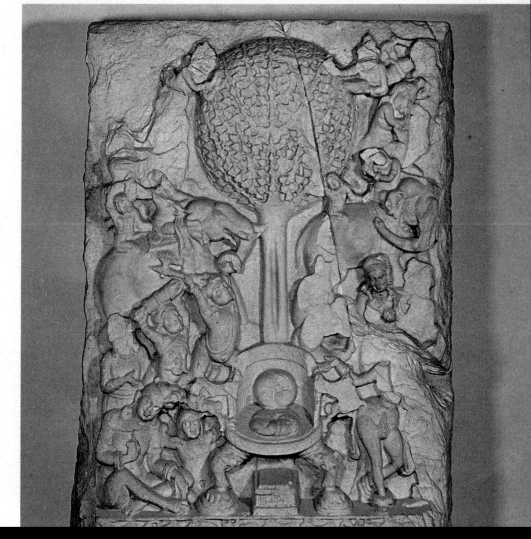

12 (next page). **Head of Buddha.** Amarāvatī school. *c.* 2nd century. Marble. h. 8¼ in. (21 cm.). Musée Guimet, Paris. The Buddhas of the Amarāvatī school display a certain elongation of the facial features which is characteristically Dravidian. Here the cranial protuberance can clearly be seen. Like the rest of the head, it is covered with small flat curls, arranged according to ritual from left to right.

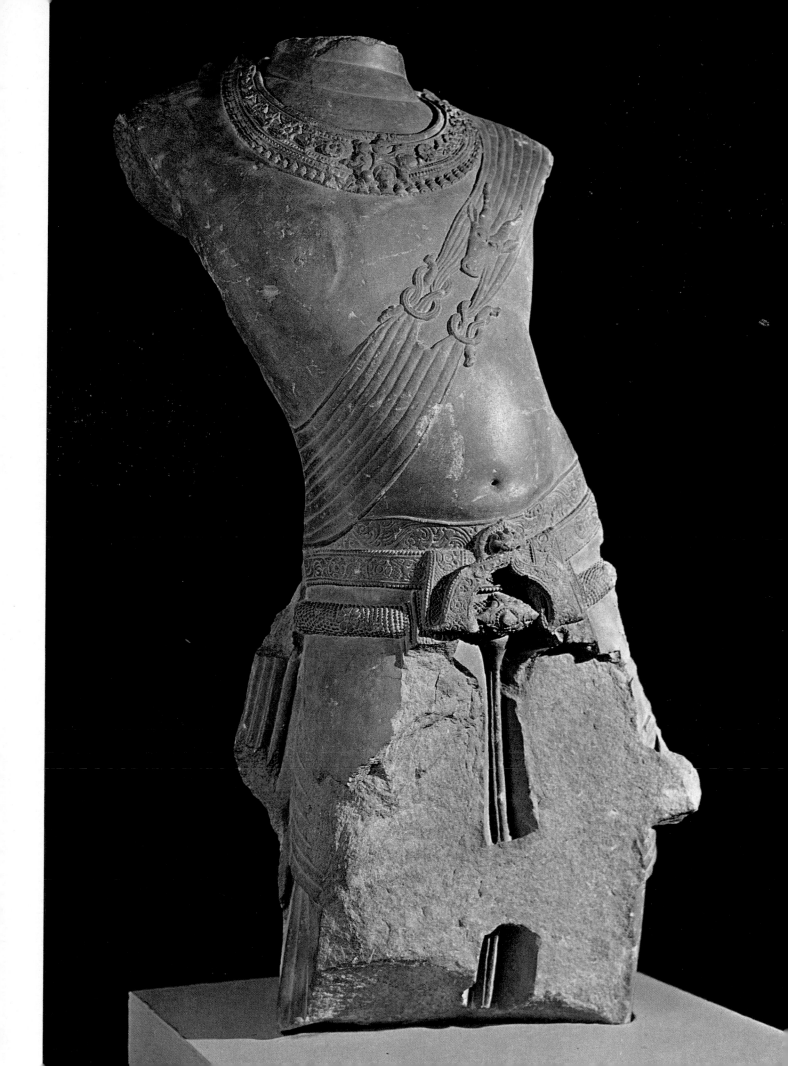

13 (previous page). **Torso of a Bodhisattva.** Gupta style. 5th century. Red sandstone. h. 2 ft. 10¼ in. (87 cm.). Victoria and Albert Museum, London. The sacred images of the Gupta reflect this style at its purest. Here all the stylistic features are blended together in a perfect whole. The curve of the figure is as subtle as the softness of the modelling, and in its balance it demonstrates the consummate skill of the Gupta sculptors.

14 (right). **Head of the Bodhisattva Avalokitesvara.** Gupta style. *c.* 5th century. Red sandstone. h. 5⅞ in. (15 cm.). Musée Guimet, Paris. The cult of Avalokitesvara, the merciful Bodhisattva, was one of the most popular, spreading not only throughout India, but also to the other countries which adopted the Buddhism of the 'Great Vehicle'. He is shown here wearing a magnificent diadem. On top of this a small Buddha is seated in the Indian fashion, flanked by two lions, with garlands of pearls streaming from their mouths.

15 (opposite). **Great Bodhisattva.** Fresco in Cave I at Ajantā. 6th century. This is one of the two great Bodhisattvas which frame the entrance to the sanctuary of Cave I. With his gentle expression and calmness of attitude the Bodhisattva shows his compassion towards man. The technique used at Ajantā was a kind of tempera which amounted almost to *fresco secco*, that is to say, the pigment was applied to dried plaster. The painting was done in four stages. First the surface was prepared, then the outlines of the design were sketched on to the plaster. The paint was then applied to bring colour and modelling to the basic shapes. Finally touches of gold were added, the contours were sharpened, the decorative details emphasised and the whole surface was burnished.

16. **The Mriga Jatāka.** Detail of fresco in Cave XVII at Ajantā. 5th–6th centuries. The composition of the Ajantā frescoes seems at first sight overcrowded and complicated. But when one grows accustomed to looking at them, the different groups of figures become distinct from one another, a pattern emerges, a harmony is revealed. Each detail is fascinating in itself, as for example this servant who is holding a dog on a leash. He is part of the suite of King of the *Mriga* in pursuit of the sacred deer (see also plate 1).

17. **The Sutasoma Jātaka.** Detail of fresco in Cave XVII at Ajantā. 5th–6th centuries. This detail forms part of a hunting scene illustrating a previous life of the Buddha *(jātaka)*. The bounding deer are full of vigour and movement, reflecting the Indian artist's delight in animal life, a characteristic which was already evident as early as the Indus valley civilisation of the third millennium BC (see figure 2).

8. **Detail of a handrail, Bhārhut.** *c.* 2nd century BC. Sandstone. h. 17 in. (42 cm.). Indian Museum, Calcutta. This detail from the balustrade of the stūpa at Bhārhut illustrates part of a narrative which is identified by the short inscription in the frieze immediately above. Each episode is enclosed within a garland of curving branches decorated here and there with flowers, fruit or even jewels. The upper frieze combines little merlons, or fortifications with lotus blossoms. This relief demonstrates not only an interest in rendering narrative but also a taste for the picturesque, a preoccupation with minute detail and a finished execution.

Kushans, who had come from Khotān in central Asia, and had affinities with the people of eastern Iran. Under able and well-advised leaders they conquered the Parthians, seizing Kabul, Arachosia and the whole of the Punjāb, and thrust out towards the east and south. Their empire extended from the Oxus to the Ganges plain, thus uniting under their authority the former possessions of the Indo-Greeks and the Sunga. The height of their power coincided with the reign of Kanishka, their third sovereign. Although his dates are not precisely known, he seems to have lived for about forty years in the middle of the 2nd century. Eclectic in his tastes, he applied himself to the spread of Buddhism, to which he was converted, but also gave protection to Jainism and Brahmanism. He was the first Indian sovereign to depict the figure of the Buddha on his coins, but he also depicted Iranian deities on them. He adopted the Indian imperial title of Mahārāja, or 'Great King', the Parthian title of Rājatirāja ('king of kings') and the Chinese title of Devaputra ('son of heaven'). In his official portraits he retained his tribal costume: Iranian tunic, Scythian cap and the tall boots of the nomadic horseman. We learn from an inscription written in Eteo-Tokharian, which was derived directly from the spoken Greek in use in Iran in the Parthian period, that he founded the temple of Surkh Kotal, a dynastic temple built at the top of a hill and which was approached by three successive terraces. Yet the Buddhist art contemporary with his reign, which is particularly that of Mathurā, continues in the style of the earlier period, without bearing the marks of any outside influence.

THE KINGDOMS OF THE DECCAN

As in the north, the Dravidian territory of south India saw the rise of kingdoms that were to enjoy great brilliance. Most of these had been founded in the preceding period and the most important was that of the Āndhras, who inhabited the region situated between the lower reaches of the Godavari and the Kistna. Traces of a brilliant civilisa-

9. **Medallion from the balustrade at Bhārhut.** *c.* 2nd century BC. Sandstone. d. 19½ in. (49 cm.). Indian Museum, Calcutta. This medallion, in which a human head is placed within a circle of lotus petals, shows the decorative skill of the Bhārhut sculptors.

10. **Medallion with a peacock, Bhārhut.** *c.* 2nd century BC. Sandstone. d. 19½ in. (49 cm.). Indian Museum, Calcutta. This exquisite stylised peacock again reflects the decorative skill of the Bhārhut artists. Such medallions decorated the upright members of the balustrade.

18 (opposite). **The story of Prince Mahājanaka.** Detail of fresco decorating the left-hand wall of the entrance to Cave I at Ajantā. (Photograph taken from a copy of the fresco by G. C. Haloi.) 5th–6th centuries. This is one of innumerable scenes in Indian iconography depicting dancers and musicians. The instruments consist of two transverse flutes, two pairs of cymbals, a pair of bulbous drums, another drum shaped like an hour-glass, and an arched harp (which can only just be distinguished). The dancer moves her hands in ritual gestures or *mudrā*, which symbolise in mime mystical power or action.

11. **Detail of the eastern torana, Stūpa I, Sāñchī.** 1st century BC–1st century AD. On the upper lintel of the torana the previous lives of the Buddha are illustrated—the Buddha of the jātaka being represented as a flowering tree surmounted by a parasol. Each 'tree' is flanked by a pair of worshippers and

12. **Reliefs from the northern torana, Stūpa I, Sāñchī.** 1st century BC–1st century AD. These two panels from one of the upright members of the torana show episodes from the life of Buddha—the Enlightenment symbolised by a throne placed beneath the sacred tree, and the crossing of the Ganges. The second episode relates to the Buddha's journey to Banāras to preach the doctrine. Having no money to pay the boatman he leaps across the river in a single bound.

above hover two winged genii. The lower lintel shows scenes from the life of the Buddha Sākyamuni—the prince Vessantara who, in his renunciation of the world, not only distributes gifts but also abandons his wife and children to the Brahmins.

13. **Yakshinī on the eastern torana, Stūpa I, Sāñchī.** The theme of the tree woman who symbolises fertility is connected with the popular cult of tree worship which was drawn into the Buddhist iconography. This Yakshinī is finely sculpted and possesses all the grace of Indian womanhood. She is shown in the canonic pose of the *tribhanga* or triple flexion, one of the attitudes laid down in the treatises of the time.

14. **Yaksha from Patna.** 2nd century BC. Sandstone. h. 5 ft. 11½ in. (182 cm.). Indian Museum, Calcutta. The earliest cult statues to have come down to us are the Yaksha, popular deities which derive from ancient animistic cults and which were adopted by Buddhism. They are characterised by their hieratic stance, a corpulent body and rather static quality. A delight in rendering detail is reflected in the careful observation of the costume and the jewellery.

15. **King Kanishka.** School of Mathurā. Probably mid-2nd century AD. Sandstone. h. 6 ft. (1 m. 85 cm.). Archaeological Museum, Mathurā. Thanks to the inscription engraved on the skirt of the garment, this statue can be identified as that of the Kushan King, Kanishka. Although the Kushans had been established in the north of India for over a century, the King still preserves in his official portraits the costume of his tribe. He wears a conical cap, a long frock-coat and heavy felt boots —the apparel of a mounted nomad of the steppes.

tion, centred on Amarāvatī, testify to the existence of a strong state in this region. They may have had as vassals the powerful Satavāhana who ruled over a large part of the Deccan stretching as far as Malwa and Mahārāstra.

TRANSITIONAL STYLES

Although Brahmanic art, which had hitherto played no part in Indian culture, now made its appearance, the art of this period was still almost exclusively Buddhist. It continued the ancient traditions, represented at Bhārhut and Sānchī, but at the same time foreshadowed the new style that was to follow. Qualified as 'transitional' it was a highly productive period in which new iconographical themes were invented, and a new aesthetic quality developed. Art reflected most accurately not only the political complexity

of the time but the triumph of Buddhism to whose glory it was dedicated. Throughout India, Buddhist art was in full flower, preserving the narrative character that makes it so valuable for a study of this period. The most important feature of this art is the appearance of the Buddha's image, which is represented now for the first time. There were three, roughly contemporary artistic schools: that of the former Indo-Greek possessions (present-day Pakistan and Afghanistan), known as the school of Gandhāra, that of Mathurā and the Ganges plain—corresponding to the territory conquered by the Kushans—and, in the south-east, the school of Amarāvatī, which corresponded to the territory of the Āndhras.

The image of the Buddha seems to have made its appearance simultaneously in Gandhāra and Mathurā; it ap-

16 (above left). **Buddha preaching.** From Loriyan Tangai. Gandhāra school, *c.* 2nd century. Schist. h. 2 ft. 9½ in. (85 cm.). Indian Museum, Calcutta. Indo-Greek syncretism is particularly well borne out in Buddha figures of this type, in which Hellenistic and oriental features are intermingled. The grave, pensive face with its faraway look reflects majestically the Buddhist ideal of an upright and charitable life, in which all desire is suppressed and total detachment achieved.

17 (above). **Standing Buddha from Nāgārjunakonda.** *c.* 2nd century AD. Madras Museum. This Buddha of the Amarāvatī school is dressed in a monastic robe leaving the right shoulder bare. The raised left arm lifts the drapery so that it falls in regular curving folds.

18 (left). **Female figure in the Greco-Buddhist style.** *c.* 2nd century AD. Schist. h. 4 ft. 3½ in. (131 cm.). Archaeological Museum, Mathurā. Although found at Mathurā, not Gandhāra, this is undoubtedly a Gandhāran piece. The facial features, wavy hair and treatment of the drapery recall Hellenistic sculpture. The statue is thought to be of the deified Kambojikā, queen of the Rājuvula satrapy.

19. **Interior of the chaitya at Kārlī.** 1st–2nd centuries AD.
The evolution of the chaitya was a slow one. Gradually the
structure acquired larger proportions—the nave at Kārlī is
59 feet high, 121½ feet long and 43 feet wide. The chaitya was
originally a timber construction (see also figure 6) and the

structural features though stylised now still reflect this ancestry
of wooden architecture. The bases of the columns are of vase
form. The elaborate capitals, with their combination of human
figures and animal heads, remind one of Achaemenian art.

peared in Amarāvatī a little later. It is possible that the
idea was Greek and that the image itself was created by
Greco-Roman artists from western Asia. It introduced a
focal point into the composition of scenes, which became
increasingly symmetrical, although the general repertoire
of motifs did not change noticeably.

THE TYPES OF THE BUDDHA

In the so-called Greco-Buddhist school of Gandhāra, the
figure of the Buddha possesses from the start all the usual
Hellenistic characteristics, blended with a few more speci-
fically Eastern features. He is represented as a young man
of Apollonian type, with a straight nose continuing the
line of the forehead and a firmly drawn mouth, but with
heavy eyelids half obscuring the very protruding eyes; a
fleshy face with the lobes of the ears lengthened by the
weight of jewels. He bears the distinctive signs of his sacred
nature: between his eyes is the *urna*, or coil of hair, and he
holds in the palms of his hands the *chakra*, the sacred wheel
that symbolises the progression of the Buddhist law. His
evenly waved hair is gathered at the top of his head in a tight
knot secured by a gold cord. The knot was later misunder-
stood and came to be represented by a cranial protuber-

ance *(ushnīsha)*, which has been included in all the images
of the Buddha throughout Asia down to our own time. He
wears the monastic robe and cloak of flowing drapery.

The school of Mathurā also had this Apollonian type of
Buddha, but there was also a very different type, quite
peculiar to this school. He has a round head and a smiling,
doll-like expression. On his shaven head he wears a skull-
cap that hides the topknot. His monastic dress is of a finer
material than at Gandhāra; it clings closely to the body
and the light relief is rendered by parallel folds bordered by
a faint double outline; the right shoulder is left uncovered.
He is fairly heavily built and makes simple gestures that
were later to become the ritual gestures or *mudrā*. This
Buddha is close to the image of *yaksha* of the previous
period and belongs entirely to Indian tradition.

Like that of Mathurā, the Buddha of the school of Amarāvatī is profoundly Indian in appearance, inheriting the
lessons of the past. However, from the very beginning, it is
more highly developed and closer to the type that was to be
adopted by later schools. The long face is characteristically
Dravidian. The cranial protuberance, like the rest of the
head, is covered by small, flat curls arranged from left to
right in accordance with ritual conventions. His monastic

38

20 (above left). **The young Ekashringa.**
Detail from the upright member of a
Buddhist balustrade. School of Mathurā.
c. 2nd century. Pink sandstone. h. 2 ft.
7½ in. (80 cm.). Archaeological Museum,
Mathurā. The simple modelling and the
clear lines of this piece bring emphasis to
the facial features which are much more
individual than was the case with
sculpture of preceding periods.

21 (above). **Kushan coin.** Gold. d. $\frac{13}{16}$ in.
(2 cm.). Musée Guimet, Paris. Kushan
rulers are represented on the obverse of
their coins while on the reverse Iranian
or Indian deities are depicted. Here the
god Siva is shown standing before his
mount, the bull Nandin.

22 (left). **Three Yakshi.** Detail from a
Buddhist balustrade at Mathurā. School
of Mathurā, *c.* 2nd century AD. Pink
sandstone. h. 3 ft. 11 in. (120 cm.).
Indian Museum, Calcutta. The use of
such profane figures for the decoration of
religious buildings may seem to us
inappropriate. But these sculptures, with
their marvellous understanding of balance
of form and harmony of line, reflect the
artist's belief in the importance of grace
and vitality.

17 cloak again leaves the right shoulder bare and falls in regular folds, held in at front and back, from the left shoulder to the chest. The right hand makes the gesture of fearlessness *(abhaya-mudrā)*. In the reliefs of this school, one notices the use of two iconographies, that in which the Buddha is replaced by symbols and another in which he is represented without the traditional signs. Amarāvatī seems to have played a particularly important role in exporting Indian works of art to the countries of the South Seas. Buddhas in the Amarāvatī style have been found scattered over such countries as were reached by Indian navigators and local imitations of these Buddhas have also been found, particularly in northern and central Thailand.

DIVERSITY AND SIMILARITY OF STYLES

A real unity is to be found in the art of this period in spite of its variations. There are elements common to all three schools: the architectural forms and the characteristics of sculpture and painting were only slightly affected by differ-
4,5 ing local customs. But the school of Gandhāra is nonetheless outside the main stream of Indian aesthetic development on account of its attachment to the Hellenistic world. Whether executed in schist or in stucco, a whole repertoire
6,18 of classical decoration is perpetuated in the treatment of the subsidiary figures accompanying the Buddha. These figures represent with great liveliness the physical types that then peopled the Eurasian world. This Hellenistic style from India's north-west frontier was to be particularly influential throughout Asia, where it was drawn into the repertoire of Buddhist art and continued long after the disappearance of the political structures that had given it birth.

Rock-cut architecture is practically the only type of building to survive. The sanctuaries retain the same ground-plans as before and still imitate the forms of wooden
19 constructions, although with some stylisation (Kārlī, Kanherī, Nāsik III). The stūpa, of which unfortunately only fragments remain, were larger than usual. We know from relief representations that they were taller, the base being higher and the dome more spherical.

9 It was sculpture that achieved true perfection, as much from the aesthetic as from the technical point of view. It is
20 very varied, because each school was imbued with a different artistic feeling and also because of the size and diversity of the materials used. The art of Mathurā reproduces both
15 the grave majesty of the Kushan kings and the delightful sensuousness of Indian women whose ample bodies are
22 shown in the graceful ritual pose of the *tribhanga* or triple flexion. The red sandstone used by this school gives its
7,8 sculpture an additional charm. Carved and engraved ivory
23 plaques, discovered in Afghanistan, at Begrām or Kapisa, the former Kushan capital, seem to share the same style. The technical and stylistic refinement of these plaques confirm the reputation of the Indian ivory workers, who were so widely praised in ancient literature.

The Amarāvatī school is quite different: the style of this school was at once more dynamic, yet less robust and more
24,25 refined than that of Mathurā. It was in the narrative relief that it reached its height: executed in the marble-like lime-
10,11 stone of the region, this is often of great beauty, not only in the subtlety of the composition but also in the confidence of the modelling. The figures are most elegantly posed—the attitude of prostration being among the most beautiful in
26 Indian art.

These differing characteristics are also to be found in the pictorial art, in the paintings of Cave X at Ajanta for example, where one can observe the same confident modelling and the same dexterity in the attitude of the figures.

This period of transition, so rich in new achievements and experimentation, carried to a peak of perfection the qualities inherited from the past and paved the way for the full flowering of the Gupta period.

23. **Girl playing with a goose.** Incised ivory plaque from Begrām. *c.* 2nd century AD. 3 × 2½ in. (7·5 × 6·5 cm.). Kabul Museum, Afghanistan. This graceful girl is naked apart from her jewellery. In her right hand she holds a flower which seems to attract the goose, whose head is raised towards it. Geese are numbered among many domestic animals which lived in the private apartments of the women.

24 (left). **The subjugation of the elephant Nālāgiri.** Balustrade medallion from the Amarāvatī stūpa. 2nd century AD. Marbled limestone. d. 31½ in. (80 cm.). Madras Museum. The sculptor has rendered with consummate artistry this episode from the life of the Buddha. The naturalness of the postures, the balance of the composition, the mastery of the perspectival planes all combine to make vivid the story of the miracle.

25 (below left). **The conversion of the serpent-king.** School of Amarāvatī, *c.* 3rd century. Marbled limestone. This relief from Nāgārjunakonda, shows the conversion of the Nāgarāja, or serpent-king, by Sāgata, one of the Buddha's disciples. On the right the serpent-king is seated among the slender, graceful women of his harem. He appears in human form, only the cobra hood behind his head signifying his true nature. On the left, the monk Sāgata subdues and converts the king.

26 (below). **Woman prostrating herself.** Detail from balustrade at Amarāvatī. *c.* 2nd century. Marbled limestone. The sculptors of Amarāvatī took advantage of the lessons learned at Sāñchī, developing that style, and perfecting it particularly in the rendering of the female form. The attitude of prostration, in particular, is among the most beautiful things in Indian art.

The Classical Styles: Gupta, Post-Gupta and Pāla-Sena

The brilliant period of transitional art described in the last section was followed by a time of political discord that seems to have weakened the intellectual and artistic vigour of India. In about 320, however, a new power emerged, that of the Gupta. This dynasty originated in Magadha, the holy land of Buddhism, where, in the old Maurya capital, Pātaliputra, the palace of Asoka could still be seen. It is probably no coincidence that their founder, Chandragupta, bore the same name as the founder of the Maurya dynasty, to which he wished to attach his own dynasty. His successors were to extend their empire over a large part of India and their influence in southern Indian in the South Seas was considerable.

The dynasty reached its height in the reigns of Chandragupta II (c. 375–414) and Kamārgupta I (c. 414–55). India then enjoyed one of the most brilliant periods in her cultural history. Music and sculpture attained their classical forms and were practised by the Indian elite from the king downwards. An extreme refinement and a remarkable unity of style was achieved. There was also an unparalleled flowering of literature and philosophy. Great developments occurred in drama, for it was then that the great poet Kalidasa wrote his most famous plays, including *The Recognition of Sakuntala*. A broad religious toleration allowed all sects to flourish freely: the religion of the time was marked by a strong tendency towards mysticism and to a growing syncretism. Philosophy shone with equal brilliance among Buddhists and Hindus. The principal Hindu philosophical systems were developed and elaborated, and the works of Asanga and Vasubandhu were to form the basis of the Buddhist beliefs of the Great Vehicle (Mahāyāna) for centuries to come. Moreover, Buddhism, now in full flower, was peacefully to conquer the farthest lands of Asia.

Building upon past experience, the Gupta style nevertheless was an expression of new preoccupations: the absolute idealism of Buddhist philosophy, the pre-eminence of mind of the Hindu systems and the idealisation of the human form reached a new height. Never, perhaps, was so much importance attached to purity of form and line, to the relationship of masses and the harmony of proportion. Aesthetic treatises were written that defined the canons on which all future rules were based.

Unfortunately, the White Huns from Bactria now appeared on the frontiers of the Gupta empire. In c. 455–67 Skandagupta succeeded in repulsing them but their incursion was nonetheless the beginning of a weakening of Gupta power. A state of confusion reigned in the imperial family, which seems to have been divided into several branches and was incapable of checking the destructive advance of the barbarian hordes who had returned in force and were surging on towards the Ganges valley. The next fifty years were to witness a series of horrifying scenes: Buddhist monasteries and universities were razed to the ground and the monks persecuted. The Gupta dynasty

27. **Main stūpa at Nālandā** (after restoration). Nālandā, was founded in 467–473. It was the seat of a famous university, and many monasteries were erected there. Among these monasteries, the ones built by Sumatrans show how important were the relations between India and the East Indies. Chinese pilgrims who came to India to visit the Buddhist holy places studied the philosophy of the Mahāyāna at Nālandā. The most distinguished of these were Hsüan-tsang and Yi-tsing who stayed there in the 7th century.

survived but its princes were now little more than local heads of state. However, the influence exerted by this period on culture was so great that it persisted long after the dynasty itself had disappeared. The northern states, taking advantage of the weakening of the Gupta, consolidated their own power. Among these was Thanesar, situated at the eastern end of Doab (a region between the Ganges and its tributary the Jumna) of which Kanauj became the capital. In the reign of King Harsha of Kanauj (605–47), northern and central India was rejoined under a single ruler for the last time before the medieval period. For a time, this empire preserved the intellectual and artistic traditions of the Gupta. The personality of Harsha, whose own role was of prime importance, is known to us from the accounts written down by the Chinese Buddhist pilgrim, Hsüan-tsang. He was a ruler very much in the Indian tradition: the protector of religious culture, eclectic and tolerant. The grandeur of imperial India that he had restored did not survive him; after his death his empire was broken up.

28 (above). **Façade of Cave I at Ajantā.** *c.* 6th century. Cave I is a monastery. It has a square plan, opening on to a veranda. The columns supporting the roof have richly carved capitals and brackets worked in great detail.

29 (above right). **Interior of Cave I, Ajantā.** *c.* 6th century. The main hall is surrounded by columns forming a square, the shafts and brackets of which are richly sculpted. The flat ceiling is painted to resemble coffering. On the walls, between the doors which lead to the chapel, are the frescoes which are numbered among the masterpieces of Indian art (see plates 15–18).

30 (right). **Façade of Cave XXVI, Ajantā.** *c.* 6th century. Rock-cut architecture reached its peak in the Gupta period. The sanctuary preserves its essential characteristics but is now covered with sculpture and decorative motifs which invade every surface including the columns.

Meanwhile, the kingdoms of the Deccan continued to increase in power, particularly the Pallava in the Tamil regions and the western Chālukya in Mahārāstra. The Chālukya and their successors, the Rāshtrakūta, filled their kingdom with priceless art treasures, the most famous of which are to be found at Ajantā, Aihole, Bādāmī, Nāsik, Elephanta and Ellūrā. In the 7th century, in the south-east, the Pallava erected the remarkable architectural complex of Māmallapuram. Thus the splendour of the Gupta was sustained until the medieval period.

GUPTA AND POST-GUPTA STYLES

From the artistic point of view, the Gupta period is marked by the emergence of a new style that is nevertheless related to the styles that preceded it. It forms one of the most important stages in Indian aesthetic development. Looking at its many masterpieces one can appreciate fully the system of gradual change that is so typically Indian, in which a single decorative repertoire may cover a wide variety of interpretations. In sculpture the Chālukya and Pallava **23** styles adopted Gupta themes, transforming them according to the laws of mutation that characterise Indian art: but they betray a different spirit, owing, perhaps, to the development of Brahmanic art. Indeed, the distinction between the aesthetic conceptions of the Buddhists and of the Hindus was to widen: the first being dominated by a spirit of peace and serenity and the second by dynamic power and a feeling for divine majesty. This difference is naturally more apparent in the narrative compositions than in decoration and single figures. Hindu high relief in particular reveals a remarkable sense of the monumental.

As in previous periods, architecture consisted of stūpa and rock-cut sanctuaries. But a great change came about: for the first time, free-standing structures were built out of durable materials.

The Huns destroyed practically all the stūpa of this period; the oldest of these (Chārsada, Mirpur Khas), built of brick covered with stucco, were a continuation of the Gandhāra style. Others (Sārnāth, Rājagriha, Nālandā) are of **27** brick and stone, sometimes braced by iron tenons. The outline of these buildings changed considerably: the dome became bell-shaped or bulbous and merged into its circular base. It was this type, brought to the Indianised countries by the Gupta, that was to be perpetuated throughout South-East Asia.

The rock sanctuaries resumed their previous shape (square or apsidal in plan), but with much more carved decoration, particularly on the abaci of the capitals. The **8, 29, 30** most famous are those of Ajantā, several of which are decorated with admirable frescoes, Bādāmī and Ellūrā.

The earliest free-standing sanctuaries varied in form, but were always simple and quite small. The solutions that were to be used by the architects of the medieval period can already be discerned. These involve either square cellas covered by a flat roof and preceded by a pillared porch (Cave XVII at Sāñchī), ground-plan covered by a barrel

31. **Temple of Lakshmana, Sīrpūr.** 6th–7th centuries. This temple appears to have been the prototype for the sanctuary with an inward curving silhouette that was to become widespread during the medieval period (see figures 42, 43, 44). This was partly achieved by placing ribbed cushions *(āmalaka)* at the corners of the building, thereby softening the angles.

vault (as in the temple of Kapotesvara at Chezarla, the temple of Trivikrama at Ter and the temple of Durgā at Aihole), or square towers surmounted by a pyramidal roof in two parts (as in the temple of Gop, in Kāthiāwād). The architectural style is characterised both by the transformation of certain ornamental forms and by the elaboration of certain themes such as that of the roof. Thus the horseshoe-shaped bow window, translated at a very early date from wood into stone, finally became a decorative motif in its own right and the different 'storeys' of the roof were embellished with miniature buildings. The undeniably original effect obtained seems to be more within the province of a sculptor than of an architect; furthermore it reflects the cosmos in following the dictates of the sacred texts. In spite of the importance which was attached to sculpture at this period, architecture and sculpture are always complementary and perfectly balanced, one with the other. The rocks of Māmallapuram, hewn to the shape of a temple, hollowed out and carved, are really enormous **19** sculptures in the round, as is also the case with the Kailāsa- **22** nāth of Ellūrā which stands within the quarry from which it was carved, enclosed by walls of living rock.

Another type of sanctuary with a square plan seems to have appeared in about the 6th and 7th centuries. Prompted, perhaps, by the use of brick, its 'storeyed' roof gradually curves inwards towards the summit and is decorated with finials in the form of ribbed cushions *(āmalaka)*. One of the oldest of these is the temple of Lakshmana at Sīrpūr **31**

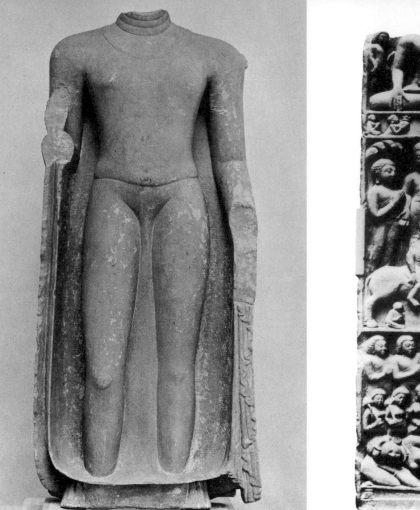

32. **Buddha in the Gupta style.** 4th–6th centuries. Sandstone. h. 2 ft. 11½ in. (90 cm.). Musée Guimet, Paris. Gupta art took the human body as its principle theme. This was treated with great simplicity, while preserving the sturdiness of the form. The Buddha's garment is rendered with a total absence of folds in the drapery, so that he appears to be naked.

34. **Head of a Gupta Buddha.** 4th–6th centuries. Sandstone. Musée Guimet, Paris. The classical Gupta style can be seen to perfection in the smiling detachment of this Buddha, with his reflective and mysterious expression.

33. **Relief from Sārnāth.** Gupta style. 5th–6th centuries. Limestone. h. 2 ft. 11 in. (89 cm.). National Museum of India, New Delhi. This relief, which illustrates the main episodes in the life of the Buddha, dates from the end of the Gupta period. The lively invention and fertile imagination of the Gupta sculptor was giving way to a more conventional approach. This stele illustrates the conception, birth, first steps, the great renunciation, the cutting of the hair, and the Enlightenment. The Earth's witness of his approach to Buddhahood, and the first sermon are illustrated in the top register, now badly damaged.

that may be regarded as the archetype of the sanctuaries with curved roofs *(sikhara)*.

Between about 600 and 750, regional styles began to develop covering vast areas of territory. The sikhara make their appearance in Orissa. At the same time, the Dravidian order, characterised by its pyramidal roofs, developed under the Chālukya (Bādāmī, Pattadakal), then of the Rāshtrakūta (Ellūrā). It also developed in the kingdom of the Pallava (Māmallapuram, Kāñchīpuram). Versions 19, 29 of the same temple were to develop increasingly differing forms.

In sculpture, as in painting, the Gupta artists used the human figure as their main subject-matter. They expressed in a majestic way the tranquil detachment proper to Buddhism; the nude appears almost transfigured, yet preserves a majestic, serene expression, and an almost regal grandeur. There are two types of statue: the Buddha, which continues according to previous traditions, and the Bodhisattva and Brahmanic deities, whose princely adornments contrast with the simplicity of the Buddha.

35. **The Maheshamūrti, Elephanta.** End of the 6th–
beginning of the 7th century. The island of Elephanta, facing
Bombay, has a rock sanctuary containing the colossal effigy of
the Maheshamūrti, the Brahmanic triad, which unites on one
body the three heads of Siva. He is represented in his three
aspects: the majestic one, the feminine one and the terrifying
god. This is the most magnificent example of post-Gupta
rupestrian sculpture, as much from the point of view of size as
for its emotional effect.

36. **Detail from the Descent of the Ganges.** Relief at
Māmallapuram. 7th century. The Brahmins, most peaceful of
men, wait at the river's edge. They carry vases to be filled with
holy water, and worship the river with the rapt dedication of
priestly men.

The most beautiful examples of this art were produced
principally by two schools, those of Sārnāth and Mathurā.
32,34 The Buddhas are often very tall, have broad circular haloes
and are set against steles. From about the 5th century, the
drapery is no longer indicated by folds of material but ad-
heres closely to the body to reveal its form. The Bodhisatt-
13,14 vas and Brahmanic deities wear a simple skirt held to the
waist by a belt, leaving the upper half of the body bare;
their adornments, though few in number, are observed in
minute detail.

From the 6th–7th centuries, the Gupta style developed
into what is known as the Post-Gupta style: gradually its
qualities change, the outlines become thicker, the iconographical rules more numerous and more stringent, the
ornament more complicated and the physical types more
impersonal. The Post-Gupta Buddha nevertheless retains
the iconographical characteristics of the Gupta Buddha;
and thousands of examples of this type are to be found
throughout India and even in the countries of South-East
Asia.

In the reliefs, the narrative sense of earlier sculptors continues, but is more adroitly executed. There is less picturesque detail, but a greater mastery of composition. If Bud- *33*
dhist relief tends to degenerate into stereotypes, Brahmanic relief is characterised by a remarkable sense of the monumental, and is much affected by the taste of the period
tempered at first by Buddhist elegance and restraint. In
the 6th and 7th centuries it acquired its full power and
beauty. The great centres were Elephanta, near Bombay *35*
(end of 6th–beginning of 7th century), Māmallapuram, on *36,37*
the east coast of the Deccan (first half of 7th century), and *20*
Ellūrā, in Mahārāstra (7th–8th centuries). Each of these *38,39*
sites has its own characteristics: purity of line and form at
Elephanta, cool elegance, naturalism and dignity at Māmallapuram, power and intensity at Ellūrā.

Wall-painting also reached its height at this time, as
much through the beauty of its composition as in its perfection of form, its confident draughtsmanship and brilliant
use of colour. The frescoes of the Ajantā group are of out- *15,16*
standing quality. Those of other sites (Sīgiriya, in Ceylon; *17,18*

37. **The Sleep of Vishnu.** Relief from the Avatāra cave at Māmallapuram. 7th century. Vishnu lies upon the body of the Serpent of Eternity whose many heads form a kind of canopy about the head of the sleeping god. The majesty of the god is counterbalanced by the peaceful, marvellously rendered figure of the kneeling woman praying at his feet.

Bāgh, Bādāmī, Sittanavāsal) are less fine, although they have interesting characteristics of their own.

The themes illustrated are religious (Buddhist at Ajantā, Sīgiriya and Bāgh, Jain at Sittanavāsal, Brahmanic at Ellūrā). But these frescoes also provide us with a wealth of information about the life of the time, from the sumptuousness of official ceremonies to the intimacy of family scenes; sacred and profane were constantly intermingled in the social life of ancient India. Ajantā is the most perfect expression of the refined, elegant art of the Gupta period and probably presents a faithful picture of life at court, as described in the rather mannered literature of the time.

The painting occupies the whole of the available surface, without either linear division or any break in the continuity. Among these masses of figures and detail, it is difficult at first sight to make out a guiding thread. Gradually, however, the eye gets used to distinguishing between different groups. Led from one to another by a subtle play of gestures and planes, it finally moves freely from one to another. The link between one group and the next is achieved through the subsidiary figures, just as in relief the half-tones form a transition between light and shade.

Following age-old principles, the Ajantā artists use several vanishing points in the same composition, which gives a certain mobility to the composition. This kind of perspective is similar in every way with the idea of movement implied in a circular composition. Indeed, many of the groups are arranged within a circular or oval scheme that is apparent only in the disposition of the figures, the direction of a limb or of a glance and in the movement of curves and lines. Each group is turned inwards to a centre, like the petals of a flower on to its calyx. The artists of Ajantā handled the circular composition with incredible subtlety. It had first appeared during the Bhārhut period and was to attain ultimate perfection at Amarāvatī. Apart from its aesthetic values, this form of composition also possesses a mystical quality that is rich in meaning, for it is a magic circle, an abstraction of the *mandala*, the imagined shape of the cosmos. In this form, as in narrative relief compositions, there is one unifying idea: to penetrate towards a centre—in the mandala, so that the initiate may encounter the divine, in relief groups to discover the principal figure of the scene. In both cases, it is a question of movement, whether physical or psychological.

The favourite subject of the Ajantā artists is the female body, whose poses not only have an aesthetic value, but correspond to a vocabulary that probably derived from the theatre or from the dance and followed very closely the requirements of the canonical treatises *(sāstra)*. As in choreography, every gesture, every facial expression has a precise meaning intended to provoke precise and documented emotions. But this mimed language is full of hints and subtleties; for the initiate, a mere frown, a movement at the corners of the mouth or a half-closed eye has a particular meaning.

38 (above). **Rāvana shaking Mount Kailāsa.** Kailāsanāth temple, Ellūrā. 8th century. The Kailāsa temple was intended as a replica of the sacred Mount Kailāsa, on the summit of which Siva resided with his wife Pārvatī. With his many arms the giant Rāvana presses upwards and outwards to dislodge the foundations. But Siva with one touch of his foot restores the balance of the mountain, imprisoning the giant in the depths of the earth.

40 (left). **Stele in the Pāla style.** *c*. 9th century. Sandstone. h. 1 ft. 11½ in. (60 cm.). Musée Guimet, Paris. This stele depicts the Buddhist divinity Tārā, the female counterpart of the Bodhisattva Avalokitesvara, 'the compassionate one'. In style it is still close to post-Gupta art. Tārā is placed against a stele with a rounded top. The smaller scale rendering of her supporters accentuates the importance of the central figure.

41 (below, left). **Bronze Buddha from Nālandā.** 9th century. Formerly in the Nālandā Museum. Many bronzes have been found at the Nālandā site. They all belong to the Pāla period, or, more precisely, to the 9th century. Cast by the *cire perdue* method, the bronze alloy consists of eight different metals combined in various proportions. They have affinities with Javanese bronzes and testify to the cultural links between Bengal and the East Indies. The *cire perdue* or 'lost wax' method of bronze casting is achieved in the following way. The work is modelled in wax on a clay core, the wax corresponding to the thickness of the final bronze product. The finished wax model (to which vents and pouring channels are added) is then encased in an 'envelope' of some inflammable material which will burn when the mould is fired. In the firing process the wax melts, leaving the mould into which the metal is poured.

THE PĀLA STYLE

Bengal remained the last bastion of Buddhism, which, as it retreated before the advance of Brahmanism, took refuge in the region that had given it birth. The Pāla sovereigns (*c*. 765–1086) made the university of Nālandā prosper once again and built monasteries there. Their successors, the Sena, on the other hand, protected Hinduism. But the Muslim invasion was spreading slowly eastwards from the Indus valley, and the Pāla-Sena empire was unable to resist its pressure. At the beginning of the 13th century, the Buddhist holy places were sacked and surrounded for a time by a Muslim state.

The Pāla style of Bengal (8th–12th centuries) may be regarded as the true repository of the Gupta style, even if it was unable to revive the creative power of its progenitor. For the 350 years that it lasted, the Pāla style developed on its own, almost sealed off from any outside influence that might have revitalised its wholly conventional forms.

The great Gupta statuary culminated in those stone images which depict a tall central figure flanked by much smaller subsidiary figures, the whole group backing on to a stele. In spite of the great care that was taken to produce pure form and line, they are little more than lifeless reproductions, the work of men whose over-riding concern was to conform to the canons of the past. It is a technically accomplished art, but one that had lost all its sparkle and spontaneity.

40

From the end of the 8th to the beginning of the 10th century, the sacred images remained very close to the Post-Gupta style. In the course of the 10th century, they became more varied. The figures became taller and more slender, the facial features thicker and heavier, the modelling more slack. This style persisted up to the 11th and 12th centuries, becoming increasingly heavy, dry and mannered.

The bronze images, whose production centred around the famous site of Nālandā, were produced by the *cire perdue* method. Placed in the traditional manner against steles, they are nevertheless set forward from this background so that they can be seen in the full round. Such statues date generally from the 9th century.

41

39 (opposite). **The Cave of Rāvana, Ellūrā.** *c*. 7th century. Siva Natarāja, the 'master of dance', possesses eight arms, the symbols of his power. Here he dances to the music of drums and flutes. This particular manifestation of Siva is widely illustrated in reliefs and bronzes. He symbolises the creation of the world, or, more precisely its 'setting in motion'. At the same time he celebrates the victory of Knowledge over Ignorance.

The Medieval Period

The Gupta period, with its prolongations, gradually leads Indian art towards a medieval period (*c.* 9th–16th centuries), during which time the political map of India was constantly changing according to the relative power of the different political groups. After the dissolution of the Harsha empire, states that had developed locally made more or less serious attempts to gain control and the struggles between different alliances and coalitions began. Art, in this period, enjoyed unprecedented patronage, each dynasty wishing to outdo another in the number and size of its temples. Regional differences became more marked, and northern India pursued a different course from the south. Certain states stand out particularly—Kashmir, under the Utpāla dynasty, was responsible for some of the most interesting temples of the region. In Kathiāwād and Gujarāt, famous sanctuaries were erected under the Solanki dynasty. Malwa, under the Paramāra dynasty (about the beginning of the 10th century), witnessed a true literary renaissance, particularly during the reign of the poet-king Bhoja (*c.* 1010–65). In Bundelkhand, the Chandella dynasty built the famous temples of Khajurāho (*c.* 1000).

In south India, Mahārāstra saw a succession of great dynasties. After the Chalukya and the Rāshtrakūta, who built the Kailāsa of Ellūrā, the second Chālukya held sway until 1190, when the empire was broken up by the Hoysala,

42. **Vaital Deul, Bhuvanesvar.** 8th–9th centuries. The sanctuary of Vaital Deul is rectangular in plan, and is covered with a barrel vault. Flanked by four smaller chapels, it forms the prototype of the *panchayatana* i.e. the arrangement of five buildings in a quincunx—a central structure with four auxiliary buildings placed at the corners of the basement.

who were then reigning in Mysore. Lastly the Carnatic, already enriched by the buildings of the Pallava, saw the rise and fall of the Cholas and the Pandyas. The Cholas reached the height of their power between 985 and 1052 and built, among others, the famous temple of Tanjore.

THE DEVELOPMENT OF ART: FORMS IN ARCHITECTURE

The gradual abandonment of rock-cut architecture and the use of free-standing structures made of durable materials such as stone and brick allowed the prevailing rules of sculptural development to be interpreted more freely and broadly, gradually leading Indian architecture towards increasingly ambitions constructions.

This period saw an increasing diversity of architectural forms based, in principle, on their function and upon the nature of the site, but certain types were nevertheless to dominate in certain regions. In all of them, characteristics from previous periods are to be found. The Hindu temple preserved its characteristic of space limited on all sides, enclosed within a thick shell of masonry. Half-light reigns almost everywhere, blurs the decoration and envelops the visitor with its mystery, forming a violent contrast with the reliefs of the exterior, which, vibrant with light, tend to raise one's eyes towards the top of the building. This contrast helps to emphasise the feelings of respect and fear that overcome the worshipper as he enters the temple and impress upon him the idea of the mysterious and divine. Corbelling in horizontal layers—a type of vault adopted almost exclusively by the Indians—tends to accentuate this feeling of mystery. Most buildings have a square ground-plan, covered either by a pyramidal or a curvilinear roof. These derive from an earlier type that originated in the 7th century. It was at this time in fact that the Brahmanic temple began to reveal certain permanent characteristics. Laid out on a single base, and developing from a single support, on a single axis, are a pillared porch, a vast pillared hall, a vestibule and a square sanctuary around which runs a narrow corridor, which enables the worshipper to make the ritual circumambulation. Until the beginning of the 10th century, this plan, with some variations, was common to both north and south. The strongly angular form of its different components distinguished it from the ground-plans of the following period. Confronted with the problem of inscribing within space a work which was to be both beautiful and based on the traditional rules, the Hindu architect succeeded, with unerring taste, in creating a complex of niches, foliated cusps and pilasters that broke up any monotony in the general lines by the addition of an abundance of ornamental or architectural sculpture.

From the 10th century, particularly in Orissā (Bhuvanesvar, Konārak) and in Bundelkhand (Khajurāho), the main parts of the temple merge into each other: the porch preceded by a flight of steps that spans the basement, is covered by a roof supported by pillars and leads into a

25, 26
34, 35

(Continued on page 65)

19. **The temples at Māmallapuram.**
7th century. The craftsmen of the
Pallava Kingdom carved a long outcrop
of rock into the shape of a group of
temples and then proceeded to sculpt the
surfaces and hollow out the interior.
Side by side can be seen sanctuaries with
pyramidal roofs and those with barrel
vaults which were to lead respectively
to the most ambitious architectural
achievements of southern Indian in
medieval times.

50

20. **The Descent of the Ganges.**
7th century. Relief at Māmallapuram.
The river, in the guise of serpent-men,
is the focal point of the entire
composition, and all sorts and conditions
of men in prayer, and all kinds of
animals are moving towards it. These
converging movements give the
composition an overall unity, but each
part is interesting on its own, and the
mass of individual detail is astounding.

21. **Shore temple, Māmallapuram.**
8th century. This temple consists of a
building square in plan, covered by a
polygonal dome and with a columned
porch *(mandapa)* in front. In the Indian
fashion, an increasing number of 'storeys'
are interpolated between the main body of
the building and the summit of the roof.

22. **Kailāsanāth temple, Ellūrā.**
8th century. The various temple buildings
are composed of vast masses of living
rock which were separated from each
other by the craftsmen and carved
individually in a long slope of the
hillside. The sanctuary is 100 feet high
and represents the cosmic mountain
which was the residence of the god, Siva.

23. Sculpture at Kumbakonam.
8th century. The sculpture of the
Pallava Kingdom is rooted in the past,
but it also has affinities with medieval
Dravidian art. Its main characteristics
are the elegance of the forms, quiet
dignity and a rather cool formality.

24. The monastery at Ratnagiri.
9th century. Buddhism flourished in
Orissā, as in Bengal, in the centuries
preceding the Muslim invasion, and the
Buddhist monasteries there such as
Ratnagiri also prospered, though they
did not achieve the fame of the
Nālandā ones.

25. Muktesvara temple, Bhuvanesvar. 9th–10th centuries. This temple has a roof whose 'storeys' are very close together, giving a ribbed effect to the whole building. The *sikhara* on top of the sanctuary has a vertical feature jutting out from each of its sides, and is surmounted by a large ribbed cushion (*amalaka*).

26. Torana of the Muktesvara temple, Bhuvanesvar (detail). 9th–10th centuries. The *torana* originated in the leafy branch stretched between two posts as a sign of a festival or of homage, which developed into a gateway, first of wood, then of stone, such as the ones at Sāñchī (see plate 3), and the crosspieces were eventually joined into one arch. The arch of the *torana* at the Muktesvara temple is decorated with garlands, with *kudus* and with graceful female figures.

27. **The Bodhisattva Vajrapāni,** found at Lalitagiri. 9th century. Granite gneiss. h. 27½ in. (70 cm.). Musée Guimet, Paris. Vajrapāni, 'bearer of lightning', appears in Buddhism from the beginning of the Christian era, and is often to be found near the Buddha on the bas-reliefs of the Gandhāra school. The one illustrated belongs to the post-Gupta art of Orissā.

28 (p. 56). **Mother and Child.** 8th–9th centuries. Sandstone. h. 15¾ in. (40 cm.). Musée Guimet, Paris. This statue is characteristic of the medieval period in northern India, and expresses all the tenderness of Indian women for children. It is small in size, like most of the sculptures decorating the walls of the Orissā temples.

29 (p. 57). **Gopuram of the Kailāsanāth temple, Kāñchīpuram.** 8th century. Pallava period. This is one of the first gopura (outer gateways of a temple) in the Dravidian style. It is rectangular in plan, and has a barrel-vaulted roof terminating at each end in a horseshoe-shaped bay. A row of slender vertical features decorate the summit of the barrel vault.

31 (above). **Siva Bhairava, Tanjore.** 10th–11th centuries.
This is one of the many figures which decorate the great
temple at Tanjore. It is characteristic of the Chola period in
its proportions and restraint. The god Siva is shown in his
most alarming aspect as Bhairava, 'frightful, terrible, horrible'.
The figure is usually naked, the hair stands on end. He is
draped in garlands of skulls and serpents, and sometimes
accompanied by a dog.

30 (opposite). **Brihadīsvara temple, Tanjore.** 10th–11th
centuries. This twin-towered temple is perhaps the most
imposing example of the pyramidal from. Each roof
comprises a great number of individual 'storeys', and each
storey forms a cornice upon which miniature buildings are
placed. The ribbed cupola perched up at a giddy height can
no longer properly be called a roof, but is a crowning
decorative feature.

32 (above). **Relief from the Brihadīsvara temple** at
Gangaikondacolapuram. 11th century. King Cola
Rajendra I (1012–1044) who conquered territories as
far as the Ganges took the title Gangaikondacola: 'Cola who
took the Ganges'. He established a new capital with a
pyramidal temple like the one at Tanjore. Here he is seen
being crowned by the god Siva.

33 (next page). **Siva Vīnādhāra.** 11th century. Bronze.
h. 2 ft 1 in. (69 cm.). Musée Guimet, Paris. This
representation of the god, which comes from south-eastern
India, shows him as Vīnādhāra, the 'master of the arts'. He is
shown as a musician, because according to Indian tradition
music was not only the quintessential art, but the inspiration
of all creation. The bronze was cast by the 'lost wax' method
and is a masterly example of that technique. The grace of the
gestures and the balance of the silhouette make this figure
particularly successful.

34. Temple of Sūrya, Konārak.
13th century. The immense temple of
Sūrya at Konārak in north-eastern
India was built during the reign of King
Narashima-Deva (1238–1264).
Dedicated to the sun-god Sūrya, it is in
the form of a gigantic chariot drawn by
the seven horses of the sun. The base is
decorated with twelve wheels ten feet in
diameter, and on the entrance side with
seven horses.

35. Detail of a wheel, Sūrya temple,
Konārak. Like all the temples in
Orissā, the temple of Sūrya, sometimes
called the Black Pagoda, is decorated
with numerous sculptures of mythological
animals and persons, and with erotic
couples. Here one of the wheels can be
seen in detail, the spokes filled with
exquisite decorative carving.

36. **Chenakesvar temple, Belur.** 12th century. The
architectural style of Mysore was created by the Hoysala
dynasty. The temples are based on elaborate geometric
ground-plans of which the star form is the most original. They
have flat roofs, perhaps unfinished, or perhaps deliberately left
bare. The walls are covered with sculpture, which, although
prolific, are really only ornamental.

37. **The story of the Jain monk, Kalaka,**
(Kalakacharyakathā). Gujarāt miniature. 14th–15th
centuries. 4¼ × 2⅜ in. (11 × 7 cm.). Musée Guimet, Paris.
While Jain themes are illustrated in the miniatures of Gujarāt,
few references to that religion are to be found in sculpture.
These miniatures bear little sign of Mughal influence; they
display affinities, rather, with Persian and Chinese painting
deriving directly from the first Muslim settlements in India.

38 (opposite). **Vishnu.** Mysore style. 13th century. Basalt. h. 5 ft.
(150 cm.). Musée Guimet, Paris. The god Vishnu, 'the sun
which traverses space', is represented in Vedic religious art in
innumerable different ways, and his cult acquired
correspondingly diverse features. He is represented here as a
young god with two pairs of arms, bearing in his hands a shell,
a sun-disk, and a club.

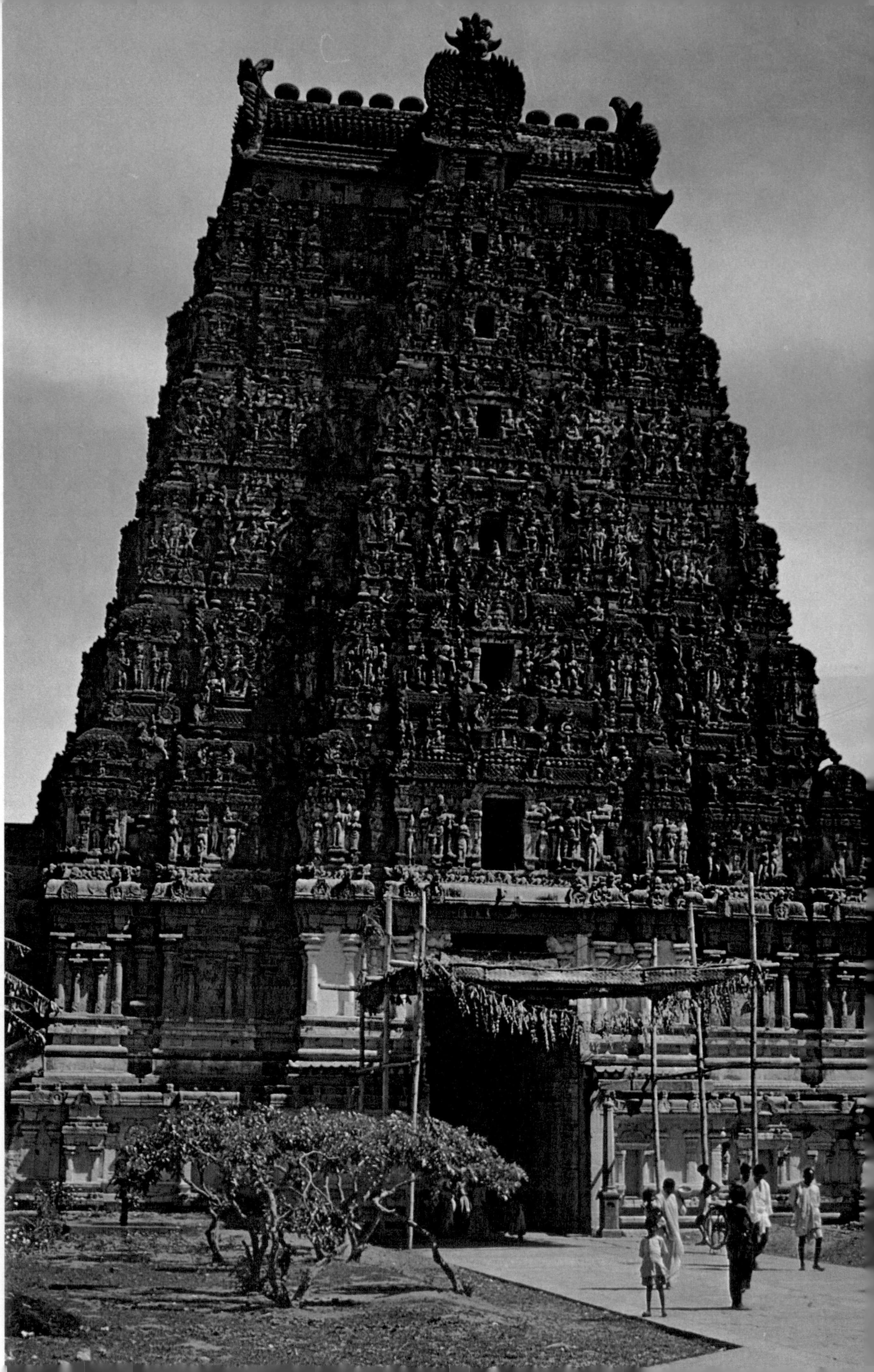

large pillared hall *(mandapa)*, which often has a transept the arms of which were sometimes used as side chapels. Opposite the entrance, the sanctuary vestibule *(antarāla)* gradually narrows until it reaches the cella *(garbha griha)*, which remained small and square in plan. There is not always an ambulatory. These parts are encased in thick masonry, which, from the outside, forms a cross of Lorraine.

An increasing number of foliated cusps mask this general outline. They disguise the angles of the transepts and give each block a circular appearance (as at the temple of Sūrya at Modhera, for example) or a star-shape (as in the **36** temples of Mysore). The main mass of the sanctuary and its subsidiary buildings are constructed of durable materials. With one type, however, separate chapels are placed at the **43** four corners of the main building (as at Kandāriya and Vishvanātha of Khajurāho). This group comprises a *pancha yatana* (five sanctuaries).

Architectural treatises have classified the temples in different ways. Some list them according to region, others to form. The first classification distinguishes three main groups: *nagara* (the provinces of northern India, comprising a region between the Himalayas and the Vindhya mountains), *vesara* (central India, stretching from the Vindhya to the river Kistna) and *dravida* (south India, situated between the Kistna and Cape Comorin). This classification has the disadvantage of restricting each type of temple to over-rigid geographical boundaries and is moreover contradicted by the facts; it may indicate no more than the origin of the different types and not their later distribution. It would seem preferable therefore to confine ourselves to the forms of the temples themselves, while referring to the texts when necessary.

The temple with pyramidal roof derives from Post-**19** Gupta sanctuaries such as those of Māmallapuram or Ellūrā. It consists of a square body whose outer walls are decorated with pilasters; its pyramidal roof is stepped inwards in imitation of a storeyed building, with miniature buildings placed around each exterior level. It is surmounted by a dome-shaped monolithic block. The miniature buildings, arranged regularly in decreasing scale one above another, echo in a simplified form the standard buildings with their connected pillars and their roofs pierced by false windows that are generally known by the Tamil term, *kudu*. Up to about the 11th century, each 'storey' or stage comprised three or four of these miniature buildings, square at the corners, rectangular in the middle. A dramatic development took place around the year 1000, when this type was enlarged to form a high multi-staged pyramid,

39 (opposite). **Gopuram of the Srīrangām temple.** South-East India. 15th century. This type of building, which is found in medieval southern India, is a development of the square-plan structure with barrel vault, a development based on the elaboration of the individual elements. Just as the ribbed dome surmounts the pyramidal roof, so here the barrel vault itself is raised to the top of the towering pyramid, no longer serving as a vault but as a cresting to the roof.

43. **Kandāriya Mahādeo, Khajurāho.** Beginning of the 11th century. This temple is one of the finest examples of curvilinear building construction. In its plan it observes the ritual exigences of Brahmanism and the majesty of medieval architecture. The outer walls of the cella and vestibule are covered with extremely fine sculpture carved in such high relief that it is almost free-standing.

the finest example of which is to be found in the great sanctuary *(vimāna)* at Tanjore. The almost continuous line **30** of thirteen diminishing storeys gives this sanctuary an emphatically pyramidal outline and enormous height (88 feet). The central kudu now has a purely decorative function, providing a pediment which breaks the monotony of the decoration of the pyramid.

On this basic principle, every region of India was to elaborate endlessly. The most remarkable are those of the south-east, which generally consist of sanctuaries with monumental gateways *(gopura)* covered by barrel-vaults. The gopuram is basically of the same form as the temple **29** with pyramidal roof. Rectangular in plan, its huge roof is crowned by a head-stone carved into the shape of a barrel-vault. Its very ancient origin is easily recognisable in the city gates depicted on the reliefs of the 2nd or 1st century BC. But according to the laws of Indian architectural development, the bold multiplication of the 'storeys' of the roof between the body of the building and the barrel-vault raises the latter to a great height and culminates in the monumental gopura that are among the most original

39,40 creations of south India. The vault that leads to the centre of the whole roof is constructed by corbelling. It is surmounted by storeys that can be reached by internal staircases and are lit by a vertical line of bow-windows placed at the centre of each side and diminishing in size towards the summit. The ribbed vault at the top is decorated with innumerable pinnacles, and with a great horseshoe-shaped gable at each end. The huge roof, often concave in profile, is punctuated by a broad foliated cusp projecting from each side and its structure is almost obscured by the quantity of carved detail. One of the finest is the eastern gopuram of the temple of Siva at Chidambaram which according to a lapidary inscription dates from the 13th century.

The type of sanctuary with a square ground-plan but a curvilinear roof also seems to appear about the 6th and 7th centuries. It may have been brought about by the use of brick; its storeyed roof gradually curves towards the summit and its angles are softened by the addition of spherical features, which look like ribbed cushions, known in Indian architecture as *amalaka*. This type of roof is called a *sikhara*. Its prototype seems to have been the temple of **31** Lakshmana at Sīrpūr, but there are numerous examples from the 7th and 8th centuries. In about the middle of the **42** 8th century, a new development occurs. The roof is composed of tiers that are much closer together than in the pyramidal type, giving the whole building a ribbed look that became more pronounced as time went on; at the corners, placed vertically one above the other, are kudu alternating with ribbed cushions (āmalaka). This superimposition forms a kind of broad beading that softens the corners and which has continued in use until the modern period. A vertical projection stands out on each side; it is decorated at the base with a large kudu that serves as a decorative pediment. The sikhara, curving inwards towards the summit, tends to adopt a tall, ogival shape. The roof becomes higher and culminates in a large āmalaka. Then everything becomes systematic: the kudu form a kind of decorative lattice and the general outline becomes particularly slender (as in the Parsvanātha of Kharjurāho, for example).

In about the 10th century, a second type emerges and it, too, gave rise to numerous variations. Small sikara *(anga-sikhara)*, corresponding to the miniature buildings on the pyramidal roofs, appear. They are placed one above the other, from the base to the summit of the roof, between the projections of each side and the cushions at the corners, as **25** at the Lingarāj at Bhuvanesvar, whose sikhara reaches to a height of 180 feet. Alternatively, the anga-sikhara are **43** placed in regular rows between the projections of each side; or, again, usually fairly large, they are placed on the middle band formed by the projection of each side of the roof and are arranged symmetrically between the projections and the beading at the corners. This type, at first rather heavy, culminates, as in the temple of Lakshmana at Khajurāho, in the magnificent flow of the curved lines of the roof.

The two main architectural types, the temple with a

44. **The Mandapa at Srīrangām.** 15th–16th centuries. During the Gupta period, the mandapa was simply a columned portico. Here, however, it has become a building in its own right, with numerous pillars loaded with sculptural decoration. The rearing horses are characteristic of the Dravidian style of Vijayanagar.

pyramidal roof and the temple with a curvilinear roof, become the main components in the composition of vast architectural complexes—the Brahmanic temples now become veritable religious cities contained within circular **40** walls. They contain several thousand inhabitants and accommodate large numbers of pilgrims. Among the permanent residents are the priests who serve the chapels and sanctuary, the temple servants, whose innumerable duties are listed in the foundation charters, the craftsmen working within the walls, the sacred dancers, whose function is the entertainment of the god, the musicians appointed to mark the hours and add to the celebration of festivals and ceremonies, and the swarming mass of beggars and tradesmen selling garlands of flowers and all kinds of votive offerings and holy relics. These architectural complexes, many of which are still in use, are astonishing accumulations of different buildings arranged in successive courtyards, in many different ways, each temple possessing its own character. The only constant factors are the internal composition of the central mass and the presence of an independent mandapa not far from the eastern gate of the outer wall. In many regions, particularly in the south, building still goes on and still follows the traditional patterns, though with an increasingly lifeless line and a debasement of form.

SCULPTURE

Sculpture has now become more than ever an integral part of architecture. The sanctuary walls are peopled by an

45 (left). **Jagadamba Devi, Khajurāho.**
Details of the decoration. 11th century.
The temple of Jagadamba Devi is a
framework to support a multitude of
sculpted figures. With their various
attributes, gestures and attitudes, these
people lend to the walls of the temple a
secret, throbbing life, exposed to or
hidden from view by the play of light and
shade.

46 (below left). **Heavenly couple from
Khajurāho.** *c.* 11th century. Sandstone.
h. 25 in. (65 cm.). Archaeological
Museum, Khajurāho. This is one of many
pairs of divinities which cover the walls of
temples, in which the life of the gods,
made in the likeness of men, is celebrated.
The tender relationship between the two
figures is suggested with wonderful
subtlety, and the rhythm, balance and
perfect proportions are astonishing.

astonishing mass of figures, statues of gods executed almost
entirely in the round, with only a small part of the back
touching the wall. The Indian sculptors of the medieval
period excelled in this technique. The temples of Khajurāho, Bhuvanesvar and Konārak (11th–13th centuries) *45, 46, 47*
are covered with sculptural groups of an exceptionally fine
quality, sometimes of average size, sometimes quite small;
they are delightfully arranged and their gestures, never
once repeated, bring the temple walls to life. They are the
swan song of Indian sculpture and their rather stylised,
exaggerated forms include the arabesques of the tribhanga
and the languid attitudes so dear to the earlier periods. The
stylisation is apparent in the facial features, in the full nose, *45*
the huge eyes sloping upwards towards the temples, the
sensual lips and an expression that is at once intense and
yet immobile. One sees vast numbers of loving couples and *46*
erotic groups. The former, known as *mithuna*, had been part
of the Indian artistic repertoire since the 1st century AD.
According to the texts that mention them, they seem to
have been symbols of good fortune. The erotic groups are
treated with a nobility which excludes any idea of coarse-
ness. Prudery was quite unknown to Indian artists, who
had no conception of 'the sins of the flesh' with which
Western civilisations were so preoccupied particularly in
the 19th century. For them, as for all Indians, the act of
love was part of Nature and therefore nothing to be
ashamed of. It was regarded as essentially symbolic of the
mystical union of the soul with the divine, and in the art of
Orissā and Bundelkhand it became a natural expression of
great beauty.

The sculpture of the southern temples is not of such a
high quality. Many of them are signed, and the best sculp- *31, 32*
tures are the bronze figures made by the *cire perdue* method. *48, 49, 33*
Sacred images, they conform to a fairly rigid iconography.
They nevertheless have great aesthetic quality and are

47. **Figure of a divinity, Konārak.** 13th century. This is one of many figures of gods and goddesses which cover the walls of the Orissā temples. The Sūrya temple at Konārak is particularly famous for its sculpture. On the terraces of the roof, punctuating the lines of the cornices, are monumental figures of female musicians and dancers. Intended to be seen at a great distance, they have a majesty beauty.

remarkable for their purity of form and sense of balance and movement.

With the Muslim invasions of the 14th and 15th centuries, a decline occurs in both north and south. Works of art seem to be executed in a lifeless way; the flame has vanished. But the custom of decorating the walls and even the ceilings with a multitude of statues continued. The structure of the gopura of south India almost disappears beneath the mass of carved decoration and, despite their rather poor quality, the effect created by this accumulation of detail makes the whole exterior throb with life. This is the baroque carried to the ultimate extreme, but it shows Indian architectural sculpture in its quintessential role—the temple is truly the support of the celestial world, and its very structure is a pulsating proof of this.

Whereas the art of relief no longer enjoyed the favour it had had in past centuries, mural painting continued to decorate temples and palaces, but it had lost most of the qualities that had brought it to its height during the previous period. It preserved a certain vigour but had become mechanical and there is a poverty of composition, an increasing stylisation in the figures, a simplification in the use of colour and a general naivety of conception. The frescoes of the 10th and 11th centuries at the Kailāsanāth of Ellūrā are marked by a peculiar stylisation of the faces: in a face seen in three-quarter view the nose, which is fairly pointed, is in profile, the eyes bulge, the eye behind the nose being particularly staring. This is a convention that is to be found again in the miniatures of Gujarāt. The frescoes of the *vimāna* at Tanjore (11th century) display quite a spontaneous sense of rhythm and supple, sensitive brush-strokes.

48. **Matrikā.** Dravidian style. 10th–11th centuries. Basalt. 43¾ in. (111 cm.). Musée Guimet, Paris. The iconography of the female form constitutes a kind of complement to the treatment of the male divinities (compare figure 49). The Seven Mothers (matrikā) illustrate this difference perfectly. Each of the seven embodies a different female power, from the most imposing to the most gruesome.

49. **Headless figure of Vishnu.** *c.* 11th century. Sandstone. h. 37⅜ in. (95 cm.). Musée Guimet, Paris. Chola sculpture continues the tradition of the Pallava. Restraint, elegance and simplicity are the characteristics of this dignified art.

Muslim Art

THE MUSLIM CONQUEST

The Muslim invasions interrupted with dramatic suddenness the cultural development of many Indian states. Islam's conquering armies arrived in the Punjāb as early as 775 and gradually reached each of the states in turn. In 1019, Kanauj was sacked by the Turk Mahmud of Ghazni; in 1021, the whole of the Punjāb passed into the hands of the Ghaznavids; and whereas, in 1199, Bihār and Bengal were incorporated into the Afghan kingdom of Ghor, the kingdoms of Banāras and Bundelkhand were included in the Sultanate of Delhi. Kāthiāwād and Gujarāt resisted longer and succumbed only in 1297. The states of the south also saw their dynasties fall beneath the attacks of the Muslims: Mahārāstra was annexed to the Sultanate of Delhi in 1317–18. The Pandyas were wiped out in 1310. Only the dynasty of Vijayanagar, which had succeeded the Hoysala in Mysore in about 1327, resisted until as late as 1565, when the battle of Talikota gave the Mughals effective power.

The Muslim advance brought with it political and religious re-organisation. At the beginning of the 13th century, Muhammad of Ghor founded the powerful Sultanate of Delhi which extended its sovereignty over several states of the south. In the 14th century, however, the Sultanate began to break up into ten or so local dynasties, until, in 1527, it was conquered by the Turk Babur, a descendant of Timur. Babur now founded the Mughal empire. His grandson Akbar (1556–1605) extended his conquests to northern and part of central India. But Akbar was not only a conqueror; he was also a great administrator, and during his reign the arts enjoyed one of their richest and most refined periods. He proved himself to be liberal and tolerant towards Hinduism. He tried to establish officially a kind of higher synthesis and protected the development of an eclectic theism. Akbar's son, Jahāngīr (1607–27), and grandson, Shāh Jahān (1627–58), were equally enthusiastic protectors of the arts. But the fierce iconoclasm of Shāh Jahān's second son, Aurangzeb (1659–1707), had grave consequences for the development of Mughal art and its decline can be dated from this time.

Developing the style they had created in Persia, the Muslims provided India with a large number of magnificent buildings, both religious and civil: mosques, tombs, citadels, palaces and monumental gateways. They varied the basic forms with great skill and each region of India developed a style of its own. The Kuwwat al–Islam and Jama'at Kana mosques and Kutb Manar minarets built in Delhi in the 13th and 14th centuries were obviously of Persian inspiration. But in Sind, Gujarāt and Kathiāwād, a style was created that can really be called Indo-Islamic, for the mosques were built with materials taken from the Hindu and Jain temples that had been partly destroyed during the Muslim iconoclastic period. In this way, the principal components of the Hindu temples—pillars and corbelled domes enclosed in thick walls of masonry—were adopted. On the outside, these buildings followed Islamic forms, while preserving within a marked Indian character.

The Mughal style was derived from the purest Islamic forms. Northern India, particularly Agra, Delhi and Lahore, was covered with buildings that were remarkable both for their size and for the richness of their materials. The most famous is the Tāj Mahāl at Agra, the mausoleum of the wife of Shāh Jahān. The architecture has an elegance and a simplicity quite foreign to Indian art proper. A dazzling surface decoration is the only indulgence, but in no way does it detract from the purity of the lines. The decoration of the buildings erected during the reign of Akbar (Sikandra, Fatehpur Sikri) is obviously the work of Indians. The south, too, developed a more or less Indianised style. The best-known buildings are to be found in Gulbarga (14th century), Golconda and Bijapur (16th–17th centuries); they are particularly notable for their bulbous, ribbed domes, which are among the largest in the world.

THE MINOR ARTS

Stone and ceramic mosaic, which first appeared in the 13th century, were used for the decoration of buildings and for floors during the Mughal period. Ceramic tile decoration which, sometimes covered surfaces of enormous size, is often very beautiful and represents animals, flowers and geometrical patterns in several colours.

On the whole, the Mughals had a favourable effect on craft techniques, though ancient Indian art had already shown great mastery of goldsmith's work, woodwork and other minor arts. Indeed, metalwork, which had been practised from early times in India, underwent a real revival in the 16th century. Iron and steel were reserved for weapons, some of which are particularly elaborate in design, gold and silver for vessels and jewellery. Usually one metal would be inlaid with another—tonal contrasts being particularly sought after. Damascening was achieved by several methods, the simplest of which consisted of making fine scratches on the surface of the basic metal and filling these with gold or silver thread, which was then carefully hammered. The metal could also be sculpted or chased. Jewellery, which was more varied than in the past, used a wide range of techniques, materials and forms.

The production of glass, which had also been brought from Persia, was of fine quality, and goblets and bowls of exquisite delicacy were carved out of rock crystal. Jade was also much used: sword hilts and jewels were often made of jade inlaid with precious stones set in gold.

Woodwork is one of the oldest arts in India, but during the Mughal period inlay and marquetry were used with great effect. Mother-of-pearl on ebony was particularly favoured; it was cut out into small pieces according to the pattern required and each piece was fixed on to the wood with tiny pins. Again of Persian origin, enamelling was completely revived under the Mughals, and some dazzling results were achieved. The finest enamels date from the 16th–18th centuries and are executed in *champlevé* on gold or silver.

50. **Ankusha, or elephant hook.** 17th century. Gilt bronze
with enamel inlay. h. 26¾ in. (68 cm.). Musée Guimet, Paris.
Elephant hooks were used by the mahouts, or elephant keepers,
from time immemorial. They can be seen, for example on the
reliefs at Sāñchī. This one is clearly a ceremonial object, not
intended for practical use. The dexterity of the Indian metal-
worker is seen at its most accomplished.

BOOK ILLUSTRATION

It was in the field of book and manuscript illustration that the Mughal occupation made its greatest contribution to the arts of India. This kind of illustration had already existed in India from an early date, although no ancient examples have survived. Until the appearance of paper, probably introduced into India from Iran about the 14th century, paint was applied to cloth, wooden panels or palm-leaves. The earliest miniatures to which precise dates can be given are no older than the 11th and 12th centuries. They belong to the school of Bengal and were obviously influenced by traditions prior to those of Islam or were only slightly affected by it. The subject-matter is Buddhist. The colours are particularly rich, red often being used as a background. The compositions are varied and although naive in spirit are executed with great skill. Landscapes are reduced to a few elements, and the stylisation—especially of the trees—is reminiscent of the ancient reliefs of Bhārhut or Sāñchī. In Nepal, there also existed a school of Buddhist painting, but one more conservative than that of Bengal; only traditional subject-matter was used, and that in an unoriginal way, with strict attention to iconography.

37 The school of Gujarāt (12th–17th centuries), which derived its themes from Jain legends, is somewhat crude in execution but has a personality all its own. With its red or blue backgrounds, its increasing use of gold and stylisation of the faces that derives directly from the Ellūrā frescoes (8th–12th centuries), it is very close to mural painting and in both style and technique serves as a transition between this type of painting and the miniature. (Much of the technique of fresco-painting was still employed, although it was quite irrelevant for the execution of a miniature.) Produced from the late 14th to the 17th centuries, first on palm leaves, then on paper, the Gujarāti miniatures reflect the various influences to which Gujarāt was subjected through its position on trade routes and on the path of invading armies. This region received influences from Chinese Turkestan and Afghanistan and was one of the first to be occupied by the Muslims. These foreign influences merged with the Indian tradition to give these miniatures a curious appearance: the landscapes and animals betray Persian and Chinese influences, the architecture and furniture are of local inspiration, Muslim figures are dressed in their national costumes and their faces are shown full-face, whereas the Jain monks, with faces shown in half-profile, wear their robes, with the right shoulder left bare. The monks have the stylised features that are to be seen in the Ellūrā frescoes (10th–11th century) and which were later used in the puppets of the shadow theatre.

The introduction of paper brought a great increase in the painting of small pictures to illustrate books for the libraries of the emperors and princes, and the influence of the Mughal emperors was to be strongest in the field of illustration. They brought famous Persian painters to their court to depict the great deeds of their heroes, the Mughal conquests and scenes of pageantry, festivals or court ceremonial—in other words, anything that would celebrate the power and wealth of the emperors. The Indianisation of the Iranian style, however, can be seen to have taken place very quickly for Indian artists gradually joined the palace studios and the collaboration of the artists of the two countries meant that their respective ideas and traditions merged. The Mughal style was, after all, 46 rather conventional. The figures were shown in profile or semi-profile, hardly ever full-face, but occasionally from behind. The Persian use of the landscape persisted even after the European influence had introduced chiaroscuro and a treatment of trees and landscapes copied from Western styles of the 17th and 18th centuries. Contrary to usual Indian practice, the Mughal miniatures are often signed.

One miniature was not usually the work of a single artist: the composition was conceived and drawn by a master and the colours applied by other members of the studio, one of whom executed the costumes, another the faces and a third the details of jewellery, weapons and other accessories. A single model was often used for several copies. They were executed from the sketch kept by the master draughtsman and on which the instructions for the colours were noted. These sketches were very highly prized and were carefully preserved by their creators who handed them down to their descendants as family heirlooms.

The Mughal school had a strong influence on all the many regional schools that flourished in the princes' courts in Rājputāna, Bengal and the Deccan. These schools do 50 not always have the refinement and technical skill of the imperial school, but drawing their inspiration from Indian traditions—religious, mythical and popular—they have greater spontaneity, sometimes bolder stylisation and they revive the narrative and pictorial sense that had been the glory of the relief sculptors of the ancient schools. The Rājput school split up into innumerable sub-groups, which were attached to two main groups: the Rājput miniatures known as Rājasthānī, and the miniatures executed 49 in the Himalaya region known as Pahārī, or 'of the moun- 48 tains'. Most of them are anonymous. The Rājput painters belonged to the guild of artisans and could paint murals for buildings as well as miniatures. Belonging as they did to a hereditary profession, they formed what was almost a caste and lived with their families. Design was the dominant element in their work, in which a taste for the picturesque was given free reign. But the general style, the costumes and innumerable other details reveal a close connection with the Mughal school.

A very special category of miniatures belongs to the Rājput school: *rāgamāla*, or music painting. This was an attempt to translate a poetic theme into pictorial terms according to a melodic mode. It is like music seen through poetry—a very Indian way of conceiving a total art.

RELATIONS WITH EUROPE
DECLINE AND RECIPROCAL INFLUENCES

It was during the period of Mughal domination that the European penetration of India, begun by the Portuguese in the 15th century, became more active. The descendants of Aurangzeb, exhausted by internecine struggles, were unable to sustain the Mughal domination and the European powers, in their efforts to re-establish throughout India an order that would benefit their trade, took firm root on the sub-continent. First, they established trading centres. These were soon followed by missionaries whose influence on Indian artists was strong and on the whole felicitous. Western influence was transmitted through copies of engravings, either Bibical or secular, and through the introduction into the Mughal miniature of Western perspective, relief and chiaroscuro imitated from the Italian, Dutch and French schools. The first copies were ordered from the court painters by the Emperor Akbar himself, to whom the Jesuits had given an illustrated Bible. From the 16th century, the Mughal miniaturists **47** often reproduced European engravings, paintings and enamels, applying themselves with praiseworthy effort to the forms and colours of a style so foreign to their own; sometimes they were content to place among the Indian and Muslim figures of their compositions, foreigners whose physique and dress betray their Western origin.

If European engraving influenced the Indian miniature in this way, reciprocally, the direct relations between India and Holland in the 17th century enabled large numbers of Indian works of art, particularly miniatures, to reach Holland. Rembrandt himself was sufficiently tempted by their novelty to make a few copies of miniatures, which are now in several European museums. One painter, Willem Schellinks, a member of Rembrandt's circle, who had many opportunities of seeing Indian miniatures, painted a curious picture, now in the Musée Guimet, Paris, which shows a kind of spectacle taking place on the stage of a theatre. Perhaps the painter wished to depict a masque, of the kind so popular in the 17th century. In doing so, he abandons himself to the exoticism of his period, but in the best sense, since he remains very faithful to his subject-matter even in the smallest details. Because of the extreme precision of the work, one can easily recognise the principle characters: Akbar, Jahangir, Shāh Jahān and his four sons. This identification is confirmed by an inscription in a scroll held by one of the minor figures in the bottom left-hand corner of the picture. Another, very similar work by the same painter has been acquired by the Victoria and Albert Museum.

Later, in the 19th century, painters of the Sīkh school, in the Punjāb, painted portraits of English and Dutch people.

Unfortunately, from the end of the 18th century, Indian painting fell into a decline and the miniaturists of the 19th century, not knowing how to distinguish the value of the European models they encountered, copied poor and superficial works in a slavish and unintelligent way. At the end of the 19th century, however, a reaction set in and an attempt was made to regenerate Indian art by freeing it from the influence of European art and returning to the great lessons of the past. A group of painters, aided by a number of Europeans, notably E. B. Havell, director of the Government School in Calcutta, tried to improve the standard of painting, which had then declined to the stage of providing popular images for pilgrimages. It needed all the conviction and enthusiasm of this movement, which originated in Bengal, to undertake the rehabilitation of Indian art in the eyes of the intellectual elite of its own country. The Tagore family played a leading part in this movement, particularly Abanindranath, the nephew of the poet, who published studies and commentaries of ancient treatises and was himself a painter, paying special attention to problems of technique. He recommended the study of ancient Indian art and a return to traditional subjects. He succeeded in creating a current of interest, and gradually progress became more apparent; a new style was born that tended to combine the technical experience of Europe and the traditional inspiration of India. Rabindranath Tagore himself took up painting at the age of sixty, producing works of great interest and astonishing modernity.

In the course of the 16th–19th centuries, in the fields of architecture and the minor arts, hybrid works were to be found in the European trading centres: and Indo-Portuguese style on the west coast, particularly at Goa; a Louis XV style at Pondicherry and other French centres; an Indo-Dutch style in the same region. Finally, a large number of objects were produced in India intended for export to Europe.

Indianism, the study of the civilisation and art of India, was born in Europe at the end of the 18th century with the foundation at Calcutta by Sir William Jones, of the Asian Society of Bengal in 1784. In 1822, the *Société asiatique de Paris* was founded and in 1862, under the direction of Sir Alexander Cunningham, the Archaeological Service of India, whose important work continued for many years until it was finally handed over to Indian archaeologists.

(Continued on page 81)

40. **The Great Temple of Madura:**
gopuram and cloister. 17th century.
The great Dravidian temple complexes,
such as Madura, consist basically of a
vast walled enclosure pierced at the four
cardinal points by monumental gateways
(gopura), and with a sanctuary at the
centre. This quadrilateral area contains
innumerable buildings arranged
apparently with no regard for order,
together with cloisters and tanks or
basins for the Hindu ritual ablution.
At the centre is an immense courtyard,
designed to hold the crowds which
gathered to see religious processions. .
It is truly a city in itself with a maze of
courts and colonnades. In this picture
the scale of the gopura which towered
over the inner city can be appreciated.

41, 42. **Carved wooden panels from processional chariots.** 17th century. Teak. h. 2 ft. 7 in. (80 cm.). Musée Guimet, Paris. The Indian craftsmen of the 17th century produced fine sculpture not only in stone and bronze, but also in wood. These panels originally formed part of the decoration of processional chariots. The god Vishnu, the second member of the Hindu trinity, was often depicted in one of the series of his incarnations *(avatara)*. There are ten main forms in which he is represented during his 'descents' to earth. On the left he is shown as Krishna, the shepherd-god, who gave birth

to a mystique based on 'trusting worship'. On the right Vishnu is shown in animal form as the boar Varahā, immersed in water in order to retrieve the flooded land.

43 (opposite). **Mughal sword hilt in the shape of a horse's head.** 17th century. Jade. l. 16½ in. (42 cm.). Musée Guimet, Paris. This magnificent jade sword hilt is encrusted with precious stones and inlaid with gold. It is typical of the Mughal style, and such pieces are often illustrated in the miniatures of the period.

44. Akbar's column, Fatehpur Sikri. Rising from the centre of the Diwan-i-Khas, the private audience chamber, this pillar supports a circular platform, which is linked to the corners of the building by four bridges. This enabled the Emperor Akbar to reach the platform without being seen, so that he could listen to the discussions between the learned religious leaders, scholars and missionaries who gathered in this chamber. The thirty-six moulded stalactite brackets, which form the capital, and the pierced balconies are of great delicacy.

45. General view of Fatehpur Sikri. 16th century. Founded by the Emperor Akbar, Fatehpur Sikri, the 'city of victory', is situated to the south-west of Agra and was completed in a very short space of time. It comprises numerous buildings, palaces and mosques, and is bounded on three sides by a wall and on the fourth by an artificial lake. The city was inhabited only from 1570 to 1585, after which it was abandoned because of a lack of water. It has remained intact to this day. On the left can be seen the Diwan-i-Khas (see plate 44), built of pink sandstone.

77

46. **The Emperor Babur with Bedi Az-Zamān Mirzā.**
Mughal miniature. End of 16th – beginning of the 17th century.
9 × 5½ in. (23 × 14 cm.). Musée Guimet, Paris. The
miniatures of Mughal India give one a vivid impression of
ceremonial at the courts of the Emperors. Not only the
architecture, but costume and domestic objects, too, are
minutely observed.

47. **Shepherds and their flocks.** Mughal copy of a
European painting. 10⅝ × 7⅞ in. (27 × 20 cm.). Musée
Guimet, Paris. Copies of European works of art by Mughal
artists are fascinating both for their careful imitation of the
European style, yet at the same time for their inability to
understand every detail. The 'Flemish' farmhouse has a
Mughal dome, and the faces of the shepherds are distinctly
Indian.

48 (left). **A Prince and his Favourite.** Miniature in the Pahārī style, school of Chambā. 18th century. 10⅝ × 7⅞ in. (27 × 20 cm.). Musée Guimet, Paris. Inspired by the Mughal court, local princes, whether allies of the Emperor or not, encouraged local schools of painting. While imitating the general style of the Imperial court, certain local differences were preserved, in colour schemes, in choice of subject-matter and in the treatment of motifs.

49 (below, left). **The Planet Saturn.** Rājasthānī miniature of the Bundi school. c. 1770. 10⅝ × 7½ in. (27 × 19 cm.). Musée Guimet, Paris. The Rājput school of painting remained faithful in subject-matter to Indian Brahmanic themes. But they adopted the Mughal interest in architecture and landscape, and abandoned line in favour of flat tones.

50 (below, right). **Couple in a garden.** Miniature of the Deccan school. c. 1750. (26 × 17 cm.). Musée Guimet, Paris. Persian influence is clearly visible here in the flowered border to the miniature, and in the decorative treatment of the yew-trees and flowering shrubs. The muted colours, characteristic of the local schools of southern India, give this painting a rather sombre feeling which is emphasised by the stiffness of the figures.

51. **Detail from a Burmese
manuscript.** 19th century. Musée
Guimet, Paris. This manuscript, which
is dated 1869, is closely allied to modern
Siamese and Cambodian styles in
painting. It shows the *Nimi Jataka*, one
of the principal earlier lives of the
Buddha. Nimi, the hero, journeys through
heaven and hell. Below, the souls in
torment are subjected to every
imaginable refinement of cruelty. Above,
the celestial hosts are entertained with
music and dance. At the top left, Nimi
can be seen in his chariot traversing the
spheres.

52. Angkor Wāt. First half of the 12th century. The temple of Angkor Wāt is the masterpiece of Khmer architecture. In the disposition of its parts it reflects the elements of the cosmos just as the Indian temples do. This relationship between the celestial and terrestrial planes emphasises the direct mystical link between god and man. The temple consists of a vast pyramid on three stages, supporting five towers linked by covered galleries, and surrounded by a moat. The masses are arranged in such a way as to give a wonderfully rhythmic balance to the whole ambitious complex.

53. Apsaras, or celestial dancer. Relief at Angkor Wāt. First half of the 12th century. One of the crowning glories of the temple of Angkor Wāt is the series of *apsaras* or *devatâ* which range along the walls of the different courts. The slim, youthful figures of these celestial dancers are placed at the base of the walls. Naked to the waist, they wear a strange kind of clinging skirt with flaring panels carefully carved with incised decoration.

Conclusion

THE GOVERNING LAWS OF THE INDIAN CHARACTER
Indian civilisation is founded upon three basic concepts:
the sacred, the universal, the ritualistic. Within its terms
of reference everything human can be related to the divine.
Art appears not as an aesthetic fact, but as a phenomenon
inseparable from the life that it tends to illustrate. It is an
image, perhaps even an emanation of the divine. Art
evolved in a religious 'climate' that has prevailed throughout history and which provided its essential qualities. It
obeys the established laws that are in perfect harmony with
the Indian character and to which India owes her real co-
hesion beneath all her paradoxes and contrasts.

The laws that govern the Indian character are basically
strength of tradition, a taste for rules and regulations and
a tendency to bring diversity into unity. The strength of
tradition has made India into a kind of religious museum;
changes come very gradually, by gradual absorption
rather than metamorphosis. The taste for regulation ex-
tends to almost every field of Indian life. It is this, among
other things, that has brought about the caste system, which
maintains the social structure in a rigid religious strait-
jacket, and the creation of a vocabulary of gestures, which
apply equally to religious ritual, the theatre and the plastic
arts. It is this that explains the peculiarly Indian concept
of the cosmos and the identification of the ideal order of the
divine and human worlds. Between these two worlds,
everything is based upon analogy and everything conforms
to a coherent scheme in which universal elements correspond to and are parallel with elements in the social order.
This identification of the human and divine enables man
to exert his influence upon the gods: the technique of
Brahmanic sacrifices is worked out to this end, as are all
the Indian ritual techniques, including those on which the
creation of works of art are based. The tendency to bring
diversity into unity is a focal metaphysical concept despite
the contradictions of innumerable sects and local beliefs,
and a slow but steady evolution has led India from apparently the most elaborate polytheism to a mystical pantheism. Very different local divinities gradually took on
the characteristics and names of great gods, and were then
incorporated in the official pantheon, acquiring some of
the characteristics of the great god that had absorbed them.

In the artistic field, these laws determined a very slow
evolution. Being almost self-sufficient, the effects of foreign
influences were minimal, and were invariably absorbed or
distorted to become utterly Indian. Canonical texts
(sastra) set down aesthetic and iconographical rules, and
artists were also guided by a whole sculptural vocabulary
composed of 'speaking' gestures (mudrā or hasta). These
were minutely classified according to subject, colour, line
and a system of comparisons or parallel images or associa-
tions of ideas, based more on the spirit of the subject than
its external qualities. In this way, an artist could create a
work that conformed exactly to the aesthetic code.

For the Indians, sculpture is inseparable from other techniques linked to ritualism and they reject the idea of separate fields which we regard as distinct. Although India
lays down a hierarchy of the arts, according pre-eminence
to music, it nevertheless affirms the existence of a total art
and the impossibility of practising one without knowledge
of the others. This interdependence of one art form upon
another can always be recognised: thus the reliefs and
paintings seem to be the faithful reproduction of theatrical
scenes, that is, divine scenes mimed by human beings, with
all their gestures, attitudes and groupings. In turn, theatrical scenes reproduce a repertoire similar to that of sculpture
with all the subtlety of its expressions.

It is also to this dual impulse to diversify the One and to
canalise the Many towards the One that some of the iconographical peculiarities created in India must be ascribed.
Seeking solutions to the plastic representation of simultaneous actions, of the union of divine opposites and equi-
valences, artists proceeded in the true Indian way, that is,
by arranging natural elements according to an intellectual
idea. They did not hesitate to indicate the omnipresence
of a god by giving him several faces. Similarly, to affirm his
omnipotence, he was given several pairs of arms. The union
of opposites is expressed very simply by a character being
divided vertically into two halves and being given a double
name: thus Harihara unites Siva and Vishnu and Ardhanari represents Siva and his female energy (sakti).

The Indian artist worked according to a mental prototype, a transposition of reality, an aspect of the thing re-
created and rethought. He did not reproduce the object
seen, but the object known. The aim of art was to manifest
and thus participate in the 'play' of nature whose forms it
exalted and whose effects it suggested. It reproduced un-
seen, but known objects, basing these upon real forms; the
artist's personal feelings were never expressed. It is neither
naturalistic, idealistic nor subjective art.

The canons which art had to obey did not paralyse the
artists, however, but provided them with a grammar from
which they could draw an inexhaustible supply of modes of
expression. Their imaginations were free to create endless
variations on a few main themes; in this way, no one work
was ever identical with another. A balance was maintained
between creative thought and the norms defined by the
treatises. Encouraged by their mission of bringing the
divine down to the world of men, the Indian artists drew
inspiration from a mass of lively popular beliefs.

A collective activity created for the community, Indian
art reflects both religious life and that of society; it perpe-
tuates the ideal existence of past times, from which incom-
parable rhythm and beauty emanate.

Appendix

51. **Relief at Barabudur.** 11th century. There are nearly two thousand reliefs at Barabudur, covering the concentric walls of the galleries which culminate in the immense pedestal of the stūpa. Astonishingly consistent in style, the reliefs illustrate scenes from the life of Buddha and edifying Buddhist stories. Here the Buddha is shown bathing in the river Nairañjanā.

THE INFLUENCE OF INDIA IN SOUTH-EAST ASIA

Indian culture penetrated the countries of South-East Asia entirely by peaceful means. This was the result of a series of enterprises by traders, adventurers, scholars and monks. Operating from Indian settlements that had been founded in about the 1st century, these men brought the highly refined culture of India to peoples whose way of life was perfectly suited to Brahmanic and Buddhist teachings.

India's interest in these countries was originally based on the trade in gold and spices that was to be found in the South Seas. The use of the monsoon winds—from at least the beginning of the 1st century—the progressive regularisation of the sea-routes and the improvement in transportation made possible a considerable increase of trade in these distant seas. An immense trade route was established linking the main coastal regions and augmented in certain parts by transcontinental tracks or sometimes by a very active river navigation.

The Indian trading settlements were dotted along the coasts and served as ports for the principalities and kingdoms that sprang up around them. Intermarriage also played a considerable role in this Indian colonisation and, according to tradition, it was to one such union that was attributed the founding in the 1st century AD of one of the oldest kingdoms in the Indo-Chinese peninsula, known as Funan, which was situated in the lower valley of the Mekong. At Oc Eo, a trading centre used by foreign merchants has been discovered. Excavations carried out on this site have yielded, apart from objects of Western origin, an Antoninus Pius gold bracteate, cornelian intaglios with typically Roman subjects, a Sassanian cabochon, a great deal of gold jewellery of Indian origin, a fragment of a Chinese mirror and sculptures in wood and stone which represents a curious mixture of Indian and Chinese influences (and which as yet have received little attention).

Bronze Buddhas in the Amarāvatī style have been found in various countries of South-East Asia, in Thailand (Korat and Pong Tük), in Java (Jember), in Sumatra (Palembang) and even in Celebes (Sempaga); but the finest example comes from the east coast of Indo-China, at Dong-duong, in Champa. It is not known whether these works are from Amarāvatī itself or from Ceylon (where this style became very popular) or even whether they were made in the Indian settlements of South-East Asia.

Throughout this area Indianisation took the form of the adoption of Sanskrit as the official and sacred language, the introduction of the Indian religions of Brahmanism and Buddhism, with their myths, philosophical systems and traditions and the establishment of a political structure very close to that of ancient India.

When works of art in durable materials appear in these countries, they are already heavily influenced by Indian characteristics, as if these regions had had no previous art of their own. Nevertheless, it is impossible to know whether the Indian influence caused a radical change or whether it was superimposed upon a pre-existent basis. It seems likely, however, that an extraordinary impetus was given to the arts by the presence of the Indians in these countries.

Architecture, to begin with, bears the unmistakeable marks of Indian influence, in both form and decoration. It must be assumed that the first 'colonists' used local labour to erect sanctuaries in the taste and tradition of their own country. These contacts were to be maintained by travellers and monks in later times.

Indian influence was soon assimilated and formed a basis upon which local work was undertaken despite the increasing resurgence of native elements. It was to be renewed consistently through the centuries. Each of the South-East Asian cultures adapted the Indian forms according to its own particular character, for their art was not a slavish imitation, but genuinely creative. Thus true works of art were produced which possess undeniably original characteristics, while remaining within the Indian tradition.

The Khmer empire was formed between the 6th and 7th centuries, from the fusion of Funan (1st–6th centuries approximately) and of the kingdom of Chen-la further north. This was followed by the establishment of royal authority first in the region of the great lakes (end of the 6th–8th centuries), then in the so-called Angkorian region and finally at Angkor itself (beginning of the 9th–15th centuries).

The first of these developments was characterised by sanctuary-towers made of brick, with square (sometimes octagonal) ground-plans, single or in groups of five within an outer wall (Sambor Prei Kuk). These towers belong to Indian tradition; they have corbelled vaulting over a Brahmanic cella, a door flanked by a pair of round sandstone columns carved with naturalistic garlands and surmounted by a sandstone lintel whose decorative theme is also Indian—a flattened ogee form ornamented with medallions, garlands and pendants, being swallowed at each end by a sea monster (makara). The walls are decorated with reliefs carved in brick which is mounted on a stucco base. The statues of this period, whether Brahmanic or Buddhist, are very beautiful and sometimes of considerable height. At first, very Indian in feeling—they observe the canonical triple flexion (tribhanga)—they soon take on a more original character.

During the Angkor period, Khmer art developed an ever increasing originality, while retaining as its basis the pre-Angkor forms. Founded on a politico-religious conception, which was probably of Indian origin and which is to be found with variations throughout the other Indianised countries, the form of the temple-mountain attained its most perfect expression in Khmer territory. Its full flower-

52. **Sanctuary of Siva.** Temple of Lara Jongrang, Prambanan. *c.* 900. The vast complex of Lara Jongrang, near the village of Prambanan, was the last great temple to be built in central Java. It consists of three main sanctuaries dedicated respectively to Siva, Brāhma and Vishnu, and three minor ones dedicated to two particular forms of Siva with his mount, Nandin. A hundred and twenty-four miniature temples are placed around this central core, and the whole complex is enclosed by three walls forming a triple square. The side of the outermost wall measures 426 yards.

ing dates from the reign of Indravarman I (877–99), with the Bakong at Roluos, not far from Angkor, and is in keeping with a series of traditions in which the king is associated with the idea of the cosmic mountain, the centre of the world and the divine residence. It consists of a stone pyramid reached by a terrace of tall steps and, with each succeeding reign, it became larger until it reached its apotheosis in the famous temple of Angkor Wāt, the temple-mountain and mausoleum of King Sūryavarman II (1113–about 1150). Its splendid plan, the balance of its proportions, the elegance of its pillared cloisters and the beauty of its decoration make it one of the masterpieces of world architecture. The temple itself is surrounded on the inside by two concentric walls of which the inner one is decorated with reliefs illustrating with an admirable sense of composition and narrative rhythm the great mythological themes of Brahmanism, such as the theme of 'Heaven and Hell' and the triumphant march of the king at the head of his army.

Single-storey buildings, both royal and private, also added considerably to the splendour of the Khmer civilisation. One could cite as an example the delightful little

54

52

53

53. **Hanumant breaking the trees of Lankā.** Relief from
the Panataran temple. 14th century. This relief shows one of
the heroes of the *Ramayana*, the monkey Hanumant.
The figure is typical of eastern Javanese art, for, while the
subject-matter is Indian, the curving stylisation is inspired by
the puppets of the indigenous shadow theatre *(wayang)*.

54. **Harihara.** Phnom Da style. *c.* 6th century. Sandstone.
h. 5 ft. 8⅞ in. (175 cm.). Musée Guimet, Paris. This statue
represents two of the principal Brahmanic gods: Siva (on the
right) and Vishnu (left). This attempt at syncretism originated
in India, but was later popular in the Khmer territories.
Vishnu is identified by his cylindrical mitre and the wheel.
Siva has the Brahmanic chignon and a trident.

temple of Bantéai Srei (967), near Angkor, whose smallest
detail reveals a perfect knowledge of the iconographical
themes of India and great virtuosity in the decoration.

Sculpture in the round, whether in bronze or stone, follows in the wake of the decorators and sometimes even
precedes them. The work of the artists of Bantéai Srei is
followed by the Baphuon style (middle of the 11th century).
This new development is marked by a certain stylisation,
great simplicity, meticulous care in the execution of details
and the appearance of a physical type that is much more
clearly native than previously.

The last phase of Ankor architecture was dominated by
the personality of the Buddhist king, Jayavarman VII
(1181–1219). He built vast temples, including the Bayon
of Angkor, which was the culmination of the architectural
style of the Khmer kingdom and the last temple-mountain
to be built in the centre of the royal city. It is a splendid
work and a overwhelming success from the point of view
of its symbolism and its sculpture.

Its fifty-four towers are each adorned on all four sides
with the half-smiling face of Jayavarman VII, represented
as the Bodhisattva Lokesvara (Lord of the World). Gazing
out towards the four points of the compass these faces symbolise the omnipresence of both god and king. The idea of
a tower with faces is not, however, entirely original: it had
occurred in India, particularly at Gujarāt, but in a less well
defined form. The Bayon combines the symbolism of the
stūpa with the Hindu formula of the cosmic temple.

The sculpture of the reign of Jayavarman VII reveals an
often admirable gift for portraiture, for it was the custom
of the king and his dignitaries to have statues made in which

they were represented as gods.

Indonesia had continuous relations with India from the
first centuries of the Christian era, and Indian influence
played the same catalytic role as in the Khmer empire.
Indonesian history may be divided into two main phases.
The first stretches from the first centuries AD to about the
9th–10th centuries and encompasses part of the Malay
peninsula, Sumatra and the western and central parts of
Java. The second phase developed in eastern Java and in
Bali from about the 10th to the 16th centuries.

In central Java no monument seems to have been built
in durable materials before 732. But from their first appearance the sanctuaries are typically Indian: a cella over a
crypt preceded by a porch with a flight of steps and pyramidal storeyed roof. The architectural decoration is of
Indian origin: a monster's head *(kala)*, linked with two
makara. This type survived to the end of Javanese art, and
was used both by Buddhism and Brahmanism.

Few temples seem to have been built in the 8th century.
Three important groups date from the first half of the 9th
century: the famous Barabudur, with the Candi Mendut
and Candi Pawon, all Buddhist; the Siva temples of the
Dieng Plateau, of which eight are more or less intact; the
Candi Sewu composed of four groups around a central
cruciform sanctuary. During the second half of the 9th cen-
tury, a fourth group was built, that of Plaosan, in eastern
Sewu. Finally, about 900, the huge Brahmanic temple of
Lara Jongrang was built near the village of Prambanan.

The Barabudur temple is exceptional in its originality of
conception and the perfection of its decoration. It is a huge
five-storeyed pyramid built around a natural hill and con-

55. **Siva.** Binh Dinh style. 12th century. Sandstone. h. 5 ft. 5 in. (165 cm.). Musée Guimet, Paris. The Cham style of Binh Dinh betrays a certain decadence which became even more pronounced at the end of the period. This statue of Siva, which comes from Tours d'Argent possesses nevertheless an undeniable grandeur.

sists of a pseudo-hemispherical mass crowned with a central stūpa, surrounded by three concentric circles of smaller stūpa. In the middle of each side of the pyramid, flights of steps placed in the same axis pass under porticos decorated with kāla-makaras and lead to the upper storeys and the top platform. This is an architectural translation of an esoteric form (mandala) which is peculiar to Mahāyāna Buddhism. This building, with its thick-set shape, is not, in itself, an architectural success, but the reliefs with which it is decorated are exceptionally beautiful. They illustrate the main episodes in the last life of Buddha Sākyamuni, events in his 'previous lives' (jātaka) and the various edifying stories (avadāna) of Buddhist tradition. They reveal both the plastic qualities of the Indian-inspired Javanese style and fidelity to the traditions acquired. The well balanced grouping of the figures, their calm and harmonious attitudes, which are reminiscent of the Post-Gupta styles of India, the taste for detail and an assured stylistic sense give this art indisputable value. If these narrative series reflect the life of their times, then their lives must have been impregnated with Indian traditions, for innumerable details of dress, hair-styles and ornament, as well as the forms of everyday objects, betray an Indian origin.

The stone sculpture and small bronze statuary of this style follow the same rules: calm attitudes and dignified gestures, fleshy bodies and moderation in ornament.

The style of eastern Java derives from the previous one, but, as it develops, it takes on Javanese characteristics to an ever more marked degree. In architecture, in which brick is often used, the tower-sanctuary is composed in almost equal parts of a high base with mouldings, a main section with a door on each side and a pyramidal storeyed roof.

56. **Dancer.** Mi-son A.1. style. 10th century. Sandstone. h. 2 ft. 5⅛ in. (75 cm.). Musée Guimet, Paris. The Mi-son A.1. style represents the apogee of Cham sculpture. Figures like this dancer possess an elegance, an idealisation of the human form, smiling countenances and lively movement, which give them especial charm.

The kāla motif surmounting the doors becomes increasingly emphasised and projects in high relief. This development is also apparent in the simultaneous raising of the basement and the roof while the proportions of the cella remain unchanged. Huge terraces decorated with reliefs (Panataran) support the sanctuaries. The surrounding walls have high, narrow doors, surmounted by high, multi-staged pyramids.

The cult statues gradually stiffen into complete frontality and are backed on to a stele, the base of which is decorated with floral motifs and subsidiary figures. It is easy to recognise the influence of the Pāla-Sena style of Bengal. On the other hand, the small limestone or clay statuary retains undeniable plastic qualities and great charm both in the faces of well-observed ethnical types and in the supple, graceful attitudes of the figures.

The strong personality of eastern Javanese art is best expressed in the bas-reliefs. These retell the epic themes of Hindu India, particularly those of the *Rāmāyana*. The sculptors created an animated style in which the figures, with their bodies depicted full-face and their heads and feet in profile, were inspired by the puppets of the shadow theatre *(wayang)*—which are still in existence—and are closely related to the dolls cut out of leather that are peculiar to certain regions of India. They move against a rich, yet stylised landscape done in low relief which occupies the entire background.

In the 15th century the Islamic architectural style appeared in Java. The mosques differed from the Brahmanic temples only in their absence of decoration with figures. Nowhere else in the world did the Islamic style adapt itself so completely to local forms.

57 (left). **Prajñāpāramitā.** Bayon style. End of the 12th century. Sandstone. h. 3 ft. 7½ in. (110 cm.). This statue shows the deified queen, Jayarājadevī, wife of Jayavarman VII, represented as Prajñāpāramitā, or 'Perfect Wisdom', as is testified by the effigy of Buddha carved on the front of her headdress. All the spirituality of Buddhism is contained in this figure, as much in the gently spreading smile on the smooth face, as in the meditative, pious, inward-looking expression which is emphasised by the closed eyes.

58 (right). **The temple of Wāt Kukut at Lamp'un.** Wāt Kukut, which was founded in the first half of the 12th century, is a brick temple-mountain, decorated at each level with images of the Buddha in a style which was inspired by the post-Gupta period in India.

59 (far right). **Standing Buddha.** U Thong style. 13th–14th centuries. Bronze. h. 3 ft. 1¾ in. (95 cm.). Musée Guimet, Paris. The Thai style of U Thong owes much to the Khmer tradition of the Bayon period. This influence is particularly evident in the realm of sculpture where the treatment of the facial features and of the body lend the figures a gentle humanity, as this figure of the Buddha testifies.

Parallel with the development in the Khmer and Javanese territories, which in the sphere of sculpture made the best use of the Indian influence, Champa (Vietnam), Burma and Thailand were also influenced by Indian art and culture and transformed these traditions according to their own temperaments.

A kingdom, known by its Chinese name of Lin-yi, occupied the Hue region about the end of the 2nd century. This was the first nucleus of a Cham political authority and it probably became the kingdom of Champa, mentioned from the 4th century in Sanskrit inscriptions found in the region.

The Champa monarchy possessed Indian characteristics similar to those of the Khmer, but its art never attained the high level of Angkor. The Chams employed neither the staged pyramid, nor the gallery which was used to such effect by the Khmer architects. Their sanctuaries were therefore reduced to isolated towers *(kalans)*, sometimes grouped, but never actually joined together. But Cham art is not without quality, particularly in the field of sculpture. The few surviving ancient works may be attributed to the second half of the 7th century and are strongly influenced by the Indian Post-Gupta style. On a fine sandstone *linga* pedestal, of the Mi-son E.1. style, are to be found architectural, decorative and sculptural elements directly derived from Indian art.

The first sanctuaries appeared from the beginning of the 9th century: these were brick towers with sandstone decoration. Sturdy and simple, crowned with multi-stepped pyramidal roofs, decorated on each side with high pilasters with foliated scrolls, with multi-lobed arcades placed one upon another, these towers are very close to the temples of

India. They attain true distinction in the 10th century, with the towers of Khuong-my and Mi-son which are built in a sober, well-balanced classical style, but are already quite different from their Indian prototypes. This difference becomes more obvious with the Ponagar temple at Nhatrang, built in the 11th century. From then on, the outline of the sanctuaries loses its elegance, the roofs their rhythm and the decoration its plant motifs.

In sculpture, the native accent becomes more apparent about 875 in the Dong-duong style, which portrays a deliberately accentuated ethnic type. Then, after a particularly rich period in the 10th century with the Tra-kieu style, which was elegant and naturalistic in a rather idealised way, sculpture gradually deteriorated, except in a series of mythical animals at Thapmam, where the Vietnamese influence revived a popular and no doubt local predilection for bold stylisation.

Apart from Cambodia and Champa, which both enjoyed political unification, the rest of the Indo-Chinese peninsula was engaged in a struggle for power. Populated by Mons, Khmers and Indonesians, the territory now known as Thailand was not politically united until the 14th century; the Thais, who had probably come from the Yünnan border, gradually infiltrated into the country from the 11th century.

The influence of India is apparent from the 2nd–3rd centuries in several sites (Pong Tük, Korat) from Buddhist bronzes of the Amarāvatī style, some of which would appear to be originals imported from India or Ceylon and others copies made locally.

The architectural remains of the 6th–7th centuries are localised in the region occupied at that time by the most

56

powerful Mon kingdom, known to us by its Indian name of Dvāravatī. They consist mainly of crypts and there is a Buddhist monument built onto a double, tiered basement (Pong Tük), decorated on each side by five Buddhas seated in niches flanked by small columns and pilasters and by large stone wheels *(chakra)* symbolising the first Sermon of the Buddha Sākyamuni in the gazelle park in Banāras. They may be contemporary with Hindu sculptures found at several sites whose style is very close to Post-Gupta art.

Under the Khmer occupation, in the 11th century, a number of buildings were erected at Lopburi. The architecture and sculpture of this period follow very closely the Khmer styles of the period. In Mon country, at Lamp'un, a brick temple-mountain, the Wāt Kukut, was built during the first half of the 12th century. This temple is related to the Sat Mahal Prāsāta at Polonnāruwa, in Ceylon (12th century). Decorated on each side with images of the standing Buddha, this monument is one of the last to be built before the Thais seized power. The Thais introduced a new aesthetic, in which, upon a Mon basis, the Indian influence was no longer a direct one, but transmitted through the arts of neighbouring peoples: the Khmers, the Burmese and the Singhalese.

Burma, which was unified as late as the 11th century, received the Indian influence together with that of Thailand, then under the Khmers. There are few remains earlier than the 9th century and these are strongly influenced by Post-Gupta India. From the second half of the 11th century, Burmese art was given a new impetus by King Aniruddha (1044–77), the greatest of the Burmese kings, who was converted to the Buddhism of the Theravada, which came from Ceylon.

The stūpa preserve the basic Indian forms, learned from models from Ceylon and the Mon-Khmer countries. At first, they were ogival in outline, then bell-shaped and were perched on top of a huge pedestal consisting of successive platforms. But the originality of Burmese art and its borrowings from north-east India, from Bihār and Orissā, is best seen in the Buddhist temples. They form a compromise between the Khmer temple-mountain, the Hindu sanctuary with its sikhara of ogival shape as it appears at Khajurāho (about 1000 AD) and the Thai stūpa, with its very slender spire.

Sculpture in the round, which is on the whole of rather poor quality, reveals the influence of the Pāla-Sena style of Bengal. The reliefs illustrate Buddhist themes with landscapes and figural elements reduced to a minimum; they are more evocative than descriptive. The many mural paintings reflect a number of influences, none of which can be said to be directly and purely Indian. Manuscripts show a delight in colour and decorative effect.

In all the countries of South-East Asia, the acceptance of Indian forms seems to have brought with it the use of durable materials. These forms took root, without eliminating local inspiration, which often reappeared again quite rapidly. Under cover of the Indian religions, a permanent artistic exchange between all these countries began. This was particularly true of the 9th–10th centuries, when the art of Java influenced that of the Khmer countries and that of Champa, and when, in turn, Khmer art influenced Cham art (end of the 10th–13th centuries) and Thai art (7th–8th, then 11th–12th centuries). But India was the inspiration behind all these developments and was present in every exchange.

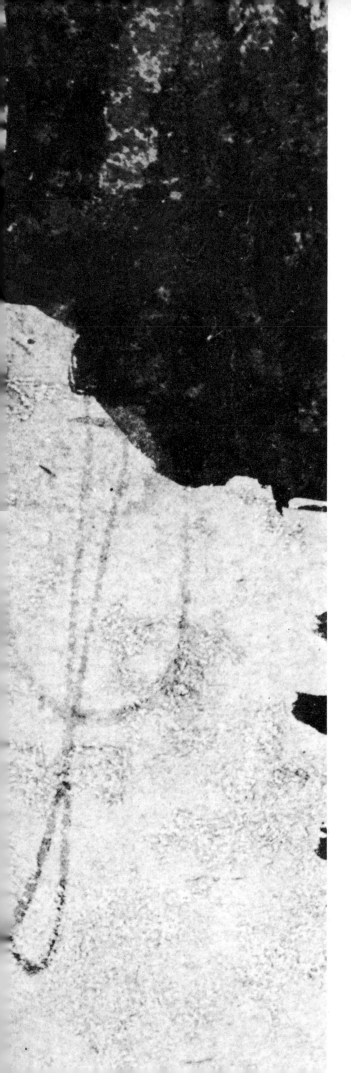

China, Korea and Japan
ROGER GOEPPER
Director of the Museum of Far Eastern Antiquities, Cologne

Introduction

Although the use of the term 'Far East' for China, Korea and Japan refers primarily to the geographical distance of these countries from the West, it also suggests a cultural remoteness that may seem hard to bridge. Until now, we in the West have been inclined to treat the various forms of Far Eastern civilisation as negative images, so to speak, of our own deep-rooted preferences. In this way we have come to regard the peoples of the Mongolian race as metaphorical as well as actual antipodeans. This view is not without foundation. In the Far East one begins a book from the back, and white is worn as the colour of mourning; in short, much occurs that is the exact opposite of our own customs.

In the light of this geographical and cultural remoteness it is understandable that the history of relations between the West and the Far East largely amounts to a series of mutual misunderstandings. One-sided ideas of East Asia have persisted even into the 20th century among educated people in the West, producing much confusion and prejudice—inevitably so as situations often arose that could not be fitted into the existing pattern of preconceptions of China and Japan.

This biased attitude appears as early as the time of Marco Polo who, despite his long stay in China from 1275 to 1292, saw some aspects of Chinese civilisation through a distorting mirror, while simply ignoring other important features. Even after the diplomatic Jesuit missionaries of the 17th and 18th centuries had succeeded in gaining a foothold in China where they even penetrated the august sanctuary of the imperial court—thus interrupting a deliberate isolation of several centuries—they succeeded in grasping only certain aspects of China's complex civilisation. Although the precision and scope of Jesuit knowledge of China as revealed by such works as Father Du Halde's comprehensive *Description de l'empire chinois* (1735) are indeed astonishing, the image of China that exercised such a deep influence on the French Enlightenment of the 18th century remained idealised and incomplete. It was based almost exclusively on Confucianism with its emphatically rational social ethic; and in fact the influence of Confucian ideas in France was so powerful that Confucius may with some justification be called the patron saint of the 18th century.

The vast area of Chinese thought that is reflected in Taoism and some aspects of Buddhism (an area which has left a decisive stamp on the art of the Far East) simply did not count for 18th-century Europeans. The influence of Japan on the revolution in Western painting of the 19th century is well known; but this enthusiasm for Japan focussed on a late form of art that was originally little prized by the Japanese themselves. It was only in the 20's and 30's of the present century that several comprehensive exhibitions at last brought the Western public into direct contact with the full range of Chinese and Japanese art.

Conversely there is no doubt that until very recent times the Oriental view of Westerners was no less distorted, for Europeans and Americans have been regarded—with some justification in an age of imperialism—as foreign devils and barbarians.

In view of the conditions that greatly restricted communication between the two extremities of the Eurasian continent—years of patient travel in the face of unbelievable difficulties and dangers were required—such misunderstandings were inevitable. Political and geographical barriers often combined to make direct contact virtually impossible. In antiquity and the middle ages the mountains, steppes and deserts of Inner Asia, crossed only by the tenuous link of the Silk Routes, lay between the West and the Far East. Of course Chinese silk was known in Mediterranean lands in antiquity, but this was traded by a chain of middle men, and thereby any direct contact with the Chinese was prevented. After the victories of the Arab armies over Chinese troops in the 8th century Islam drove Buddhism out of its earlier stronghold in Central Asia and this area became a hostile wedge lying athwart the lines of contact linking the West with East Asia. But in the course of time Islam took up the role of go-between, for the Arabs brought such Chinese inventions as paper and printing to the West, while the fundamentals of Hellenistic mathematics and astronomy were transmitted to China by Moslem scholars.

During the period of the origin, growth and first flowering of Far Eastern civilisation, between the second millennium BC and the birth of Christ, that is, during the age when this civilisation acquired its basic physiognomy, it was practically shut off from contact with other high cultures. The inhospitable steppes, deserts and rugged mountains set almost unsurmountable obstacles to the expansion of the Chinese peasantry to the north and west. These regions were only habitable by nomadic peoples, the immemorial enemies of the stationary Chinese. To the East lay the sea, which rarely tempted the Chinese to voyage into foreign parts. In the south alone was there real scope for expansion, so that during the whole course of Chinese history one must reckon with a slow and steady push southwards, a process that was seldom interrupted. In this way the whole of South-East Asia was eventually imbued with Chinese culture. Here, Far Eastern civilisation came into contact with offshoots of Indian civilisation, creating interesting hybrids in several areas.

Isolation from other high cultures combined with proximity to less civilised peoples goes far to explain the confidence of the Chinese in their innate cultural superiority. In time this proud and refined civilisation, which was unrivalled elsewhere in the world during the medieval centuries, infiltrated Korea to the north-east, important for her intermediary role, and then the islands of the Japanese archipelago.

But much earlier, in the archaic period under the first Chinese dynasties, there came into being the self-centredness of the Chinese people that is characteristically expressed in the term *Chung-kuo*, the 'Middle Kingdom'. The earliest witness for this is the *Shu-ching*, the classic book of documents which reflects the political and social ethos of the Shang dynasty in the second millennium BC, as mediated by the thought of Confucius (552–497 BC). Here we find that the lands inhabited by the Chinese are regarded as the world navel—the hub of the universe and the home of all true culture. Despite enormous social changes this attitude has survived almost unmodified among the Chinese down to our own day. Anything lying outside the fortunate central zone was barbaric by definition. An outgrowth of this conception is the Great Wall, which is even more significant as a symbol than as a physical bulwark protecting China from the destructive raids of the alien nomads of the Inner Asian steppes.

The characteristic Chinese sense of belonging to a firmly established tradition, a tradition that had forged eternally valid patterns in an earlier classical age, undoubtedly has its roots in the retrospective attitude of Confucianism. In this framework, the historical consciousness that characterises East Asia has grown up. In contrast to the indifference of various old high cultures, notably that of India, to the continuity of their past, the Far Eastern peoples reckoned their history in terms of the reigns of their sovereigns, continuing this practice from one dynasty to the next. In looking backwards into history they could depend on historical events being exactly dated; and in this way they formed a rounded picture of their own historical position and aims.

This profound sense of living at the centre of the world left its mark on the political development of the Far East where the life of the state revolved about the dominating figure of the emperor. Although he often held nominal authority only, he was still the son of heaven and enjoyed the mandate of the supreme powers. His palace stood in the centre of a fortified city and both the city and the imperial residence were planned in accordance with the directions of the universe. The dominant urban culture was at first transmitted by the feudal nobles who owed their position to the emperor, and later by a hierarchically organised bureaucracy, which was also sworn to obey the emperor. In the classical phase, membership of the ruling class of officials was theoretically open to all qualified persons; this class was flexible and could replenish itself from below and in this way could survive over many centuries. Recruits to this elite were not sought from the military class but from scholars, who had to show their ability in arduous examina-tions. With their extensive literary and general cultural education the officials were transmitters of culture, and indeed often artists in their own right, whether poets, painters, or musicians. Thus the political and social elite was synonymous with the intellectual and cultural elite—a situation unique to the Far East and one that helps us to understand many features of East Asian art. The liberal arts of calligraphy, painting and music, which were practised for the sake of personal enjoyment—arts that early acquired a subtle aesthetic—were exalted above the professional skills of architecture, sculpture and the minor arts, despite the fact that no well-defined boundary separates the crafts from the liberal arts. The concept of an art that, though certainly not practised as 'art for art's sake' was unhampered by religious ties, came into its own in the Far East between the 5th and the 9th centuries. At the same time the various arts acquired their aesthetic and theoretical foundations. An active trade in works of art developed to satisfy the needs of collectors, together with no less active an industry producing forgeries.

The origins and the real development of this fascinating phenomenon lay in China, but it passed with some modifications to the other main centres of Far Eastern culture, Korea and Japan. Geographical, ethnic, historical and social conditions produced particular developments of art in these two countries, which were stimulated and fertilised by the inexhaustible strength of the Chinese civilisation. The Korean people, because of their exposed position in the area of tension between Chinese and Japanese interests, were only occasionally able to develop their own powers undisturbed. By contrast the Japanese in their island home quickly assimilated Chinese influences and made them their own. Hence they created a culture distinguished from the Chinese example in many ways. The various phases of receptivity to foreign influences were followed by periods of Japanese isolation, which brought into being a special type of cultural introversion and self-sufficiency.

The aim of our study is to trace the main lines of the development of art in the Far East against the background of the society that produced it. In view of the richness and longevity of this culture this is not a task lightly to be undertaken. Our account will be mainly confined to the historical epoch, for little is yet known about the social structure of the prehistoric period.

China

The first organised state known to us arose in China in about 1500 BC—or in the opinion of Chinese scholars, who follow the date of traditional histories, as early as 1700 BC—from the neolithic phase, which is now relatively well documented by archaeological finds. The culture of this state, which is called Shang or Yin after the two names current for the dynasty, long retained many neolithic traits, at the same time developing an art of bronze casting that is astonishing in its technical excellence and artistic sophistication. Among the neolithic predecessors, the Lung-shan culture in the north-east of the later Chinese area seems to have been particularly remarkable in its contributions to the formation of Shang culture.

It is characteristic of this early historical phase of Chinese development (and indeed for the preceding neolithic and palaeolithic periods) that the culture is largely indigenous, having been pioneered on Chinese soil, in all likelihood by the Mongolian or proto-Mongolian peoples, who preceeded the later Chinese. The geographical centre of the Shang kingdom lay in the northern half of the province of Honan in the great fertile plain of the Yellow River. Until 1373 BC the capital was the walled city of Ao near modern Chêng-chou; thereafter until the fall of the dynasty it lay about 200 miles north-east in the vicinity of modern An-yang. Because of their military and cultural superiority the power of the Shang kings and their vassals spread from the political and cultural centre around the capital far into the central Chinese provinces—and indeed their cultural influence reached much farther.

Characteristic of the phases of the Shang period in so far as they are known to us from archaeological finds is the emergence of an urban culture firmly based on the peasantry who tilled the land. The social pyramid culminated in the person of the all-powerful king, who also acted as the high priest of an agrarian religion with a strict ancestor cult. The divine origin of the ruling family placed the king in a middle position between the powers of nature and creation on the one hand and the peasantry who depended on the fertility of the land on the other. Thus there developed an incipient feudalism, for the king bestowed fiefs and retainers on the members of his house, as well as on the men who served the state.

Beneath the king stood the various ranks of military and civil officials, forerunners of the bureaucrats who were so characteristic of later China. Their chief was a kind of chancellor. The scribes represented a special group that was essential for the working of the state apparatus and for the preservation of tradition. The complex ideographic script, from which the modern characters directly descend, was one of the most important features distinguishing the Shang culture from its neolithic ancestors and competitors. In all probability the Shang capital included a central archive with administrative documents and historical records. But of this material we only know at present the questions inscribed or painted by the priests on bone and tortoiseshell (the 'oracle bones'), together with reports of the results. The king headed a large college of augurs, oracle priests with shamanistic traits within the framework of the agrarian religion. Of course there was a separate class of artisans, among whom bronze founders serving the priesthood and the feudal nobility enjoyed special status. But the vast majority of the population of the Shang kingdom belonged to the peasantry, who did not contribute to the cultural life of the community. Every day the peasant farmers streamed out of the villages to the fields under the direction of overseers; they generally used primitive stone tools, which were distributed from government storehouses.

The centres of power and residence of the Shang kingdom were the walled cities planned in accordance with the heavenly directions. Excavations have shown that as in neolithic times the people normally lived in covered pit-dwellings and that only the platform-based palaces and temples were wooden structures, the exterior walls of which were reinforced with rammed earth and surmounted by double roofs.

As has been explained, this period of high culture was monopolised by the ruling house and the feudal nobility. The remarkable ritual bronze vessels, which rank as China's earliest works of art, were cast for the ancestor cult of the king and the feudal lords. The question of whether the technique of bronze casting was imported from the outside or developed in China itself is still unresolved. The earliest known vessels show a remarkably advanced technique and artistic quality, being cast from clay moulds and subsequently finished with tools. Possibly the smiths responsible for this work had the semi-priestly status known in other ancient cultures.

During the early phase of the Shang dynasty the ritual vessels of the ancestor cult often imitate pottery both in form and decoration, particularly that of Lung-shan ceramics. The vessels are thin-walled, the ornament is sparing and generally confined to a narrow band. Even in more recent Shang pieces the ceramic form sometimes 61 shines through. For the angular vessels of the later An-yang phase, however, wooden prototypes have sometimes been assumed, because the geometrical and animal decoration spreads over the whole surface of the object. The decoration 55 of these containers of sacrificial wine would provide a veritable catalogue of the symbols of ancestral religion and fertility cult—if only we understood its language better. The outstanding motif is a glowering mask, the so-called *t'ao-t'ieh*, or 'glutton', made up of various animal elements. The mask may have served to ward off evil or was a potent symbol of the powers of nature, comparable to the later Tao. The *t'ao-t'ieh* appears at the centre of a flat incised or raised relief decoration surrounded with dragons and feline animals, buffaloes and birds. Although we can sense immediately the magical force of these figures, we can only guess at their particular significance. Especially effective are the offering vessels that take figural shapes, such as

61. **Bronze ritual vessel of the chia type.** Shang period, 12th–11th centuries BC. h. 9¾ in. (24 cm.). British Museum, London. This vessel which dates from the An-yang period is decorated with both flat and raised ornament. *Chia* vessels, used for warming wine, are round or rectangular in shape with splayed legs and with two pillars rising from the lip.

60. **Ritual vessel of the ho or yu type.** Shang period. 14th–12th centuries BC. Bronze with shiny black patina. h. 13¾ in. (35 cm.). Musée Cernuschi, Paris. This offering vessel in the form of a tiger protecting a man may represent an ancestor spirit in animal form embracing the oldest member of the clan. The bodies of both the tiger and the man in this expressive group are covered with animal motifs: snakes, dragons and masks. These motifs, which relate to some indigenous fertility cult, stand out in relief from a ground of spirals.

those of owls or tigers, which are overlaid with symbols. *60* These may have been regarded as totemic embodiments of the ancestor spirit who protected the founder of a clan. A good many of these ritual bronze vessels bear short inscriptions dedicating them to a particular ancestor.

With some reservations, the Marxist theory of the slave-holding stage of society can be appropriately applied to this earliest Chinese state. Archaeological finds have shown that as part of the ceremonies accompanying the erection of temples and the outfitting of royal tombs a large number of men—mostly slaves and prisoners-of-war—were killed and buried as a sacrifice. In many cases the individuals were beheaded, perhaps with the huge heavy axes that **54** have been found. Too unwieldy to be weapons, the axes display magical decorations that would suit them to this grisly function.

Limits of space forbid more than a passing mention of such other aspects of Shang art as the powerful stone sculpture and the refined jade carving.

After the Chou people, who had been living east of the Shang kingdom to which they were more or less tributary, overran the Shang state with their 'barbarian' allies (be-

62a, b. **Ritual vessel of the Kuei type.** Early Chou period, late 11th century BC. Patinated bronze. h. 7½ in. (19 cm.). British Museum, London. While the dedicatory inscriptions on ritual bronzes of the Shang period are generally limited to a few words, many vases of the Early Chou period, which are stylistically quite similar, bear long inscriptions. The text on the

inside of this *Kuei* states that it was made on the occasion of an award by the Duke of Chou to Marquis Hsing, who was given lands and vassals of three classes in recognition of his services. The Marquis' speech of thanks and a short donation formula complete the inscription.

tween 1100 and 1000 BC), they completely adopted the superior Shang culture, which indeed they seem to have known considerably earlier. The warrior caste of the Chou made use of the expertise of the Shang priests and artisans, so that the archaeological record of the early Chou shows no break from the preceding Shang period. The rationalisation of the feudal system under the new dynasty led to a strengthening of cultural unity in the territory controlled by the Chou king. The Chou king's followers, whom he settled throughout the country as his feudal vassals were instrumental in spreading the culture over a wide area.

Like the Shang, the Chou lords concentrated their might in walled cities. The cultural superiority of the nobility rested on the traditional lore known as the 'six accomplishments' *(liu-i)* or the rites: ritual music, the script, which served to guarantee the continuity of tradition, the art of calculation, important for keeping the calendar in order, chariotry and archery—these last two being indispensable for hunting and war. The Chou period saw a consolidation of religious and political ideology and achievement that was to prove crucially important in the unfolding of Chinese civilisation. The prevailing ideology was finally codified by Confucius (551–479 BC) in a body of detailed ritual prescriptions, the *li*.

The bronze vessels of the ancestor cult (which retained some of the magical repertoire of earlier days but with an increase of distinctively Chou features) must be seen against this background, for it was found that they could be turned into a kind of historical document. The often lengthy inscriptions, whose language is related to the Chou texts of classical Chinese literature, inform the ancestors of the *62a, b* deeds of posterity and the decrees and largesse of the Chou rulers. But the highly developed political organisation of

the Chou bore with it the seeds of the dynasty's own disruption. The increasingly powerful magnates, who had become only nominally dependent on the central authority of the Chou king, fought ceaselessly among themselves. A shift of the Chou capital to the east in 770 BC seems to have brought no lasting benefits. The changing fortunes of the feudal states gave rise to a 'proletariate of the nobility', from which a new social class arose, the so-called *shih*, a mixture of political advisers, scholars, philosophers and knights errant. Confucius was the most famous representative of this group. It is symptomatic of the new social order that was coming into being that he took as pupils not only scions of the nobility but also sons of the common people.

In the last phase of the Chou period, the age of the Warring States (Chan-kuo, 475–222 BC), the central authority completely collapsed, but even under semi-chaotic political conditions the highly competitive feudal states were able to create a rich and distinguished culture. Economic growth and an increase of trade between the states brought the once despised merchant class into its own. The western Chinese state of Ch'in increased its power through astute economic policies. Even merchants could become ministers exercising effective political control.

It is not surprising that in these times of changing social, material and intellectual conditions art also should adopt a new path. As early as the Middle Chou period the magical intensity disappears from the decoration of the ritual bronzes. Then, in the period of the Warring States, the 56 surface of bronze vessels was covered with a luxuriant small-scale decoration, the effect of which was heightened by inlays in such precious materials as gold, silver and turquoise. Scenes of some complexity, including hunts with figures, also appear at this time.

Despite the relative homogeneity of Chou civilisation the archaeological finds from later phases give evidence of the rise of regional cultures, especially in the southern part of the Chinese area in the valleys of the Huai and Yangtze Rivers. These include the culture of the state of Ch'u with its characteristic lacquer industry, and, on the fringe of Chinese civilisation, the recently discovered Tien culture of Yünnan province with the extraordinary naturalism of its bronze work.

THE UNIFIED HAN STATE AND THE PERIOD OF DISUNION

In the centuries of warfare among the Chou feudal states the western state of Ch'in finally imposed itself through skilful polical manoevering and ruthless energy. In 221 BC its prince proclaimed himself the 'First illustrious Emperor of the Ch'in Dynasty' (Ch'in Shih-huang-ti). Supported by advisers from the severe legalist school of philosophers he pushed through strict reforms and standardised procedures not only in the political and administrative field, but also in cultural and intellectual matters. The rather old-fashioned Ch'in style of writing was decreed as the single script throughout the empire and the classic books, which mirrored conditions under the Chou, were forbidden and burned. In a gigantic engineering project the various small defensive walls of the old Chou states were linked into a monumental fortification in the north-west to secure the frontiers menaced by the barbarian nomads and at the same time to serve as a powerful symbol for the self-confidence and superior civilisation of the Chinese people.

But the achievements of the Ch'in were to have no lasting success. Shortly after the death of the gifted and powerful First Emperor, the dynasty was overthrown and from the general confusion there finally emerged a soldier of peasant origin by the name of Liu Pang, who founded the Han dynasty (206 BC–AD 220). A reaction set in against the tyranny of the Ch'in emperor. The Confucians won influence at court and their classics were henceforward to provide the basis for all education. Towards the end of the Han dynasty the edited and purified text of the Classics was engraved on sixty stone tablets, an undertaking carried out by an academy of officials under imperial order. Although the local administration was at first managed in accordance with feudal precedent, in the course of the Han dynasty a centralised bureaucracy was gradually built up under Confucian influence. Thus there merged a new 'gentry' or cultivated class, recruited from all ranks of society according to natural gifts and abilities. In 165, for the first time, the state subjected aspirants to office to an examination; this procedure became standard practice in the centralised Chinese state, serving to consolidate tradition and promote the longevity of the administration. The academy of the capital, which was responsible for training the higher officials, guaranteed a unified education and culture through the length and breadth of the enormous Han empire, which at its height stretched far into Central Asia. Thus lacquer objects produced in the south-

63. **Model of a pavilion.** Han period, 206 BC–AD 221. Glazed pottery. h. 15¾ in. (40 cm.). Musée Cernuschi, Paris. The small figurines which were placed in Han-dynasty tombs were supplemented by other gifts, most notably these terracotta models of buildings. Such models are of great value, for they give us a clear idea of the architecture of the period. Set in an enclosure, the open pavilion stands on piers that were probably made of wood in the prototype. The roof, with its tower-like projection, was covered with tiles.

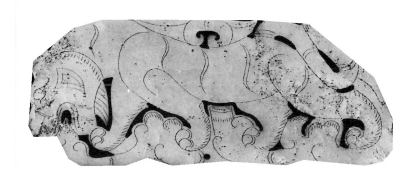

64. **Amulet in the form of a tiger.** Han period, 206 BC–AD 221. White jade. l. 7½ in. (19 cm.). Musée Guimet, Paris. As early as the Neolithic epoch, jade was recognised in the Far East as a precious stone endowed with extraordinary symbolic and magical powers. Here the artist has carved a white jade plaque in the form of the White Tiger, the mythical animal identified with the west. Notice the elegant engraving delineating the parts of the animal's body.

western province of Szechuan, the ancient centre of the industry, were used in the military colony of Lo-lang in the far north, in Korea, as archaeological finds attest.

Alongside the definitive establishment of the text of the Confucian classics there emerged that veneration of the written word that was destined to become so characteristic of Chinese culture. Tradition has handed down the names of high officials who were renowned for their calligraphic style; thus Ts'ai Yung is supposed to have written the texts of the stone classics in AD 183. In the Han period, familiarity with the classics and proficiency in the art of calligraphy foreshadows the later role of the Chinese 'man of letters' as the leading exponent of artistic culture. From calligraphy's sister art of painting we also know the names of important masters, though no work by them has survived. Descriptions in the Han dynasty histories indicate that the palaces contained impressive wall-paintings. The great halls were embellished with pictorial cycles of moral and didactic character: scenes of good rulers and faithful civil servants provided ever-present reminders to officials. A more convivial note was struck by scenes of feasts and banqueting, which reveal the extraordinary prosperity of Han China. There were also fine paintings on silk, which the emperor gave to subordinates as a mark of favour. A special bureau established in 29 BC for the care and preservation of paintings and calligraphic works of the court shows both the esteem in which works of art were held, and at the same time demonstrates the equal status accorded to painting and calligraphy. Nevertheless, the painters of the Han dynasty (and for a long time thereafter) did not belong to the social class of the *literati*, but, as in the earlier phases of western art, were craftsmen.

A reflection of the great wall-paintings of the palaces is provided by the frescoes that have survived in tomb chambers, such as those discovered in Liao-yang in southern Manchuria and in Wang-tu in Hopei province. In these paintings the artists first drew the contours of the picture and then filled in the colours. The well-known painted tiles from a tomb chamber now in the Boston Museum of Fine Arts show a type of line drawing that is closely related to calligraphy. The repertoire of subject-matter found in the rare fragments of Han painting is supplemented by the many stone engravings in their tombs, particularly in the Shantung province, and by the tiles with lively relief scenes of daily life that have come to light in Szechuan.

The sculpture of Han China is also known from funerary art. Work of this kind includes the monumental, but still primitive stone sculptures of the avenue of approach, the so-called 'spirit path' *(shên-tao)* leading to the tomb of general Ho Ch'ü-ping, as well as the winged lions at the tomb of Kao I in Szechuan, a motif that reached China from western Asia, though exactly how they arrived is not yet known. Symbolic figures of fired clay which replaced the earlier sacrifices of men and horses: glazed vases, jewellery and other offerings, are outstanding in the rich inventory of grave goods. The wealth lavished on burial and

on the cult of the dead by officials and their families led to such a weakening of the otherwise unassailable economy of the late Han dynasty, that after the break-up of the dynasty into smaller states, successive rulers imposed a ban on luxurious tomb furnishings.

Although no single monument of architecture has survived, extensive excavations in the old metropolis of Ch'ang-an, together with the evidence supplied by terracotta models provide us with a clear idea of Han building. 63 A basic feature of architecture, and one which was to remain important in later periods was a rectangular hall placed on a podium with wooden pillars and a trussed frame to support the heavy, projecting tile roof. The walls formed screens between the pillars but had not structural function. These halls, grouped around a sequence of courts or following one another along a central axis and with the entrance on the long side instead of on the narrow gable front provided the main feature of the extensive palace compounds. Even the various kinds of tower took the form of houses one placed on top of the other with a separate roof crowning each storey.

The sophisticated way of life of the Han society is reflected in various crafts. Bronzes lose the magical quality of the archaic phase: forms become simple, clear-cut and often rather sober. The most frequently occuring shape is the holder for toilet articles. There are also incense burners with pierced covers taking the form of a hill with animals, a scheme that reflects the Han affection for nature and landscape. Elegant gilded specimens of these incense burn- 58 ers survive, sometimes inlaid with precious stones. A speci- ality of the Han dynasty is lacquer work, which was pro- 57 duced commercially in the provinces of Szechuan and Hopei under state supervision. Silk was a Chinese monopoly and its products were exported westwards across Central Asia along the Silk Routes leading to Syria and Rome. The highly sophisticated art of jade carving continued the traditions of the Chou period; from this famous precious stone of the Far East the craftsman produced elegant pendants for ceremonial costumes and powerfully designed animal amulets. 64

The three and a half centuries between the final break up of the Han dynasty and the reunification of China under the Sui and T'ang dynasties are an age of change and new beginnings, culturally as well as politically. Admittedly the teachings of Buddhism had already entered China during the Han period and found some adherents, but in art the new faith began to make itself felt only during this period of transition.

At the beginning of the 4th century non-Chinese people pushed into the weakened north Chinese area, becoming the rulers of the native population that was culturally more sophisticated. The prestige of Chinese civilisation, however, soon cast its spell over these invaders and after a few generations they became largely absorbed into the Chinese way of life. Several states emerged, the most important one

(Continued on page 113)

54 (above). **Ceremonial axe.** Late Shang period.
12th–11th centuries BC. Bronze 11¾ × 13¾ in. (30·4 × 35 cm.).
Ostasiatische Kunstabteilung, Staatliche Museen, Berlin. This
axe is rare among Shang bronzes because it shows a human
mask in fairly high relief upon both sides. The usual motif
was a more or less abstract animal ornament. The piece is
too heavy and unwieldy to have been used as a weapon for
practical purposes, but it may have been employed for ritual
executions.

56 (above). **Ritual vessel of the hu type.** Middle Chou
period. 8th–7th centuries BC. Patinated bronze. h. 2 ft. 4¾ in.
(73 cm.). Musée Guimet, Paris. Owing to a decline in belief
in the magical religion, the decoration of animal motifs
characteristic of the Shang and Early Chou periods gave way
in the Middle Chou period to a ribbon and interlace decoration
incorporating animal heads and other zoomorphic elements.
The function of this new repertoire seems to have been
largely aesthetic. It is significant that Confucius's rationalistic
doctrine was formulated only a little later.

55 (left). **Ritual vessel of the lei type.** Late Shang period.
13th–12th centuries BC. Bronze with green patina. h. 20½ in.
(52 cm.). Staatliches Museum für Völkerkunde, Munich. The
vessel, which bears a character on the inside made of the
components 'bird' and 'halberd', served as a container for
the fragrant wine offered to the ancestors. It reputedly comes
from the tomb of a Shang king of the bird clan near An-yang,
the final capital of the first Chinese dynasty. It is cast with
consummate mastery and the surface teems with a whole
catalogue of magical motifs, including a large t'ao-tieh mask,
and rows of dragon-like animals and birds.

98

57. **Covered toilet box, or lien.** Han period. Lacquer. h. (with lid) 4 in. (10 cm.). British Museum, London. The astonishing water-resistant quality of lacquer led to its use on a whole range of objects during Han times. It was applied either to wood, or to wood covered with hemp cloth, or to the cloth alone. This toilet box, obviously a luxury object, was made by applying successive layers of lacquer to a hemp core. Originally black, it has now acquired a greenish tone, and is decorated with animals and delicate scroll patterns in yellow and red, some motifs (e.g. the armed rider) being inlaid with silver.

58 (right). **Incense burner.** Han period. 2nd–1st centuries BC. Gilt bronze inlaid with stones. h. 6⅞ in. (17·5 cm.). Freer Gallery of Art, Washington, D.C. The design of openwork censer covers of this type symbolises the land of the immortals with animals running through the mountains and genii staging hunts. This so-called *po-shan-lu* in the Freer Gallery with its fine decoration and inlay is a key example of the metalwork of the first half of the Han dynasty.

59 (opposite). **Stele with Sākyamuni and Prabhūtaratna.** Wei period, dated 518. Gilt bronze. h. 9⅞ in. (25 cm.). Musée Guimet, Paris. The group represents the mystical conversation between Prabhūtaratna and the historical Buddha Sākyamuni. This elegant piece displays the mature style of the Wei period, which results from a Chinese transformation of elements from the Buddhist art of Central Asia. Characteristic of the developed Wei style are the subtle play of the drapery and the stylised flames of the two haloes, as well as the slender, graceful figures with their 'archaic' smile.

60. **Bodhisattva.** T'ang period. Probably 8th century. Sandstone. h. 3 ft. 3⅜ in. (101 cm.). Rietberg Museum, Zurich. The figure comes from the rock sanctuary of T'ien-lung-shan in the province of Shansi. In contrast to the linear austerity of the sculpture of the Wei period (see plate 59) this Bodhisattva seated in the 'pose of indolence' *(lalitasana)* represents the mellow and full-bodied style of T'ang sculpture.

61. **Silver plate with gilding.** T'ang period. 618–906 AD. Diameter 8½ in. (21·5 cm.). Musée Guimet, Paris. The prosperity of the T'ang civilisation is reflected in its fine gold- and silverwork. Decorative motifs derived from Persia are common. But the lobed plant forms and the pair of mandarin ducks betray the Chinese style of the second half of the T'ang period.

62 (opposite). **Seated court lady holding a mirror.** T'ang period. 618–906 AD. Fired terracotta with coloured glazes. h. 12½ in. (31·8 cm.). Victoria and Albert Museum, London. The practice of providing the dead with ceramic figures of women, entertainers, horses, dogs and so forth as symbolic companions in the after-life replaced the custom of human and animal sacrifice several centuries before Christ. In this small figure the elegance of the T'ang way of life speaks to us with astonishing freshness.

63 (p. 102). **Lotus and Ducks.** Hanging scroll. Late Sung or Yüan period. 13th–14th centuries. Colour on silk. 4 ft. 2⅜ in. × 2 ft. 6¾ in. (128 × 78 cm.). Ostasiatische Kunst-abteilung, Staatliche Museen, Berlin. Paintings of this kind are not simply views of natural scenes, but a particular type of Buddhist cult image. The pure lotus growing up from a swamp is a prime symbol of Buddhism. Professional painters executed these pictures in pairs or sets for temple use.

64 (p. 103). **The Great King of Mount T'ai.** Hanging scroll. Late Sung or Yüan period. 13th–14th centuries. Ink and colour on silk. 33½ × 19⅞ in. (85 × 50·5 cm.). Ostasiatische Kunstabteilung, Staat-liche Museen, Berlin. This painting comes from a series showing the ten infernal rulers of Chinese Buddhism. In the foreground sinners are tortured, while a demon takes the soul of a woman with her child to the terrible judge, wearing a collar of shame about her neck. In the 13th and 14th centuries Hell pictures of this kind were made by particular guilds of painters in the neighbourhood of the city of Ning-p'o, in Chekiang province.

65. Kuan-yin, the Bodhisattva of Mercy. Yüan or early Ming period. Late 14th century. Wood, partly gilded. h. 5 ft. 7 in. (170 cm.). Private Collection, Lucerne. On loan to the Rietberg Museum, Zurich. This magnificently sculpted piece probably dates from the Yüan or early Ming period, for it possesses a sleekness and attenuation not usually found in sculpture of the Sung period. The Kuan-yin or Avalokitesvara is represented with all the gentleness and compassion associated with that deity. The beautifully rendered drapery adds to the serene air of the figure.

66 (opposite, above). **The Hall of Supreme Harmony.** Inner City, Peking. Ming dynasty (1627), restored and rebuilt under the Ch'ing. This main ceremonial hall, the *T'ai-ho-Tien* or Hall of Supreme Harmony, stands on a double-tiered marble terrace approached by two flights of steps and ramps of white marble. It was here that the Emperor sat enthroned at the great mass audiences of the year. The building style of the Imperial City was based on the disposition of ceremonial halls along an axis, separated by wide courtyards. If the decoration is sumptuous, the basic plan is simple enough, and is typical of Ming or Ch'ing structures. It consists of a simple oblong, the columns inside set out on the chancel-and-aisle principle. The overhanging roof covers a pillared portico, and is surmounted by a second roof, both of curved section and covered with blue tiles.

67 (opposite, below left). **Chün ware bottle.** Northern Sung dynasty. 960–1127. Stoneware with blue glaze and purple stippling. h. 11½ in. (29 cm.). Percival David Foundation, London. The best Sung ceramics are characterised by a supreme elegance of form. One-colour glazes were generally preferred, accompanied by flecks in another colour that appear to have been distributed almost at random. In this way they adhered to an ideal of simplicity that was especially prized by Japanese adepts of the tea cult.

68 (opposite, below right). **Vase in Mei-p'ing form.** Tz'e-chou ware. Sung dynasty. 960–1279. Stoneware with incised decoration under a green glaze. h. 15⅜ in. (39 cm.). British Museum, London. In many pieces of this north Chinese ceramic group, T'ang traditions persisted, and their latent effects were felt as late as the Ming period. The brightness of the colours, the solidity of the form and the elegance of the decoration achieve a harmonious balance in this piece.

69 (above). **Wu Pin.** *The Coming of Spring*. Detail from a handscroll. Late Ming period, dated 1620. Ink and colour on paper. Size of entire scroll 1 ft. 3 in. × 4 ft. 3⅜ in. (38 × 131.5 cm.). Cleveland Museum of Art, Ohio. In this work, one of the so-called individualists of the late Ming period unfolds with epic breadth and in minute detail a whole panorama of landscape in which he captures the lively activity of towns and villages at the beginning of spring. Wu Pin was a secretary in the government and a court painter, but he also belonged to the social elite of the literary artists who were not obliged to earn their living by their craft.

70 (left). **Shoulder jar.** Ming dynasty, Chia-Ching period. 1522–66. Porcelain with yellow glaze and iron-red pigment. h. 8¼ in. (21 cm.). Ostasiatische Kunstabteilung, Staatliche Museen, Berlin. This piece, which was fired in several stages, bears a powerfully drawn dragon, an emblem indicating that it was made in an Imperial factory. Porcelain decoration of this kind preserved its freshness and immediacy into the middle of the 16th century.

71 (p. 107). **Ch'iu Ying.** *Emperor Kuang-wu fording a river.* Detail of hanging scroll. Ming period, first half of the 16th century. Colour and ink on silk. Size of entire scroll 5 ft. 17⅜ in. × 2 ft. (171 × 65·5 cm.). National Gallery of Canada, Ottawa. An ideal landscape with steeply vertical mountain peaks in the manner of the Sung master Chao Po-chü shows in the foreground an Emperor of the Han dynasty with his retinue, fording a river. In typical Chinese fashion the figures are subordinated to, and absorbed into the main theme of the landscape. This strongly coloured landscape style was favoured by professional painters, of whom Ch'iu Ying was one; historically, Chinese taste has generally preferred the landscapes of the literary dilettante painters.

72 (opposite). **Offering Hall at the Altar of Heaven,** the *Ch'i-nien-tien,* Peking. Ming period. First built in 1420, reconstructed in 1889. This hall, in which the Emperor offered seasonal sacrifices to the God of Heaven, stands on a triple terrace symbolising heaven. Eight flights of steps approach the terrace from the eight cosmic directions. The hall itself is full of numerical symbolism. In accordance with the *yang* number of heaven the building has a three-stage roof, the twelve supporting columns representing the months of the year. In early Chinese history the *Ming-t'ang,* or Imperial ancestral hall, was built on similar cosmological principles.

73. **Offering Hall at the Altar of Heaven: interior of the dome.** First built in 1420. Reconstructed 1889, restored early 20th century. The magnificent interior of the Offering Hall is painted in a glowing mixture of blues, red and gold. The coffered dome encircling the lantern is covered in gold leaf, while the brackets are painted blue against a red background. Although the paintwork is much restored, it gives an accurate impression of Chinese Imperial splendour during Ming and Ch'ing times.

74 (opposite). **Seated figure of Lo-han.**
Ming period, 16th century. Light
grey terracotta with coloured glazes.
h. (without base) 3 ft. 1 in. (94 cm.).
Ostasiatische Kunstabteilung, Staatliche
Museen, Berlin. The figure belongs to a
set of sixteen or eighteen Lo-hans, the
chief disciples of the Buddha. These
groups were generally arranged on
stone benches along the side walls of the
hall of Chinese temples. In them the
rigorous iconographic prescriptions of
later Buddhist sculpture were relaxed
in favour of a relatively free and
naturalistic rendering.

75. **Lacquer throne.** Ch'ing dynasty,
Ch'ien-lung period. 1736–96. Wood
core with carved red lacquer decoration.
h. 4 ft. (122 cm.). Victoria and Albert
Museum, London. An outstanding
document of the Imperial majesty of the
Ch'ing, the throne originally stood in the
Nan-hai-tze before the Yung-ting Gate
in Peking, the hunting palace of the
Manchu Emperor Ch'ien-lung. The
piece is covered with good luck symbols,
which are carved deep in the thick layer
of red lacquer, exposing the underlayers
of olive-green, brown and yellow lacquer.

76. **K'un-ts'an.** *Landscape.* Ch'ing
dynasty. Ostasiatische Kunstabteilung,
Staatliche Museen, Berlin. The monk-
painter K'un-ts'an, also known as
Shih-ch'i, lived *c.* 1625–1700. He
entered the priesthood as a young man and
spent most of his life in Buddhist
institutions, becoming friends with many
of the *literati* who had gone into
voluntary exile at the fall of the Ming
(1644). His work is characterised by a
rather sombre atmosphere, and a
complicated brushwork which gives his
landscapes, with their jagged mountains
and twisted trees, a restless quality. He
appears to have been a simple,
unambitious man of great piety. In this
work a Buddhist priest is shown in his
mountain retreat. The landscape, although complicated, is totally un-
mechanical and reflects the painter's
deep feeling for nature.

77. **'Famille Rose' bottle.** Ch'ing
dynasty, Yung-chêng period. 1723–35.
Porcelain with coloured enamel
decoration. h. $11\frac{1}{2}$ in. (29·4 cm.).
Percival David Foundation, London.
During the reign of the Manchu
Emperor Yung-chêng, the porcelains of
the Imperial factories of Ching-tê-chên
reached an unsurpassed peak of
technical refinement and brilliance.
Pieces of the quality of this bottle
were probably not intended for export
but were made for use in the Imperial
palace.

being set up under the leadership of the Toba clan as Northern Wei (386–534). Many Chinese nobles and with them members of the bureaucracy fled before the barbarian inroads south of the Yangtze River. In the south too a number of states arose, the most important of which had its capital at Chien-k'ang, modern Nanking. Here the educated classes strove to maintain cultural and intellectual life according to the traditional pattern.

The political collapse and the breakdown of the old social order dealt nevertheless a heavy blow to traditional Confucianism and encouraged the growth of Taoism, especially in South China. Thinkers of this school had always regarded Confucianism as an over-rationalistic system; in its place they preached a return to the simple ways of nature. In general, a certain vaguely Taoist kind of escapism seemed to catch the spirit of the times in the south.

Scarcely less attractive than Taoism—and indeed more so for the common people—was the new religion of Buddhism with its elaborate metaphysics, a dimension that was lacking in the classical religio-philosophical systems of China. From the Central Asian trading cities, which were also flourishing centres of Buddhist missionary activity, the new faith trickled into north China via the Silk Routes. In South China it came by way of South-East Asia with its own active cradles of Buddhism, notably the kingdom of Funan.

The monastic aspect of Buddhism, which was utterly alien to the traditional Chinese social system, offered comfort and security to the rootless and dispossessed from all sectors of society. And the unaccustomed practice of honouring cult figures with religious rites and ceremonies produced a flood of pious foundations to shelter the holy images. In sculpture and painting as well as in architecture, artists had to come to terms with models from Central Asia and from India herself; the acquisition and spread of these forms created whole new branches of Chinese art. The earliest known examples of Chinese cult images in bronze for Buddhist use depend closely on Central Asian prototypes

59 and were generally small in size. But the native Chinese capacity for assimilation and transformation brought about a fusion with earlier Chinese forms so that a new and homogeneous art emerged. This constitutes the so-called 'archaic' stage of Buddhist sculpture in China which is usually **65** termed the Wei style after the dynasty founded by the Toba clan.

In accordance with the monastic rule of Buddhism the monks used to spend the summer months in missionary work begging for their food in the countryside, while they passed the winter in the monasteries. Following Indian precedent and Central Asian prototypes their *viharas*, or monasteries, often consisted of a series of caves cut in the side of rocky cliffs. The Toba nobles vied with one another in founding these cave sanctuaries and in providing them with a wealth of painting and sculpture; such works of piety were encouraged by the nature of Buddhism which was a religion of salvation. The caves of Yün-kang and Lung-mên with their thousands of sculptures are justly famous.

65. **Maitreya.** From the cave sanctuary at Lung-mên, Honan province. Wei period, early 6th century. Limestone. h. 21¼ in. (54 cm.). Rietberg Museum, Zurich. Like a statue from a Romanesque church portal the Buddha of the future sits with crossed legs on a lion throne. The slenderness of the figure and head, the archaic freshness and the linear manner of execution make the piece an outstanding example of the early phase of Chinese Buddhist sculpture. Hundreds of figures of this kind were carved as pious offerings on the walls of the cave sanctuaries.

By contrast the sanctuary on the mountain of Mai-chi-shan **66** in the south-west corner of the western Chinese province of Kansu lay forgotten for many years and was only recently rediscovered. While the cave temples of the central area boasted stone sculpture of large, even colossal dimensions, here the images were moulded in stucco following Central **67** Asian practice. The need to make the figure accord with iconographical rules formulated in India was new to the Chinese artists. But they soon adjusted themselves to this idea and in the 6th century created forms of an astonishing **65** inner force and beauty that recall the sculpture of the earlier middle ages in Europe. In the predilection for the sinuous folds of the draped figure the Chinese feeling for **59** calligraphic line took on a new life. In cases where the iconography called for nude forms, however, as in the fierce guardian figures, the sculptors were tempted to exaggerate the musculature and to ignore softness of the human **68** body. In painting also Buddhism brought new elements. The paintings of the cave temples of Tun-huang (executed

66. **The cave temples of Mai-chi-shan, Kansu.** 6th century AD. Mai-chi-shan was a holy site as early as the 5th century. The sanctuary comprises over 190 separate caves hollowed out of the rock. The work began in the Northern Wei period and continued until 1000 AD. Since the type of rock was unsuited to sculpture, the innumerable figures which decorate the sanctuary were modelled in clay over stone or wooden cores. The name 'Mai-chi' derives from the shape of the mountain which resembles sheaves of corn.

67. **Detail of sculpture, Mai-chi-shan.** The sculpture at Mai-chi-shan represents an important stage between the early examples at Lung-mên (see figure 65) and the full flowering of the T'ang style. The figures are far more naturalistic than at Lung-mên. The huge figure of the Buddha was constructed by inserting wooden armatures into the walls so as to support the projecting members such as the arms.

68. **Dvarapāla.** From Pei Hsiang-t'ang, Hopei-Honan border district. Northern Ch'i period, second half of the 6th century. Limestone. h. 3 ft. 6⅞ in. (109 cm.). Rietberg Museum, Zurich. This figure is one of a pair of door guardians from the famous cave sanctuary of Pei Hsiang-t'ang, where their fierce forms flanked one of the entrances, to ward off devils and evil influences. The musculature of the athletic figure has been turned into a kind of ornamental pattern that betrays the uncertainty of the Chinese sculptor (who was accustomed to making draped figures) as to how to render the naked human body.

69. **Ta-yen-t'a, the Great Gander Pagoda.** Sian-fu, formerly Ch'ang-an. T'ang period, *c.* 704 AD. This brick pagoda, one of the most important remains of the T'ang capital Ch'ang-an, was erected in honour of the famous pilgrim Hsüan-tsang in his monastery of Tz'e-ên-sze. The building, which originally had five storeys, was rebuilt about 704 with seven storeys. Its simple, clear forms are generally regarded as the classical expression of T'ang-period building. Pagodas of this kind were erected more as commemorative monuments than for any practical purpose.

between the last quarter of the 5th and the first half of the 8th century) show clearly the way in which the Chinese gradually brought their own aesthetic to bear on Buddhist religious painting.

Alongside this Buddhist world, the indigenous tradition of wall-painting lived on, as we know from examples in Manchuria and Korea. In the south, in Chien-k'ang, numerous painters and calligraphers were at work under the patronage of the Eastern Chin dynasty (317–420). We can get some idea of their art from a scroll in the British Museum ascribed to Ku K'ai-chih (*c.* 344–406). This period saw the appearance of the typical Far Eastern scroll which took the form of an ancient book or rotulus. Painting was now freed from bondage to architecture and brought into the intimate setting of the refined connoisseur who would unroll the scrolls for his own pleasure. This was part of the cultivated life of the nobles and literati of the southern dynasties who enjoyed and themselves practised the fine arts—poetry, music, calligraphy and painting. Painting no longer played the didactic role attributed to it in Confucian thought, for it was no longer intended for the instruction of the general public, but was the special preserve of a social elite, whose members derived exquisite pleasure from its practice and enjoyment. Consequently in about 500 we find the first indications of a conscious critical theory of art. At the same time political vicissitudes and the growth of Taoism promoted an interest in nature—an interest reflected both in the poetry of T'ao Yüan-ming (365–427) and in the beginnings of pure landscape painting, of which unfortunately there are no surviving examples. The architecture of this period blended the form of the Indian *stupa* with the indigenous tower to produce the characteristic Buddhist stone pagoda. Monastery and temple layouts made use of the old Far Eastern hall type, placed in and around courtyards. In the crafts the creation of proto-celadon ranks as an important innovation.

78

116

THE CLASSIC AGE OF THE SUI AND T'ANG DYNASTIES

The reunification of the far-flung Chinese territories under the short-lived Sui dynasty (581–618), followed by the consolidation and extension of the state to the gates of Persia under the rule of the T'ang emperors (618–906), may justly be regarded as the golden age of Chinese culture. The initial toleration, even support of the Buddhist faith—with its almost bewildering variety of sects—on the part of the imperial house, produced a flowering of Buddhism that was unprecedented in the Far East. The art of block printing which began during the T'ang period and which was practised with great dedication and outstanding ability by Buddhist monks, played an important part in spreading Chinese versions of the creeds and texts of the faith throughout the empire. The number of monks who had renounced their families and society for the meditative life in a monastery, grew rapidly, much to the disgust of the worldly and practical Confucians. Through pious donations the great monasteries acquired vast holdings of land worked by tenant farmers. In the same way bronze suitable for coinage flowed into the temples where it was made into cult images which lay outside the grasp of the imperial treasury. Not surprisingly the Buddhist monasteries took on the role of banks, accumulating large funds from the high interest rates they charged on loans to members of the commercial and agrarian classes. The Buddhist church was on the way to becoming a state within a state, thereby gravely undermining the basic Confucian structure of the government. When Buddhism penetrated the heart of the palace, it became the focus of family intrigues. The situation eventually reached a breaking point and the Confucian state apparatus reacted with a drastic measure: an imperial edict of 845 let loose an avalanche of compulsory secularisation. As a result of this persecution some 4600 large temples and 40,000 shrines were destroyed and an incalculable number of monks and nuns were forced to return to the world. This blow destroyed the power of Buddhism to control the development of society; when tolerance or support returned, as they did in later times, the earlier vigour could not be recaptured.

Our only picture of the imposing temples of the capital of Ch'ang-an in the first half of the T'ang dynasty comes from contemporary literary descriptions. Some stone pagodas of typically Chinese form alone escaped the fury of destruction. The lost palace halls must have abounded in sculpture in wood, dry lacquer and, most notably, bronze; their classic style is echoed in some pieces of the same period that have survived in Japan. Wall-painting, too, achieved a style of international standing characterised by harmonious design and balanced compositions. This style reached far beyond China's borders, as is affirmed by the examples of 711 in the Japanese temple of Hōryū-ji—unfortunately largely destroyed in a recent fire. Such renowned painters as Wu Tao-tzŭ (active 720–60), who was attached for a time to the imperial court, created pictorial cycles on temple walls, but unfortunately none of these have survived.

70 (above). **Eleven-headed Bodhisattva Kuan-yin.** Found at Toyoq, Turkestan. 9th–10th centuries. Wood, formerly mounted. h. 15 in. (38 cm.). Indische Kunstabteilung, Staatliche Museen, Berlin. Though found outside China proper, this small, finely carved piece may be regarded as a good example of Chinese sculpture between the late T'ang and early Sung periods, of which hardly any large-scale wood sculpture survives. The eleven-headed Bodhisattva of compassion was probably originally revered in the cult ceremonies of a Tantric sect under Indian influence.

Provincial versions of the great wall-paintings of this period appear among the wall-paintings of the Tun-huang caves, which lie on the edge of Central Asia, far from the hot-houses of classical culture in such great cities as Ch'ang-an and Lo-yang. As the finds show, designs were transferred on to the walls from pricked cartoons. This device facilitated the execution of carefully measured iconographical compositions, but it tended also to restrict the artists' imagination. Stipulations of this kind explain the attitude of disdain felt by the literati-artists towards religious work of this kind.

Stone sculpture lined the walls of cave sanctuaries or took the form of the ever-popular steles or cult images. It **60** reveals a maturity and fullness of form partly achieved through a natural process of evolution from the styles of the 6th and 7th centuries, and partly through the new wave *70* of influence from the Indian homeland of Buddhism.

In its heyday the T'ang imperial court showed a liberal cosmopolitanism only rivalled, if at all, under the Mongol rulers of the 13th and 14th centuries. The metropolis of Ch'ang-an, which had some two million inhabitants according to the census of 742, formed the eastern end of the long caravan route passing through Central Asia; at the same time it was linked with the Chinese coastal regions as far as Canton through a network of natural and artificial waterways. Here, at the heart of the administrative system and the seat of the emperor, foreign tribute goods both from home and abroad arrived in a ceaseless flow. The city teamed with merchants, monks, craftsmen and artists from Central Asia and points farther west. Western motifs ap-*71* pear in ceramics even before the founding of the T'ang dynasty as well as in the gold and silverwork of which we **61** have a number of examples showing a fusion of Sassanian stylistic features with native decorative elements. Until the persecution of 845, Zoroastrians, Nestorians, Manichaeans, Jews and Moslems could practice their religions freely in Ch'ang-an.

The sophisticion of life under the T'ang still speaks direct-**62** ly to us in the lively modelling of the ceramic figurines, partly glazed with colour, which were made as grave goods: elegant harem ladies, Central Asian merchants and camel drivers, noble breeds of horses imported from *72* Ferghana for hunting and polo, dwarfs employed as court entertainers and many other subjects.

The aim of the first T'ang rulers, who came from a north Chinese family, was to achieve a homogeneous culture for the whole far-flung empire, which was to be based mainly

71 (opposite). **Pilgrim's Bottle.** Sui or early T'ang period, 6th–7th centuries. Heavy stoneware with bright green glaze. h. 7¼ in. (18 cm.). Ostasiatische Kunstabteilung, Staatliche Museen, Berlin. So-called 'pilgrim's bottles' of this type show Western influence in shape and generally in decoration as well. The pearl band and the bird in a roundel on this piece recall Sassanian metal objects, though these are somewhat later; this disparity may indicate a common Central Asian origin. The motifs testify to the cosmopolitan spirit of this period.

72. **Horse.** T'ang period, 618–906. Ceramic with colour glazes. h. 24⅜ in. (62 cm.). H. König Collection, Cologne. Although the majority of the terracotta grave gifts of the T'ang period were mass-produced from moulds, some of the larger pieces reach the status of independent works of art. The 'blood-sweating' horses of Ferghana, which were used in polo and equestrian displays, were among the most popular imports into the T'ang empire. It is therefore not surprising that these horses occur frequently among the tomb figures.

upon the continuing traditions of the refined south. Particularly effective were the measures of the emperor T'ai-tsung (627–49), who sought to consolidate and purify the lately rather muddled tradition of the Confucian classics that had persisted in the south; he held this revitalised tradition up to the nobility and the bureaucracy as an eductional model. T'ai-tsung was an almost fanatical admirer of the calligraphic school of the southern dynasties that had grown up around the figure of Wang Hsi-chih (c. 307–65). To his favoured academy of Hung-wên-kuan in Ch'ang-an he summoned as leading scholars and calligraphers the literati Ou-yang Hsün and Yü Shih-nan, both of whom had reached a venerable age. The theory and aesthetic of calligraphy were firmly grounded in the T'ang period, though in the second half of the dynasty a certain reaction took place against the traditionalism of the dominant Wang school. Characteristic are the severe writing style of Yen Chên-ch'ing (709–85) and the rather fantastic expressive script of the monk Huai-su, who seems intentionally to have flouted the classical rules. While the calligraphers became well established in the upper ranks of the social hierarchy, the painters were still unable to free *73*

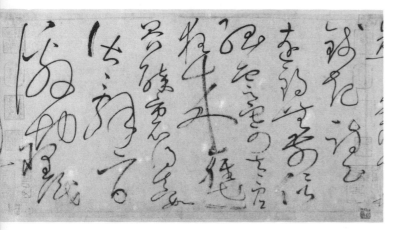

73. **Huai-su.** Part of an autobiography. Dated 777. Handscroll. Ink on paper. h. 9⅝ in. (24·4 cm.). National Palace Museum, T'apei, Taiwan. Huai-su (725–c. 787) of the T'ang period practised an idiosyncratic version of the *Ts'ao-shu* or 'Grass Style'. His characters, which tend to be joined, have an extraordinarily expressive quality.

74. **The Emperor Hui-tsung.** *Beginning of a poem on autumn flowers.* Handscroll. Ink on silk. h. 10¾ in. (27·2 cm.). National Palace Museum, T'apei, Taiwan. Hui-tsung (1082–1135; reigned 1101–25), the last ruler of the Northern Sung dynasty, was a gifted poet, painter and calligrapher. This example is written in 'Slender Gold', an aristocratic variation he created from *Hsing-shu* or the 'Running Style'. The elegant strokes often end in a hook—a characteristic feature of Slender Gold.

themselves entirely from the fetters of craft work. On the one hand such painters as Wu Tao-tsŭ and Li Sze-hsün enjoyed esteem and were able to acquire official recognition—the latter was a minister of state—but on the other the head of the Ministry of Works, Yen Li-pên bitterly complained of the imperial commissions he had received and he cautioned his son against taking up such an occupation. Unfortunately no signed work survives from these artists' hand nor from that of the poet-painter Wang Wei (699–759), who seems to have played an important role in the development of brush drawing and who had a great reputation as a landscape painter. In general, the T'ang dynasty saw the appearance of the distinctively Chinese artistic figure—men who belonged to the social elite and were not obliged to earn their living by painting.

THE FIVE DYNASTIES AND THE SUNG PERIOD

Like the Han before it, the T'ang empire split into a number of successor states. And just as before this political fragmentation was accompanied by a shift in the cultural centre of gravity towards the Yangtze River and farther south. While the north was risen by chaotic economic and political conditions, the south at first enjoyed an economic resurgence based on an increasing production of rice, tea and salt and extensive trade connexions.

Under the last ruler of the short-lived Southern T'ang dynasty, the sensitive poet Li Yü (937–98), (reigned 961–75), the refinement of life reached new heights. The academy of Li's court was illuminated by such figures as Chou Wen-chü, who painted elegant figure scenes in the style of the great T'ang period. At the same time the ruler fostered a new category of painting, a kind of 'nature still-life' with scenes of plants and animals acutely observed and finely executed. Other figures at work in this period include the founders of a branch of monumental landscape painting, Ching Hao, Kuan T'ung and the monk Chü-jan. Another monk Kuan-hsiu, became famous for his expressive pictures of Buddhist saints.

The aesthetic refinement of the court of Li Yü was also reflected in the art of print making. The paper produced in the imperial workshop was long regarded as the best and commanded high prices. Ceramics also enjoyed a new flowering in southern China.

After reunification had been achieved once more, the new Sung rulers sought to recreate the state and culture of the T'ang, though less effectively. The new bureaucracy and leisured classes of the Sung came, however, mainly from the civil population and not from the military aristocracy as under the T'ang. The art and culture of the Sung dynasty (960–1279) was marked by the rise of a new urban bourgeoisie. Often the members of this bourgeoisie, who might hold high office within the government hierarchy or occupy themselves with trade matters, were also big landowners with estates worked by peasant farmers under the supervision of a bailiff. This double aspect—urban society with its burden of community responsibility on the one hand and carefree life in the country on the other—typifies the life on the educated class under the Sung. In the early part of the dynasty several men of strong personality left a decisive stamp on the image of the literati. These figures include the politically somewhat unfortunate Su Tung-p'o (1036–1101) and the successful Mi Fu (1051–1107). Alongside their official duties these men cultivated in their private lives the liberal arts of poetry, calligraphy, painting and music. Their critical and theoretical writings proved decisive in establishing the concept of the literary artist *(wên-jên)*, which later became almost a cliché. Firmly linked to the state hierarchy was the artist who belonged to the Academy of Painting *(Hua-yüan)* of the imperial court and who bore official titles. Under the patronage of the politically weak emperor Hui-tsung (reigned 1101–1126) the academicians produced detailed pictures of plants and animals as well as landscapes. But there were also schools of painters comprising largely anonymous masters who continued a long-established tradition in this

74

75 (above). **Hsü Tao-ning.** *Fishing in the Mountain Stream* (detail). Northern Sung period, *c.* 1000. Handscroll. Ink on silk. Whole size 19 × 82½ in. (48 × 210 cm.). William Rockhill Nelson Gallery of Art, Kansas City. This is one of the finest landscapes that have come down to us from the Sung dynasty. It was painted by a former herbalist who, under the protection of a minister, made a name for himself in aristocratic circles as a painter. The artist develops and varies his landscape theme like a musical composition in a sequence of motifs running from right to left; the work was intended to be enjoyed, not only in its entirety, but also in sections as it was unrolled on a table in the privacy of a scholar's study.

genre. These were professional artists organised in corporations or guilds who often worked for Buddhist patrons. **63** The increasing artistic influence of the bourgeoisie is evident in the figure of the painter Hsü Tao-ning, who lived in the first half of the 11th century. Originally an apothecary who only painted in his spare time, Hsü eventually received a flood of commissions, ultimately becoming a minister's protege. Although to our eyes his powerful land- *75* scape paintings seem to belong among the most effective works of their kind they were characteristically considered 'vulgar' by the contemporary art critic Mi Fu.

Another feature of Sung painting—especially during the second half of the dynasty when the Chin dynasty established by the nomadic Jurchen usurped the north, forcing the Sung to move the capital to the southern city of Hang-chou—is the increasing influence of the Ch'an (Zen) sect of Buddhism. Many literati were attracted by its teachings and particularly towards the elegantly simple way of life of this meditative school. In the first half of the 13th century several monks of the Ch'an sect became famous as painters; they developed a style of their own characterised by immediacy of expression, simplicity of means and individuality of brush-stroke. Outstanding among the Ch'an painters is Liang K'ai, who at first worked at the imperial *76* academy in Hang-chou. When he was awarded the Golden Belt by the emperor he left it hanging in the hall of the palace and quit the capital. He spent the rest of his life in the solitude of Ch'an temples, where his art acquired the style so characteristic of the monk painters. Also standing apart from official painting were such local schools as that of Ning-p'o in Chekiang province—a school famous for **64** its scenes of hell.

In sculpture T'ang tradition persisted, but the weakening of links with Buddhism is unmistakeable. Wood sculpture in particular freed itself almost entirely from Indian tutelage; it tended either towards excessive elegance or **65** towards naturalism.

Ceramics offer the finest witness of the technical and artistic achievements of Sung crafts. The vases produced in the state factories for palace use possessed a classic per- **67** fection of form and colour scarcely rivalled anywhere else in the world. At the same time factories in northern China adapted the old traditions of colour glazing and painting to the taste of the age. The cult of the tea ceremony which **68** had grown up in association with Ch'an Buddhism created

76 (left). **Liang K'ai.** *Ch'an Patriarch Cutting a Bamboo Pole.* Sung period, first half of the 13th century. Hanging scroll. Ink on paper. 29⅝ × 12½ in. (72 × 32 cm.). National Museum, Tokyo. Liang K'ai, who first worked as an academic painter at court, later withdrew from the world to live according to the spirit of Ch'an (Zen) Buddhism. Not only did he take the themes of his painting from the school, but his style itself, with its immediacy and simplicity, accords with Ch'an ideals. This work represents the sixth Chinese patriarch Hui-nêng, whose enlightenment was no obstacle to his carrying on everyday activities.

77. **Huang Kung-wang.** *The Fu-ch'un scroll* (detail). Yüan period, dated 1350. Handscroll. Ink on paper. Whole size 13 in. × 20 ft. 10¾ in. (33 × 673 cm.). National Palace Museum, T'apei, Taiwan. This famous scroll is the artist's masterpiece and it can appropriately be placed at the forefront of the later phase of Chinese painting. After a short official career Huang lived as a Taoist priest in the mountains near Hang-chou; in this painting he offers a panoramic view of these mountains. Stylistically he depends on masters of the early Sung period, yet in his work the mountain and rock formations take on a crystalline character that found much favour among later literary painters.

its own aesthetic with a tendency to simplicity and unobtrusiveness, which may have influenced the so-called Temmoku ware.

THE RECENT PERIOD: FROM THE MONGOL PERIOD UNTIL THE PRESENT TIME

Through its incorporation in the vast Eurasian empire of the Mongols, who ruled in China under the name of the Yüan dynasty from 1260 to 1368, China emerged from its isolation as never before or since. The cosmopolitan atmosphere of the Mongol imperial court in Peking led to the introduction of foreign ways of thinking, particularly in the natural sciences. Since the Mongols, especially under the reign of Kubilai Khan, sought to assimilate as much as possible of the culturally superior Chinese civilisation and since the Eurasian 'Pax Mongolica' assured a period of tranquility, many of the literati decided to collaborate with the conquerors. Pre-eminent among them was the calligrapher, painter and connoisseur Chao Mêng-fu, who exercised a great influence on the cultural life of his time, ultimately becoming director of the Han-lin academy.

Other Chinese literati and artists, however, true to their Confucian heritage, practised a kind of passive resistance to the 'barbarian regime'. They refused to accept offices and lived as outsiders in temples or on their estates according to their means. Among these was Huang Kung-wang (1259–1354), whose Taoist leanings prompted him to wander over the countryside expressing his feeling of union with nature in landscape paintings. Together with three other artists he can be regarded as the founder of later Chinese painting. In Huang's pictures the rendering of immediate perceptions yielded to an emphasis on individual brush-work, and a manneristic tendency to reduce landscape forms to a series small repetitive devices. His friend Ts'ao Chih-po (1272–1355) at first held a minor office but later he too adopted a life of leisure. In contrast to Huang, this artist's landscapes and trees are still fairly close to the style of the Sung period.

The national Chinese dynasty of the Ming cast off the foreign domination of the Mongols, initiating an uninterrupted rule of almost three centuries (1368–1644). Its

78. **Ts'ao Chih-po.** *Pavilion with Ancient Pines*. Yüan period, first half of the 14th century. Hanging scroll. Ink on paper. 18¾ × 17⅝ in. (47 × 45 cm.). Musée Guimet, Paris. Unlike the revolutionary Huang Kung-wang, his friend Ts'ao Chih-po (1272–*c.* 1362) followed the style of the Sung masters in his landscapes and tree pictures. Initially, the painter served an official bureau under Kubilai Khan, but he later retired to devote himself to Taoist studies and to painting.

79 (below). **The Sacred Way heading to the tomb of the Emperor Yung-Lo.** Ming dynasty, *c.* 1403–1424. His tomb lies some twenty-five miles north of Peking at Nan-k'ou. A broad avenue leads to the tomb, lined with monumental figures of warriors and animals carved in limestone. Among these are lions, camels, elephants and horses. Although these sculptures derive from T'ang models, they lack, perhaps because of their size, some of the delicacy and subtlety of T'ang examples.

80 (right). **Limestone figure of a warrior.** One of the sculptures lining the Sacred Way (see figure 79), this official is dressed in a coat of mail with a helmet reaching to his shoulders. In his right hand he holds his baton of office and with his left he clasps his sword hilt. The rich surface decoration of this figure makes it particularly splendid.

81. **Burial temple of the Emperor Yung-lo, near Peking.** *c.* 1424. This interior is typical of the temple halls of the Ming dynasty. The traditional Chinese system of beam and pillar construction is observed, the beams being morticed and tenoned together so that the stress on the massive columns is reduced. As this is a broad building, additional columns are needed within the hall. The overhanging roof protects the exterior walls from the weather so that these can be light and insubstantial.

rulers sought to return to older Chinese ways and to reject the cosmopolitan spirit of Mongol times. During the second half of the dynasty, however, European traders succeeded in gaining a foothold on the south China coast and then, towards the end of the Ming period, large-scale exports of such Chinese goods as porcelain and silk began to flow to the Middle East, Europe and Latin America.

The imperial majesty of the first Ming rulers is still proclaimed today in the imposing tombs approached by *79, 80,* **72** avenues lined with colossal stone statues, and by the *81, 66* grandiloquent architecture of their ancestral halls.

The dictatorial attitude of the earlier Ming emperors towards the artists attached to the court is notorious. Some seventy or eighty artists worked in loose association in the palace workshops which were supervised by eunuchs. There was not academy as such; instead the authorities hit on the expedient of giving military ranks to many of the painters. Some artists of the imperial workshops paid with their lives for conspicuous lack of application or zeal.

A real advance in the art of painting could not occur in this oppressive setting; rather the progressive spirits flocked to the old centres of the fine arts in the south. The city of Suchou in Kiangsu province sheltered not only such important professional painters as Ch'iu Ying, who was **71** obliged to make his living from the sale of his pictures and whose works as a result were often tailored to meet the customer's requirements so that they cannot be regarded as evidence of the true dilettante painting, but also a circle of famous literati painters who played an important part in *82* the development of the genre. Although the members of this group are often known collectively as the 'Wu school' after an old name for Suchou, they form more of a literary circle, held together more by common interest than by the bonds of a regular artistic school. Many regarded painting as the least of the arts they practiced, and consequently even today they are better known in China as calligraphers and poets. They generally belonged to well-to-do families; consequently few of them were obliged to accept office in order to live. The central figure of the Wu school, Shen Chou (1427–1509), consulted an oracle when an office was offered him, rejecting the post when a negative answer was forthcoming. In his landscapes the natural atmosphere is even less evident than in the work of Huang Kung-wang, which he took as his model. His highly personal brush-work is of particular interest and the landscape elements become taut and stylised.

This new tendency was carried to an extreme by Tung Ch'i-ch'ang (1555–1636), a calligrapher, painter and critic active towards the end of the dynasty; he served as head of the Ministry of Rites and reflected the official taste of the time. Tung Ch'i-ch'ang was responsible for the theoretical elaboration of the concept of the literary painter (wên-jên). Another group of artists was at work in the last decades of the Ming period: the so-called 'individualists'. The outward appearance of their landscape paintings ranges from tranquil reserve to a conscious striving for monumentality.

Craft productions reached new heights, reflections in their richness the exalted claims to majesty made by the dynasty itself. In the province of Kiangsu the flourishing state porcelain factories of Ching-tê-chên supplied not only the national market, but were also able to meet an increasing volume of orders from the West. The same is true of the flourishing lacquer industry.

The weakness of the Ming empire in the first half of the 17th century could not fail to tempt the Manchu, a people stemming from Jurchen stock, who first occupied Manchuria with their strong cavalry forces and then the whole of China. For two and a half centuries they ruled the country under China's last imperial dynasty, the Ch'ing (1644–1912) The Manchu tried from the beginning to absorb the most important elements of Chinese civilisation and in this they were more successful than earlier conquerors. Some of the early Ch'ing rulers painted pictures in Chinese style and the Emperors K'ang-hsi (1662–1722) and Ch'ien-lung (1736–95) became fanatical enthusiasts of Chinese art and culture. Although a certain latent hostility towards the conquerors persisted among educated Chinese, a real understanding developed between the two peoples, giving rise to a new flowering of art and culture.

Nevertheless one cannot help noticing a certain tendency towards empty display and self-conscious rigidity in the official art of the court. The traditional Chinese court ceremonial, which was intentionally fostered by the conquerors, called for a worthy setting; and this necessitated the expansion and luxurious outfitting of the Peking palace

82. **Shêng Mao-yeh.** *Noble Pines and a Venerable Tree of Life.* Late Ming period, dated 1630. Hanging scroll. Ink and pale colours on silk. 5 ft. 1¾ in. × 3 ft. 3 in. (156 × 99 cm.). Ostasiatische Kunstabteilung, Staatliche Museen, Berlin. A native of Suchou, this artist was one of the 'individualists' of the late Ming period. This 17th-century painting shows the persistence of the tradition of close attachment to nature—the literatus' sense of absorption into the natural environment.

83. **Shên Chou.** *Scene from Tiger Hill, Suchow.* Ink and colour on paper. Cleveland Museum of Art, Cleveland, Ohio. Shên Chou (1427–1509) is generally regarded as the founder and outstanding member of the Wu school of painting, the name deriving from that of the province in which he worked; Wu is modern Kiangsu. Shên Chou came from a family of scholars. He led a reserved life surrounded by congenial friends, refusing always to take payment for his work. His paintings are characterised by the boldness of their lines.

complex, which was organised according to an old pattern as a series of halls on imposing stone terraces placed along a central axis through a sequence of courts. In the work of the imperial porcelain factories, on whose industrial methods we are well informed thanks to the report of a Jesuit missionary, we are again struck by the almost incredible technical perfection and the elegance and richness of the vases and other containers. The Manchu productions 'in the Chinese style' recall the rarified luxury of the Byzantine court and seem more Chinese than the Chinese art itself.

Lacquer-work also supplied the demand for courtly display, though the details of the ornament have lost the pleasant softness of the earlier Ming pieces.

The establishment and rapid growth of the trading posts of the British East India Company in Canton caused a sudden increase in the export of porcelain and lacquer to Europe. Many Chinese merchants made their fortunes as middlemen in this trade. But the volume of export and the differing taste of the European market led in the course of time to a decline in technical and artistic quality.

Western influence was felt even at the court, where Jesuit missionaries had succeeded in gaining entry, taking advantage of the Emperor Ch'ien-lung's curiosity. Some of the Jesuits worked in the palace workshops, where they made clocks and astronomical instruments, painted and even designed palace buildings in the rococo style of Europe. But Chinese society remained strongly nationalistic, and withdrawn under Manchu rule, and the initiative taken by Manchu rulers were to have no lasting effects on later Chinese culture.

In the Peking palace workshops of Ju-i-kuan and Yang-hsin-tien Chinese and Manchu painters were enlisted and invested with court titles, although they did not form an academy as in Sung times. The Emperor Ch'ien-lung took an active interest in their work, which he liked to criticise and correct. Under this well-intentioned, but too rigorous and one-sided control, the court painters generally drifted towards an empty eclecticism, repeating and varying standard motifs until their work became mechanical and meaningless.

As had happened several times before, the driving forces in the evolution of the art of painting were at work far from the court in the provinces, where circles and schools of in-dependent painters appeared. While many of them lived in the usual way on the generosity of their families, and did not have to serve the official hierarchy to make a living, others did accept appointments. But many chose the modest but unrestricted life of the Buddhist monastery—often as a protest against foreign rule.

Among the monk painters were some remarkable individuals, such as Pa-ta-shan-jên or Chu Ta (c. 1625–1705), who came from a branch of the imperial Ming family, but preferred to live an eccentric and remote life under the Manchu usurpers. Whether his madness was genuine or feigned is difficult to say, but in his expressive painting he mocked every rule of the classical tradition. More normal in his personal life and artistic style was the monk K'un-ts'an or Shih-ch'i (1617–c. 1680), who preferred the quiet retreat of a monastery where he could commune with nature, though he was often in financial difficulties.

The two basic tendencies, on the one hand towards eclectic traditionalism and on the other to decisive rejection of time-honoured forms in favour of individual expression, characterise the development of Chinese painting in the 18th and 19th centuries. The increasingly uncompromising attitude of the educated classes produced a greater formality and rigidity in the art they patronised. In the 19th century, however, the focus of interest of the literati was directed less towards the cultivation of the liberal arts than towards a antiquarian interest in China's past. Scholars concerned themselves with collecting old texts and with studying the primitive beauty of obscure or newly rediscovered forms of script with the aid of the sciences of palaeography and archaeology. In this scholarly preoccupation with China's historical traditions, revolutionary ideas found favourable soil, eventually leading to the overthrow of the empire in 1912. Even under the communist regime scholars of this kind still play an important role in shaping cultural policy.

Chinese art of the 20th century, however, oscillates between a cultivation of classical tradition, which has no real social validity and a still tentative effort to adopt and develop cultural stimuli from Western Europe and Russia. Under present circumstances a satisfactory solution to these problems and dichotomies is probably not yet to be expected.

84. **Chu Ta.** *Rocks with plants and fish.* Ch'ing period, late 17th century. Handscroll. Ink on paper. Size 11½ in. × 5 ft. 2 in. (29 × 157 cm.). Cleveland Museum of Art, Cleveland, Ohio. Like many earlier calligraphers and painters, Chu Ta usually created his works under the influence of wine. He is best known for his ink paintings of birds and flowers. The economic means of expression, the skilful use of space, the apparently spontaneous brush strokes give his work immediacy and particular charm.

Korea

The history of Korean art was shaped almost entirely by the country's geographic position at the meeting point of the power and interests of the gigantic Chinese empire with those of Japan's island kingdom, which repeatedly sought to establish a continental bridgehead in the Korean peninsula. The Tungus element dominates the make-up of the Korean people, whose language is a remote branch of the Altaic family, overlaid since the 8th–9th century by a Sino-Korean literary and cultivated speech derived from T'ang China.

In the neolithic culture of the centuries before Christ we find objects imported from the steppe art of Inner Asia and the transitional stage leading to the metal age is characterised by two types of dolmen. During the late Chou period the north-eastern Chinese state of Yen made its influence felt in part of the peninsula.

In the time of the powerful Han empire the whole peninsula was incorporated into China, being divided into four prefectures, which were finally (*c*. 75 BC) combined into the single province of Lo-lang with its centre at the present city of P'yongyang. Rich finds in this area have brought to light characteristic Han objects of high quality. The lacquer pieces, which have become famous, were imported from their place of manufacture in south China. Other objects such as the splendid jewellery in granulated gold- and silverwork may have been produced in Korea itself. Although these products of an advanced civilisation may have been exclusively intended for the use of the Chinese ruling class, they exercised an influence over the indigenous culture of the peninsula as a whole – an influence that reached as far as Japan.

Aggressive nationalist states finally drove the Chinese out of Korea, freeing Lo-lang in 313 and initiating the period of the Three Kingdoms (313–668). The most powerful of these kingdoms was the northern Koguryo, which extended its sphere of influence far into Manchuria. The patrons of art belonged to a privileged military nobility, which fell under the intellectual spell of Chinese Confucianism in the second half of the 4th century of our era. Buddhism, however, was the state religion. (It will be recalled that this is the period of the great spread of Buddhism in north China). The most important evidence of Koguryo culture is found in the tombs in the plain of T'ung-kou on the Manchurian border and in the vicinity of P'yongyang; many of these tombs have chambers containing well preserved wall-paintings. Although subject-matter and technique were undoubtedly borrowed from contemporary Chinese art, these paintings give us a fascinating glimpse into the daily life of the feudal nobility of Koguryo in the 5th and 6th century with its numerous hunts and festivities.

In the south-western corner of the peninsula several hereditary principalities coalesced to form the kingdom of Paekche. In keeping with its geographical location this kingdom played an important part in bringing Chinese culture to Japan. The peasantry, and the craftsmen who

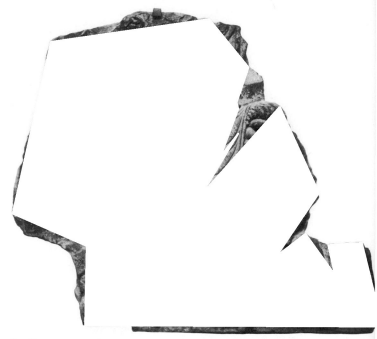

85. **Fragment of a tile, with a Buddhist figure.** Old Silla period (668–918). 7th century. Terracotta. h. 21 in. (53 cm.). National Museum of Korea, Seoul. This tile comes from the temple of Sach'onwang-sa, near Kyong-ju. Buddhism probably came to Silla in the 5th century, but it was only accepted officially under King Phophung (527). This figure, which perhaps represents a Bodhisattva, shows how the Korean sculptor adopted the decorative and iconographic features of Buddhism, while giving the relief a liveliness which is characteristically Korean.

were organised into guilds formed the economic basis of the country and were ruthlessly exploited by the nobles to support a courtly culture influenced by China. From what must have been richly furnished tombs of the Paekche princes only terracotta tiles decorated with reliefs have survived; with their landscape scenes, these show an astonishing similarity to earlier Chinese tiles. There are also well-executed figural examples. The advanced Buddhist art of Paekche exercised a strong influence on the sculpture of Japan. The ethereal Paekche sculptures in turn reflect the stimulus of Chinese schools, probably those of the Northern Ch'i dynasty. The gilt-bronze work was cast with great technical knowledge, showing the high level of achievement of the Korean craftsmen.

The third state, which is the most important for future development, was the kingdom of Silla in the south-east. The ruler was at first a kind of shamanistic priest-prince, who only in the 6th century took the title of king. A symbol of the old priestly kingship may be the crowns of gold or gilt-bronze found in tombs of the 5th and 6th centuries; the characteristic open-work motif may derive from the so-called shaman-tree or from antlers.

After internal warfare in Korea in the 4th and 5th centuries and the expulsion of a Japanese colony, the politically gifted Silla Kings succeeded, with the help of Chinese armies of the Sui and T'ang dynasties, in conquering first Paekche and then powerful Koguryo. Afterwards they managed to drive out the ambitious Chinese, welding the

86 (left). **Observatory at Kyong-ju.** Old Silla period, early 7th century. h. about 30 ft. (9·14 m.). This bottle-shaped observatory tower (Ch'omsong-dai), built in the reign of Queen Sondok (632–46), supported astronomical instruments on an upper platform, of which the stone frame has been preserved. It is one of the rare surviving monuments of the period, providing evidence of the highly developed astronomical science of the Far East.

87 (above). **Stone Stairs and Pavilion of the Pulguk-sa Temple near Kyong-ju.** Great Silla period, 7th–8th centuries. Apart from the two pagodas (see plate 81), only foundations remain of the old buildings of this famous Silla temple. The first section of the double flight of stairs passes over a true barrel vault in stone. Many details of the terrace façade and the understructure imitate wood construction in stone.

whole of the peninsula south of P'yongyang into a unified state (668–892).

The Silla population was organised according to a complicated class system. The dominant class of free men comprised the ruling clan and the high officials. Also free were the feudal magnates who formed the military nobility, but the mass of the people worked in conditions of near slavery. The Chinese pattern was of course adopted for the state apparatus, and land ownership was entirely in the hands of the state, that is, of the king, who conferred it to the nobility in the form of fiefs. In Silla, culture and scholarship, which flourished primarily in the capital of Kyong-ju, the influence of T'ang was dominant. Nobles and monks were sent to China to study, where they sometimes stayed to take the state examinations like any Chinese official. The calligraphy of Ou-yang Hsün was imitated throughout Korea, and the cultivated life of the nobility and the ruling clan followed the T'ang example as far as local resources would allow. The famous 7th-century observ-
86 atory tower at Kyong-ju provides evidence of their scientific ambitions. Kyong-ju and the neighbouring area became a flourishing centre of Buddhist culture, much evidence of which remains. The monks rivalled the nobles as patrons of the arts.

The terrace and the celebrated vaulted stairs of the
87 Monastery of Pulguk-sa founded in 751 in the vicinity of the capital partly imitated wooden prototypes in stone.
81 The same goes for the Prabhūtaratna pagoda (Tabo-t'ab)

of the same temple, which is unique in all of East Asia. Apart from the great monasteries which were generous patrons of art and scholarship, the Buddhist tendency to withdraw from the world was decisive in influencing the character of their architecture. Witness of this is the cave temple of Sokkul-am, founded in 752 by the minister Kim Taesong, who also founded Pulguk-sa, situated high on a mountain near that monastery. This temple was not cut from the living rock, but constructed of stone masonry and covered over with earth. It is uncertain whether the present form of the building, which was restored by the Japanese, corresponds to the original. The fine stone sculpture re-
88 calls that of the mature T'ang style in China. The ceramics of Silla developed vigorous forms, which have many points in common with earlier Chinese and with later Japanese work, perhaps representing a link between them. The grey Silla ceramic wares were hard-fired and only towards the end of the period provided with glazing. Characteristic are
89 the figural grave gifts, which seem somewhat primitive in comparison with their Chinese counterparts.

Peasant risings undermined the power of the Silla kingdom, which finally split into several small states, after which the north Korean Koryo dynasty (918–1215) was able to weld them together to form a new unified state with its capital at Kaesong. In the organisation of the state the Koryo rulers retained the Silla institutions that were of proven value, though they adopted Confucian practice by setting up an official class in place of the hereditary nobility.

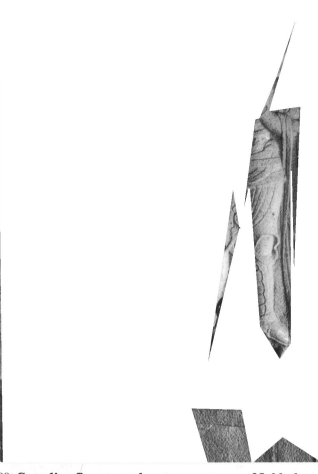

88. **Guardian figures at the cave sanctuary of Sokkul-am.** North Kyongsang province. Great Silla period, 8th century. Granite. h. *c*. 6 ft. 4 in. (193 cm.). The minister Kim Taesong, who also endowed the Sokkul-am temple, founded this sanctuary high on a mountain in 752. Unlike its Chinese counterparts, the complex was not hewn from the living rock, but constructed in masonry and covered with earth. In the interior is a colossal figure of the Buddha Sākyamuni, while the round inner wall bears reliefs of Lo-hans and Bodhisattvas. The sanctuary was protected externally by guardian figures. The style of the figures corresponds to the T'ang style of China.

89. **Vessel in the form of a rider.** From the Tomb of the Golden Bell. Old Silla period, 5th–6th centuries. Grey stoneware. h. 9½ in. (24 cm.). National Museum of Korea, Seoul. This figure of an armoured warrior on his horse imitates a vase type that was in actual use. The piece has an opening for filling behind the rider and a spout on the horse's chest. It was intended to serve as a tomb offering, rather than for practical purposes.

The practice of granting land as fiefs was now limited to the lifetime of the recipient in order to inhibit the growth of great estates. Trade, even when conducted in association with foreign partners, lay exclusively in state hands so that private initiative could not develop as a basis for a middle class. Buddhism was once more the state religion, and art and scholarship were primarily cultivated within the walls of the many great monasteries. Stone pagodas commemorated pious foundations.

During the golden age of the Koryo dynasty in the 11th century a growing Sung influence was evident, providing almost unbelievable luxury in the royal court and its dependencies, a development that was to have catastrophic effects on the economy of the country. Revolts among the dissatisfied peasantry and attempts to avoid taxation endangered the foundations of the dynasty which, although it was apparently saved by severe measures on the part of the Ch'oe family, sank into a kind of twilight existence.

The high artistic level of the Koryo period is reflected in the art of ceramics, which adopted and developed influences from the north Chinese celadon both in form and in the greenish colour of its glazes. A characteristic Korean technique is a decoration in black-and-white slip beneath the glaze, known as *Sanggam*, in which the monochrome glazing was enriched with charming colour contrasts.

In the 13th and 14th century Korea was repeatedly overrun by Mongol armies, which devastated the country, destroying much of its artistic patrimony forever. Most of the architecture of the period went up in flames. For a while a shaky Korean government-in-exile maintained itself on the island of Kanghwa, but for most of the time between 1215 and 1356 the Koryo kingdom was subject to Mongol rule.

After the collapse of Mongol power in East Asia, Korea was governed by the Yi dynasty (1392–1910), which moved the capital to Seoul, prudently recognising the overlordship of the Ming in China. On the whole it can be said that Korean art of this period is an offshoot of that of the Ming dynasty. An initial uprising of the economy, together with increasing trade with Japan and China provided the early Yi rulers with the means to create a bureaucratic state on the Confucian pattern. While Buddhism was systematically stripped of influence, its adherents being persecuted and hindered from practising their faith, state examinations were introduced for officials and

90. **Interior of the Throne Hall.**
Kyungbok-gung Palace, Seoul. Yi
period, 1395 (rebuilt 1867). The Throne
Hall stands on a double-tiered granite
terrace surrounded by carved marble
balustrades (see plate 84). The gallery
and ceiling are supported on sixteen
enormous wooden columns nearly a yard
in diameter, the centre one being forty
feet high. The throne was so placed that
when the king was seated there he could
see the broad highway beyond his palace.
In scale and in technique, the hall is an
outstanding example of Yi-dynasty
architecture.

91. **Kim Tu-ryang** (attributed to).
Autumn Landscape. Detail from one of a
pair of handscrolls. Ink and colours on
paper. $3\frac{1}{8} \times 72\frac{1}{2}$ in. (8×184 cm.).
Duksoo Palace of Fine Arts, Seoul. Kim
Tu-ryang (1698–1764) excelled in a style
of landscape painting that was clearly
based on that of the contemporary or
slightly earlier Chinese literati painters.
He often introduced scenes with many
figures into his landscapes, but more
according to Chinese tradition than to
the contemporary style of Korean genre
painting.

92. **Kang Hui-an.** *Sage in Meditation.* Early Yi dynasty. Ink and light colours on paper. 9 × 6¼ in. (23 × 15·8 cm.). National Museum of Korea, Seoul. Kang Hui-an was a man of aristocratic family, a poet, calligrapher and painter. He was born in 1419, passed the government examination in 1441, and entered the *Chiphyon-jon*, the academy to which all scholars were attached. He served under three kings and is reputed to be one of the scholars who helped to devise the Korean alphabet. He made many visits to China, and was directly influenced by Ming painters.

93. **Portrait of Song Si-yol.** Yi period, 18th century. Hanging scroll. Ink and colour on silk. Size 35½ × 26 in. (90 × 66 cm.). Duksoo Palace Museum of Fine Arts, Seoul. This portrait, by an unknown court painter, shows a high official and influential scholar who was born in 1607. Although his talents brought him to the vice-premiership, he was disgraced in 1689. The garment, which is indicated in a few precise lines, contrasts with the lively treatment of the dignified face. An inscription added later states that the picture hung in the Confucius Temple of Seoul.

throughout the land there appeared private—though state supported—Confucian academies *(sowon)*, intended to replace Buddhism as the dominant intellectual force. The cultivation of dogmatic Confucian learning was supplemented by a study of Chinese-influenced natural sciences. In 1446 scholars created the national Korean alphabet, which is still in use. Moreover, printing with moveable characters was pioneered more successfully than in China itself, where it had been invented and then forgotten again.

The ambitions of the new dynasty found an outlet in large-scale building activities in the new capital of Seoul. The Kyungbok-gung palace, a large complex with a central throne hall, is a small-scale version of a Ming-dynasty theme. This building, intended for state functions, was completed by wings containing studios, libraries and apartments for the court retinue. The adjacent palace of Ch'angdok-gung had a large secluded garden with little retreats and pavilions where the court ladies of the palace could arrange delicious outings.

The cultivated upper class dependent on the patronage of the royal family, was divided into two separate sub-classes. High officials and bureaucrats were recruited exclusively from the dominant caste of the *Yangban*. The lower class of the so-called *Chung'in* had no prospects of rising to *Yangban* status, but provided incumbents of lesser offices. The *Chung'in* were educated along Confucian lines and from their ranks came scholars and artists. Under the dominant Confucian ethos Korea developed the familiar literary-artist type, who wrote or painted for his own pleasure.

The landscapes and the flower-and-animal pictures of these painters occasionally followed the Chinese style of the Southern Sung period, as for example the work of the famous savant Kang Hui-an (1419–65) who had visited China. Later Korean literary painting was dominated by the Ming and Ch'ing masters of China. Finally in the 18th

(Continued on page 137)

78. **Mural from the Tomb of Uhyon-ni, near P'yongyang, Korea.** Koguryo dynasty, 6th–7th century AD. The wall-paintings in the tomb chambers of the P'yongyang region date from the latter part of the Koguryo dynasty. They are mainly earthern constructions with stone chambers inside. Outstanding among them is the Tomb of Uhyon-ni. Although the tomb was looted of any transportable objects, the paintings remain in a remarkably fine state of preservation. The subjects include the deities of the Four Cardinal Points: the Red Phoenix, the Green Dragon, the White Tiger and the Tortoise entwined by a Snake. Such symbols had been imported from Han China, but are depicted in a way which can be regarded as authentically Korean.

79. **Gold crown with pendant ornaments.** Old Silla period. 5th–6th centuries. Gold and jade. h. (without pendants) 17⅜ in. (44 cm.). National Museum of Korea, Seoul. In 1921 three golden crowns were found amongst other jewellery in stone tombs near Kyong-ju. This one, from the tomb now called the 'Tomb of the Golden Crown', must have belonged to a king or nobleman. It consists of an outer circle with five upright features, and an inner cap with branch- or antler-like projections. The outer part is made of cut sheet gold, ornamented with punched dots. From this, small jade ornaments dangle on lengths of twisted wire. These comma-shaped jade pieces also occur in Japan. The 'antlers' may connect with shamanist beliefs.

80 (next page). **Bodhisattva Maitreya.** Old Silla or Paekche period. Early 7th century. Gilt bronze. h. 3 ft. 2¾ in. (91 cm.). Duksoo Palace Museum, Seoul. The play of drapery in this figure seated in meditation recalls the sculpture of the Northern Ch'i in China. The comparatively high number of surviving bronze images of Maitreya from this period—this is by far the finest of them—suggests that his cult was especially popular. The type was imitated in Japan.

81 (above). **Prabhūtaratna Pagoda** *(Tabo t'ab)*. Pulguk-sa Temple near Kyong-ju. Great Silla Period, mid-8th century. Stone h. *c.* 33 ft. (10·05 m.). The westernmost of two pagodas before the main hall of the big Silla temple is unique in the history of Far Eastern art. The shape is similar to the small gilt-bronze pagodas made as reliquaries, while other features of this stone building, including the balustrade and the system of support, imitate wooden architecture.

82 (above). **Palace buildings, Kyungbok-gung, Seoul.** Early Yi period. The Kyungbok Palace was built during the third year of Yi Sunggye (1394). It consisted of nearly a hundred independent buildings surrounded by a palace wall. In this picture two of the wooden pavilions can be seen. These were restored under the Prince Regent Taewun-gun in 1867.

132

83 (previous page). **Pavilion in the
Secret Garden** *(Pi-won)*. Ch'angdok-
gung Palace, Seoul. Late Yi period. The
large garden behind the palace contains
an assortment of small villas, pavilions
and gazebos in rustic style that served for
festivals, banquets or for tranquil
gatherings of the king and his palace
ladies. In contrast to the artificial

arrangement of gardens in China, the
fine natural landscape has been left
largely undisturbed.

84. **Throne Hall** *(Keunjong-chon)*.
Kyungbok-gung Palace, Seoul. Early
Yi period, 1395 (rebuilt 1867). The
imposing Throne Hall with its heavy
double roof was originally built by the

founder of the Yi dynasty, but it was
destroyed during the Japanese invasion
in the 16th century. It was only fully
restored in 1867. The stone piers in the
paved courtyard before the hall mark
the places where the officials stationed
themselves according to rank during
audiences and ceremonies.

85. **Sin Yun-bok.** *Genre scene.* Yi period, *c.* 1800. Ink and colour on paper. 11 × 13¾ in (28 × 35 cm.). Hyung-pil Chun Collection, Seoul. This illustration is from an album by Sin Yun-bok, who worked under the professional name of Hewon and who lived from 1758 to about 1820. He was one of the leading masters of the genre trend that flourished in the Yi period. In this delightful album, one of his best works, he depicted various scenes from the Korean upper-class life of his time.

86. **Wine pitcher.** Koryo period, late 12th century. Stoneware with celadon-type glaze and slip inlay. h. 9 in. (23 cm.). Ostasiatische Kunstabteilung, Staatliche Museen, Berlin. This elegant vessel was made in the *sanggam* technique, in which the decoration was incised into the surface and filled with a slip in another colour, a practice popular in celadon ware of the Koryo period. The centre of production seems to have been in the vicinity of Kangjin in the extreme south of Korea. The flower pattern often occurs in the 12th- and 13th-century ceramics.

87 (opposite). **Japanese bell, or dōtaku.** Yayoi period.
300 BC–AD 300. Patinated bronze. h. 27 in. (69 cm.). Museum
für Ostasiatische Kunst, Cologne. The bronze bells of the
Yayoi period are evidence of Japan's short-lived bronze
culture. The production was centred in the provinces near the
present city of Kyōto, but their date is uncertain. The bells are
decorated with line ornament in low relief, sometimes
geometric, sometimes showing hunting scenes.

88. **Haniwa head of a woman.** Old Tomb period, late
Yayoi. 3rd–6th centuries AD. Fired clay. h. 7½ in. (16.3 cm.).
Matsubara collection, Tokyo. The most interesting objects of
the late Yayoi period in Japan are the *haniwa* figures which
were erected in circles around burial mounds (*hani* means
clay and *wa* circle). Among these are simple cylinders, human
figures, animals and houses. This female head has minimal
modelling, the features being indicated in the briefest manner.

89. **Pagoda of Yakushi-ji, Nara.** Nara period. *c.* 700. The
pagoda, on the right in this picture, actually comprises three
storeys, although the building gives the effect of six because of
the introduction of mezzanines *(mokoshi)* with their own roofs.
The resulting differences in scale produce an attractive
rhythmic alternation. The central mast *(shimbashira)* running
through the whole building and supported by a foundation
stone containing relics is not linked directly to the individual
storeys, but serves to stabilise the building as a whole in case
of earthquake.

94a, b. **Tea bowl.** Yi period, late 16th or early 17th century. Fired clay. d. 5⅞ in. (15 cm.). Ostasiatische Kunstabteilung, Staatliche Museen, Berlin. The simple, rather rustic pottery made in Korea during the middle Yi period contrasts strongly with the sophistication of contemporary Chinese ware. Korean pottery of this type exercised a strong influence on the forms taken by the ceramics of the Japanese tea ceremony.

85 century there appeared a characteristically Korean genre painting of great freshness and vitality.

Yi Korea had an official art bureau *(tohwa-so)* with professional painters of the *Chung'in* class permanently attached to it, but they belonged to the lowest rank of officialdom and were poorly paid. They had to execute **93** portraits of the *Yangban* to order and were not very much respected as artists.

Before long the struggles of rival political groups began to cast lengthening shadows on the Yi regime. The Japanese invasion of Korea in the last decade of the 16th century devastated the exhausted country. Cities, villages and most of the buildings of consequence were gutted and countless works of art were destroyed. Deportation of Korean craftsmen to Japan was a heavy blow and the losses almost brought ceramic production to a standstill. **94** On the other hand the rather rustic pottery of local Korean craftsmen exercised a decisive influence over Japanese tea ceramics. Moreover, the great simplicity and authenticity of their work contrasts with the sophistication of contemporary Chinese porcelain. Characteristic of this phase is the blue-and-white ware made in Korea for court use, as **95** well as the pottery painted with iron oxide.

From 1637 to 1894 Korea was a vassal of Manchu China. Renewed struggles for power, corruption in the administration, heavy taxation and repeated failures of their crops caused deepening misery among the hard-pressed Korean people. After a period of withdrawal from the outside world and some terrible persecutions of the newly implanted Christianity, the country became a pawn in the hands of foreign powers. From 1905 to 1910 it was a protectorate, then (until 1945) a colony of the Japanese empire. It is only too clear that the traditional arts could not flourish under these conditions. Now that peace seems to have been established in the divided country, the authorities are seeking partly to revive the remains of the ancient crafts and partly to create entirely anew. The future will tell whether these efforts can succeed in a radically altered social and cultural setting.

90 (opposite). **The Priest Ganjin.** Nara period. 8th century. Painted dry lacquer. h. 2 ft. 8½ in. (81.7 cm.). Tōshōdai-ji, Nara. Ganjin was a Chinese monk who, having made a number of unsuccessful attempts to reach Japan by sea, finally succeeded after he had become blind. He founded the famous Tōshōdai-ji Temple in Nara. This figure is made of linen saturated in lacquer modelled over a core that was later removed. It ranks as one of the earliest and most moving portraits in the history of Japanese art.

95. **Porcelain jar with clouds and dragon.** Yi period. 17th–18th centuries. Grey porcelain with iron-oxide underglaze decoration. h. 14⅛ in. (36 cm.). Duksoo Palace Museum of Fine Arts, Seoul. In bold, energetic strokes the potter has depicted a dragon and cloud motifs in a brownish hue before applying the transparent glaze. In a Korea impoverished by Japanese invaders the costly blue preferred in the older underglaze painting became almost unobtainable, so that potters often fell back on the cheaper iron-oxide pigment.

Japan

Until the present geological epoch, the Japanese archipelago was linked to the mainland of Asia in a crescent-shaped peninsula stretching down into the Holocene. Even after the land bridge with Asia had sunk below the sea, invaders continued to reach Japan, ultimately fusing to make up the present population. The main ethnic components of the Japanese of today come from Tungus, Sinic and Palaeo-Mongolian stocks. Traces of an originally much larger stratum of Caucasian peoples are found among the Ainu of the northern Island of Hokkaidō.

PREHISTORIC JAPAN

As a result of extensive finds from many parts of the islands we are now fairly well informed about the two main prehistoric cultures. The neolithic Jōmon culture, which apparently enjoyed more than two thousand years of uninterrupted predominance, gave way in about 200 BC before the men of the Yayoi culture who pushed in from the south (probably from Korea) via the Island of Kyūshū. Many mainland elements came in with the Yayoi people, notably bronze casting (the short Japanese Bronze age began in about AD 300). The Yayoi phase passed without transition into the semi-historical Old Tomb period; but even before this shift some of the countless Japanese principalities had come into contact with Han China. Iron soon appeared and the princes were buried in gigantic tomb mounds, the building of which may have required the toil of as many as five thousand men for a year. The ceramic cylinders known as *haniwa* with the upper part modelled in human or animal form (in an astonishing and wholly Japanese style) were set up around the mounds. Similarly Japanese in character are the so-called *dōtaku*, bronze bells that seem to have had a religious use. The social unit of this period was the clan, and craftsmen were already organised in closely-knit guilds *(be)*, in which membership was hereditary. The pottery shapes, which show a similari-

88

87

96. **The Izumo shrine.** Last rebuilt in 1744. Izumo is the most ancient sacred precinct of the Shinto religion. The great shrine or *Taisha* has been successively rebuilt since the 7th century when it became obligatory to rebuild the entire complex every twenty years. Its origins are much earlier. It is recorded that the Emperor Suinin rebuilt the sanctuary sometime in the 1st century 'in the same shape as the Emperor's palace'. In any case the ground plan and the architectural features of the latest rebuilding (1744) preserve the essentials of the archaic period, although the cross-beams above the ridge are no longer projections of the barge boards but merely scissor-shaped ornaments to the roof. Nor would the original structure have had the curved roof which suggests later Buddhist influence.

ty with those of the Korean Silla kingdom, point to close cultural links with the peninsula.

Among the numerous principalities Yamato with its centre near the present city of Nara eventually proved the strongest. Yamato created the first Japanese state system. The old shamanistic nature religion was fused with concepts of an ancestor cult and a large pantheon of nature and clan gods came into being. In the climate of this early Japanese religion of *Shintō* (but also stimulated by the Chinese emperor's status as the son of heaven), there developed the idea of the *Tennō* (exalted heavenly ruler), who was regarded as a direct descendent of the sun goddess Amaterasu Omikami. Despite powerful later influences from the well-organised Buddhist church, the native religion of Shintō ('the way of the gods') has kept many traits of a primitive nature and ancestor cult until the present day. With their simple form and structure, the Shintō temples still retain memories of prehistoric nature and ancestor shrines that constituted the holy places of the clans.

96

THE ASUKA AND NARA PERIODS

Although the beginnings and development of the Yamato state are described in some detail in the first Japanese historical chronicles written in the early 8th century, the true historical period begins only with the introduction of Buddhism. A fixed point of reference is provided by the dispatch of a statue of the Buddha accompanied by texts, from the Korean kingdom of Paekche to the Japanese imperial court in AD 552. A lively debate arose among the nobility as to the merits of the new religion, which ultimately triumphed, being firmly established under the special patronage of the ruling house. In the Asuka period (538–645), named after the first fixed capital, Yamato underwent a powerful mainland influence, which came not only from Korea, but from China itself. Confucian ideas penetrated in strength and stimulated the creation of a real governmental apparatus. Then, too, the adoption of the Chinese script greatly facilitated the introduction of Chinese ways and forms.

The extent of this process of assimilation appears in the seventeen articles of the prince regent Shōtoku Taishi (604), a kind of draft constitution for the youthful Japanese state, as well in the Taika reform of 645, which affirmed Confucian influence in the political field. Shōtoku Taishi was also an ardent supporter of Buddhism; in 607 he decided to send Japanese monks to study in China of the Sui dynasty, and he summoned Chinese artists to his court. In the same year he founded the Hōryū-ji temple as the main centre of Buddhist study and teaching. The plan of the temple, which follows a venerable Korean or perhaps even Chinese model, juxtaposes a pagoda to house relics and a main hall *(kondō)* in a rectangular court. Both of these still stand, ranking as the oldest wooden buildings in the world. The main cult image of the *kondō* is a triad with

97. **The Sākyamuni Triad.** Asuka period, dated 623. Bronze. h. (of main figure) 34⅛ in. (86·7 cm.). Hōryū-ji Kondō, Nara. An inscription states that this group is a pious offering in recognition of the recovery from illness of the Crown Prince Shōtoku Taishi. The name of the sculptor, Tori, is also given. Tori, a descendant of immigrant Chinese craftsman, was given a grant of land in recognition of his services. The style of the figure stems from Continental sculpture of the 6th century.

historical Buddha Sākyamuni in the centre. Set up in 623 in memory of Shōtoku Taishi, the group's dedicatory inscription mentions the name of the sculptor Tori, the grandson of a craftsman who had emigrated from Korea. As a reward for the successful casting of this outstanding work, which clearly descends from the Chinese Wei style, the empress gave Tori the noble rank of *Daijin* and an estate in Sakata. This shows the high value attached to outstanding artists even in this early period.

After the shift of the capital to Nara, which gives its name to the following Nara period (710–84), the influence of the rich culture of T'ang China became dominant. The new capital was a copy of the Chinese metropolis of Ch'ang-an on a smaller scale in a rectangle measuring 2¾ by 3 miles. Since it was now possible to deal directly with the great mainland civilisation which had reached the height of its glory, and Korean Paekche was no longer needed as a go-between, influences were received in a fresh and undiluted form. Intense curiosity prompted the dispatch of a series of embassies. With one of the official missions the famous Chinese monk Ganjin (Chinese: *Chien-chên*), who had become blind as a result of repeated attempts to reach

98. The Hōryū-ji temple complex at Nara. 7th century. This picture shows the Hōryū-ji complex from the south-east. The pagoda and kondō are enclosed on three sides by covered corridors and on the fourth by the Lecture Hall (extreme right). A single entrance gateway pierces the southern corridor (left). The complex is unusual in that the kondō and pagoda are not placed on the axial line but alongside each other. This asymmetry is compensated for by the placing of the entrance gateway one 'bay' nearer the western end. (See plate 89.) The 10th-century Lecture Hall replaces an earlier dormitory building which must have been set further forward to complete the originally simpler rectangular form to the compound.

Japan for the faith, arrived at Nara in 754, where he became high priest in the great temple of Tōdai-ji. The portrait made a few years after Ganjin's death in the complex 'dry-lacquer' technique ranks among the earliest and most effective Japanese portrait sculpture. An eloquent witness of the highly cosmopolitan character of Nara art and culture is the collection in the Shōsō-in treasury attached to the Temple of Tōdai-ji, founded in 756 and completed in 760. Here thousands of objects were assembled, comprising the entire personal property of the dead Emperor Shōmu, willed by this widow to the temple of the imperial house. The furniture, works of art and domestic objects in this oldest museum in the world included the products of China, Japan and even Persia. They give an impressive picture of the luxurious and cultivated court of a Japanese emperor at this period.

The intellectual and practical influence exercised by Confucianism resulted in the elaboration of a bureaucracy along Chinese lines, which was intimately linked to the feudal aristocracy, whose members held an exclusive right to high office, as well as to the brilliant retinue of the emperor himself. More strongly than in China, where from T'ang times onwards the hierarchy of the officials fluctuated and could be replenished from below through the examination system, in Japan privileges of office were reserved for definite social groups bound together in noble clans.

In the Nara period, Buddhism consolidated its position as the leading faith of the land. Buddhist priests were accorded a special position in society. The imperial house was especially devoted to the religion that had come from the west, perhaps because the highly developed ritual practices of the faith offered almost unlimited scope for

pomp and ostentation, a feature that was lacking in the more primitive Shintō cult. The imposing Nara Tōdai-ji temple, of which only a gateway survives from the 8th-century constructions, became the official temple of the imperial house and was richly furnished. A special bureau within the temple was responsible for the work of outfitting and decoration. In the Zōbutsu-jo (sculpture department) many sculptors and their assistants were employed in making cult images. A system of division of labour was in force. An unusually expensive undertaking even for such a wealthy temple, was the casting of a Roshana Buddha image fifty-three feet in height, which was finally dedicated in 752 in an impressive ceremony witnessed by the reigning empress. Often restored in the course of its eventful history, the great figure sits today in the main hall of the temple. The Shōsō-in preserves many objects used in the dedication ceremony.

An imperial decree of 741 ordered the building of 'official provincial monasteries' (kokubun-ji) throughout the realm; these monasteries were placed under the jurisdiction of the Tōdai-ji administration. The temples in the capital were particularly splendid. A good example is the Yakushi-ji, dedicated to Yakushi, the Buddha of healing, which was established as early as 680 in Asuka as a thank-offering for recovery of an empress from illness, and transferred to the new capital in 710. Of the old buildings one of the two pagodas has survived (718). Built in wood with plastered walls, the three stories of the building look like six because each storey has a kind of mezzanine with its own roofing. With its clear articulation and harmonious proportions, the Yakushi-ji pagoda ranks among the finest examples of its kind in East Asia. The chief cult image, a triad with Yakushi in the centre, dominates the main hall of the temple. The three figures, originally gilded but now showing the soft brilliance of a dark lacquer patina, were cast in bronze about 720. In their perfection of form they descend directly from T'ang dynasty models which influenced all areas of Japanese culture at this time. The figures of the triad are rare in Far Eastern art in their mastery of sculpture in the round, without resource to linear aids. (Similarly, the paintings of Hōryū-ji—unfortunately almost completely destroyed by fire in 1949—embody the international style dominant in the Buddhist art of East Asia.)

It is possible that the casting of the giant Buddha of Tōdai-ji, which consumed enormous quantities of bronze, explains the fact that many of the sculptures of the first half of the 8th century in the same temple were modelled in terracotta or in dry-lacquer technique instead of being cast in metal. A characteristic example is the Shukongō-shin, who brandishes a thunderbolt in his right hand, a guardian divinity of fierce aspect executed life-size in terracotta and painted in colours.

Under the pressure of the preeminent Buddhist church (a significant indication of which is Emperor Shōmu's abdication in favour of his daughter in 749, in order to become a monk) it is not surprising to see the first hints of Shintōism's later effort to imitate or even fuse with the ritual and organisational apparatus of its more powerful rival.

THE HEIAN PERIOD

The increasing might of the Buddhist monasteries in Nara finally induced the emperor to move his capital once more. After preparations had been under way in Nagaoka for a decade, a different site was finally chosen at the present Kyōto, where the new city of Heian was founded in 784. Ten years later the emperor moved to his new residence, but work continued there for a long time. Here again the layout followed the Chinese model: a grid of broad main streets and smaller parallel ones divided the city into a regular chequerboard plan. At the centre were the imperial palace and the big new monasteries. The years from 784 to 1192 are named after this city, which was the cultural and political centre of Japan throughout this long period.

After the aboriginal Ainu had been driven northwards into Hokkaidō the whole of the main island of Honshū was subjected to the central government, which was organised according to Chinese practice. Peace prevailed in the country for a long time, so that social and cultural life were able to develop freely. Of course the stream of civilising influence from the mainland did not diminish, but the Japanese were no longer content with uncritical imitation of things Chinese. Political unrest and the decline of the T'ang empire did not go unnoticed by Japanese visitors and a sense of national identity took root in the islands. After the 838 embassy to the T'ang emperor, official contacts were discontinued and upon the return of this embassy

99. **Yakushi Nyorai.** Nara period, c. 720. h. 8 ft. 4⅜ in. (2·55 m.). Yakushi-ji, Nara. The triad with the Buddha of healing in the centre flanked by two standing Bodhisattvas is surely one of the most beautiful bronze groups in the world. The pliant modelling of the figures betrays the influence of Chinese sculpture of the Sui or early T'ang period, when the metropolitan style of Buddhism centred in Ch'ang-an stimulated the entire Far East.

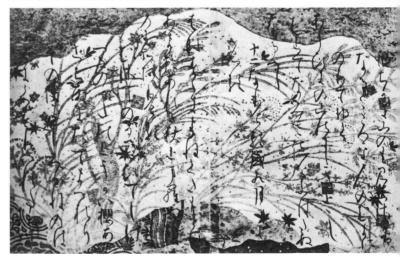

100. **Poem on Decorative Paper.** Heian period, 12th century. Ink on paper prepared as a collage. h. 7⅞ × 12⅝ in. (20 × 32 cm.). Nishi Hongan-ji, Kyōto. The elegant line of the Japanese *Hiragana* script, which contemporaries dubbed the *Onna-de* 'Women's Style', was especially suited to short poems. The collection in the Nishi Hongan temple comprises some 3,000 leaves, none quite like another. The fine calligraphy of this specimen is doubtless from the hand of an aristocratic writing-master. The paper in this example was first wood-blocked with a design of flowers and plants and then overlaid with coloured papers to form a sky-line and foreground The poem was written across the background 'landscape'.

101. **The Animal Scrolls** (detail). Heian period, 12th century. Ink on paper. h. 11⅞ in. (30·2 cm.). Kōzan-ji, Kyōto. The detail comes from the finest of the four scrolls preserved in the Kōzan-ji that were formerly ascribed to the priest-artist Tōba Sōjō. With a sure sense of line the artist shows animals engaged in human activities. The choice of subjects indicates that the scrolls are a satire on late Heian society, focusing particularly on abuses in the Buddhist Church. Although there are overtones of caricature elsewhere in late Heian painting, these scrolls are nevertheless unique in the art of the Far East.

to Japan, the imported Chinese goods were distributed for the last time in a special sale attended by members of the court. Certainly private contacts with the continent continued through the activity of Chinese and Korean merchants, but diplomatic relations were only fully resumed after about AD 1000, when the powerful founders of the Sung dynasty had firmly established their line in China.

The phase of imitation of Chinese models by the nobles and the Buddhist church in Japan between the 6th and the 9th century, was followed by a period of progressive naturalisation of imported models in every field of art, a process that was to remain characteristic of Japanese culture. Phases of assimilation and transformation of foreign stimuli have generally occurred in periods when Japan retired into seclusion from her neighbours, turning her entire attention inwards.

A characteristic development from this point of view is the flowering of native Japanese syllabic scripts during the Heian period. Even in earlier times the Japanese had used Chinese characters according to their sound value to write Japanese texts phonetically. Thus through a refinement of rapidly written Chinese characters, the so-called *Hiragana*, a highly cursive type of syllabic script arose in court circles in the 8th and 9th centuries. Then towards the end of the Heian period the angular *Katakana* was created by abstracting individual graphic components from regular Chinese characters. The former script remained dominant in as much as it was much more attuned to the elegance of contemporary taste. Since it was extensively cultivated by court ladies who largely determined the literary atmosphere of the time, and who wrote some of the most important works, and since its form fully met the needs of the precious letter-writing style of amorous dalliance, the *100 Hiragana* is also called the *Onna-de*, or 'Women's Style'. Different coloured papers were arranged in collage fashion to produce delightful effects in which the elegance of the narrow swooping line achieved its full value, contrasting strongly in its feminine delicacy with the more robust Chinese script.

After the first emperors of the Heian era, who were gifted and successful rulers, the effective power of the sovereign declined: he was caught up more and more in the pomp of official ceremonies, while the machinery of government fell into the hands of ambitious nobles. In the general struggles for power at court and in the government, the Fujiwara clan gained the upper hand through its marriage ties with the royal family; ultimately the Fujiwara occupied almost all important offices. From this clan came not only leading politicians, but also great scholars, poets and artists. Behind the façade of imperial majesty the real affairs of state took place among the regents and councillors *(sesshō-kampaku)*. The greatest and most capable of the regents was Fujiwara Michinaga (died 1028), who retained his position through a number of brief imperial reigns. The domination of the entire spectrum of official and cultural life by the Fujiwara became so obvious that the second part of the Heian era is justifiably termed the Fujiwara period (967–1192).

The less fortunate noble families retired into the provinces, where they succeeded in acquiring vast tracts of land that were exempt from taxation. These provincial nobles, including the competing clans of the Taira and the Minamoto who rose to prominence at the end of the Heian period, were constantly increasing their economic powers. In the eastern provinces their autonomous tendencies were particularly evident. Since taxes and compulsory labour were appreciably lighter there than under the severe and often corrupt control of the central government, the peasants tended to flee to the protection of the powerful clans.

Towards the end of the Heian era these families, notably the above-mentioned Taira and Minamoto, became the real political power. Rival factions of the Fujiwara fell into civil strife and violence, losing all control over the country.

As a consequence the emperor regained political stature after the voluntary abdication of Shirakawa Tennō in 1087 to become a monk. For over forty years, under three emperors, Shirakawa Tennō was successful in controlling politics from behind the scenes, working methodically towards the destruction of Fujiwara power. But the real victors in this struggle were the Minamoto, and with them there emerged a new social group made up of their followers, who formed the basis for the warrior class that was to determine the character of the succeeding Kamakura period.

As a result of these changes, the art and culture of the later Heian period was more strongly influenced by the taste of the aristocracy than had previously been the case. State and private academies, which favoured a Chinese-oriented curriculum, were open only to aristocrats; a few of the public schools maintained after 828 by the new Buddhist sects were accessible to other classes, but there the training imparted was, of course, predominately Buddhist.

Japanese national trends made themselves felt even in the official architecture of palaces. Instead of being paved, the floors of the courts were covered by mats; the buildings were raised slightly above ground level on posts, and the roofs no longer displayed glazed tiles as in China but were covered with a thick layer of fine shingle. The houses of the nobles also took on a new character. The style known as *Shinden-zukuri* called for the arrangement of buildings in a garden setting with an artificial lake, the various pavilions being linked by covered passageways.

Courtly and aristocratic life reached a peak of luxury in the capital of Kyōto. Exile from the city was a much-dreaded punishment for the courtiers and nobles, for whom it amounted to a loss of human dignity. The pursuit of luxury and refinement became a conscious 'cult of the beautiful'. A lyrical, slightly melancholy note permeated all aspects of this civilisation. An almost sentimental sympathy with 'things' *(mono no aware)* is a characteristic feature of its highly feminine nature. Amorous dalliance became the preoccupation of social life and cultivated ladies were the arbiters of literary taste. From their ranks we have sensitive diaries, which provide us with many details of daily life, as well as the first narrative works, the most famous of which is an enormous novel dealing with the loves and adventures of Prince Genji and his descendents, written about 1000 by Lady Murasaki as a faithful mirror of the courtly life of her own time. Such books were well suited to illustration in a congenial Japanese style, the *Yamato-e*. Although this depends ultimately on Chinese sources, it followed its own paths from the 9th century onwards. One of the triumphs of this category of painting was the cycle of illustration made in the first half of the **93** 12th century for the *Tale of Genji* in which the brilliance and melancholy of the late Heian period are blended.

Poetry is possibly even more important for Heian literature, and this medium also saw the flowering of a native Japanese form, the *waka*, a kind of lyrical poem. Correspondence was often conducted in this form, and was full of tender allusions. Those who could not write poetry were regarded as uneducated. The emperor himself arranged anthologies of such *waka* and a bureau, the *Waka dokoro* was set up in 951 to preserve and collect them. Poetry competitions were set in either Japanese or Chinese style *(uta-awase* and *shi-awase)* in the palace on the occasion of the spring flower show or during the ceremony of moon-viewing. The finest works produced were written on screens and sliding doors in the palace and commonly supplemented with illustrative paintings. The aesthetic appreciation of this verse is reflected in the development of poetic theory.

The rapid growth of the Japanese *Yamato-e* style of painting took place in close association with the illustration of novels and poems. This was practiced at court in the Painting Bureau *(e-dokoro)* founded in 886. From painting on walls and sliding doors the court artists turned to the illustration of horizontal scrolls *(e-makimono)*, where text and image blend to make a single whole. Alongside the courtly and elegant manner, which was decorative in the best sense, exemplified by the brightly coloured and flatly designed Genji scrolls, court painters turned their attention also to scenes of popular life, which they often burlesqued in broad caricature. Expressive line was an important feature of such pictures. A famous example, and indeed a unique achievement of Japanese art, is represented by the satirical animal scenes of the 12th century from the *101* Kōzan-ji Temple, which probably satirise abuses among the Buddhist priesthood.

Lacquer objects offer eloquent testimony of the refined and luxurious life of the Heian nobility. They, too, are emancipated from Chinese tutelage, following a highly decorative manner that is all their own. The contrast of gold, silver and mother-of-pearl inlays against a black ground makes a rich impression. **94**

The brilliant opulence of the aristocracy and the imperial court was supported on a basis of peasant labour. Grinding poverty led to outbreaks of banditry not only in the provinces, but also in the capital reaching the walls of the imperial palace itself.

Only two decades after the foundation of the capital of Heian, two Buddhist sects newly imported from China obtained a powerful following: the *Tendai* school of the monk Saichō, which strove to reconcile the various contradictory Buddhist divisions and which enjoyed the patronage of the imperial house, and the *Shingon* school of Kūkai with its esoteric doctrines *(mikkyō)* and its rich pantheon of gods borrowed from Indian Tantrism. Secret mystical rites and the veneration of images played a large part in the cult practices of these sects, leading to a new flowering of Buddhist art. Not only craftsmen but also the monks themselves worked in the monastic workshops as priest-painters *(e-busshi)*, where they made the elaborate diagrams of the celestial spheres, *(mandara)*, and the often terrifying, even demonic figures of gods with many heads **95** and hands.

144

102. **Bodhisattva (Bosatsu).** Fujiwara period, middle of the 12th century. Wood with remains of gold lacquer decoration. h. 3 ft. 4 in. (101·5 cm.). Ostasiatische Kunstabteilung, Staatliche Museen, Berlin. This sculpture was probably the side figure of a Buddhist Triad, and may represent the Bodhisattva of Mercy, or Kannon Bosatsu.

A third important new trend in Heian Buddhism was the Amida cult of the priest Genshin (942–1017). This school emphasised spiritual sincerity and the believer's genuine, if rather simple-minded faith in the Buddha Amida. Promising even the humblest of believers a rebirth in the Paradise of Amida, the sect found a ready response not among the aristocracy, but among the generally literate middle-class. This tendency only became really effective under the priest Hōnen at the inception of the following Kamakura period, but many Heian nobles founded Amida temples for the salvation of their souls. Thus in 1052 the regent Fujiwara Yorimichi converted the estate of his father at Uji near Heian into the Byōdō-in Temple, of which the Phoenix Hall or Hōō-dō represents one of the few remaining examples of Heian architecture. The building, whose proportions are of great subtlety, is set at the edge of a lake; in form it depends upon palace architecture rather than upon 11th-century temple construction. 96,97

Buddhist sculptors of the Heian period worked mainly in wood. At first they were accustomed to carve statues from the single trunk of a tree but later they joined several blocks of wood together in the so-called *yosegi* technique. The rather heavy, massive style of early Heian times ultimately gave way to a 'Japanese style' *(wa-yō)* in keeping with the elegant taste of the age; this reached its peak in the work of Jōchō (died 1057) and his school. Many pieces of the 10th and 11th centuries are signed by the sculptors, which in itself is significant since it reflects their improved social status. The Buddhist sculptors *(busshi)* were often not just craftsmen, but monks in workshops run on guild lines *(bussho)*. The prestigious Jōchō, in addition to enjoying the favour of the nobles, was the first artist to receive the high ecclesiastical title of *Hokkyō* (Bridge of Doctrine). His gentle but distinguished style was widely diffused and imitated in Japan. 102

In spite of the militant attitude of a few of the Buddhist monasteries, Heian Buddhism is generally characterised by its tolerance, and aspects of Shintōism were drawn into its orbit. In the so-called *Ryōbu* Shintō, which was especially favoured by the Shingon sect of Buddhism, the old Shintō nature gods were welcomed into the Buddhist pantheon as manifestations of Buddhist divinities. From the second half of the 9th century this amalgamation of beliefs was reflected in sculpture. Although the attributes are Shintō, the style follows contemporary Buddhist sculpture. Obviously the 103

(Continued on page 161)

91 (opposite). **Biwa.** Nara period. 8th century. Wood with inlay in mother-of-pearl, amber and tortoiseshell. l. 3 ft. 8½ in. (113 cm.). Shōsō-in, Nara. This handsome five-stringed lute comes from the household furnishings of Emperor Shōmu, given after his death to the imperial temple of Tōdai-ji in Nara. The diverse origin of the pieces included in the gift—they range from Persia through China to Japan itself—and the refined craftsmanship of many of them attest to the luxury of Nara court life.

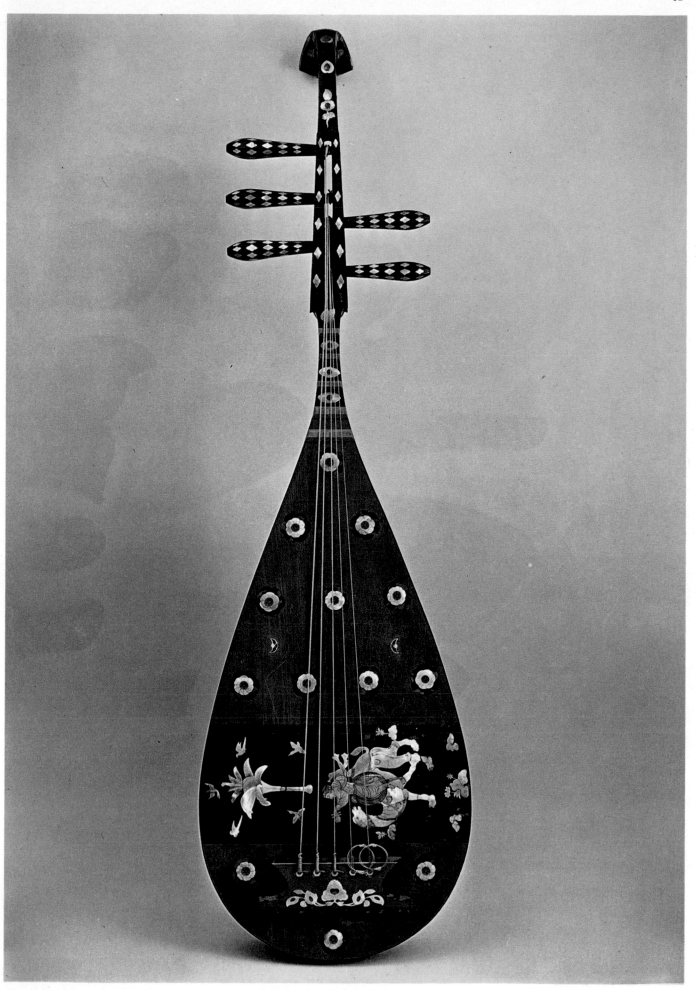

92 (opposite). **Shukongō-shin.** Nara period. 8th century. Painted terracotta. h. 5 ft. 6 in. (167·5 cm.). Hokke-dō, Tōdai-ji, Nara. Since this figure of Vajrapāni wielding a thunderbolt was formerly locked up in a shrine as a 'secret image', it is well preserved, despite the fragility of the material. The piece represents a fierce guardian deity of Buddhism, in full armour and with swirling drapery.

93 (above). **The Tale of Genji.** Detail from the Genji scroll. Late Heian period. h. 8⅝ in. (22 cm.). Tokugawa Museum, Nagoya. The surviving pieces of the Genji scroll are attributed to Takayoshi, a mid-12th-century painter who lived a century after the death of Lady Murasaki, the author of the story. This section illustrates the illness of Kashiwagi, who dies of love for Genji's consort, Nyōsan.

94 (below). **Cosmetic box.** Heian period. 12th century. Wood with *maki-e* decoration and mother-of-pearl inlay on black lacquer. h. 9 in. (13·5 cm.). Commission for Protection of Cultural Properties, Tokyo. Against a background of alternating blue-black and reddish gold tones, the groups of wheels half submerged in the water *(katawa-guruma)* provide a rhythmic pattern. The cosmetic box is a fine example of Heian luxury objects.

95 (opposite). **Batō Kannon.** Heian period. 11th century. Colour and ink on silk. h. 5 ft. 5⅜ in. (166 cm.). Museum of Fine Arts, Boston. Kannon, traditionally the goddess of compassion, is seen here in her more terrible aspect with a small horse's head surmounting three human heads: she has become one of the esoteric deities of the Tantric *Shingon* sect. The figure comes from a series depicting six different manifestations of Kannon.

96, 97. **The Phoenix Hall** (Hōō-dō), Byōdō-in, Uji near Kyōto (and detail). Heian period, erected 1053. After the Regent Fujiwara Yorimichi had transformed the villa of his father into a Buddhist monastery dedicated to Amida, he built the Phoenix Hall there in 1053. The name refers either to the bronze figures on the roof or to the plan which suggests a bird with outstretched wings. Within the middle block is the famous Buddha image by Jōchō. The sophistication of the building's design with its lateral pavilions and linking corridors suggests a palace rather than a temple.

98. **Amida Buddha.** Kamakura period,
mid-13th century. Bronze. Height 42 ft.
6 in. (12·95 m.). Kōtoku-in, Kamakura.
Voluntary contributions collected by the
monk Jōkō made possible the casting of
this colossal image of Amida. It was
erected in Kamakura, the seat of the
military government, as a counterpart to
the giant Buddha of the Nara period in
Tōdai-ji. The temple hall that originally
contained the cult image was destroyed
centuries ago.

99 (above). **The Adventures of Kibi in China.** *Kibi Daijin Nitto E-Kotoba* scroll (detail). Late Heian—early Kamakura period. Late 12th–early 13th century. Scroll painting in colour on paper. h. 12⅝ in. (32·2 cm.). Museum of Fine Arts, Boston. This scroll illustrates the story of the Japanese courtier Kibi no Makibi who was sent as an envoy to T'ang China. He was set a series of intellectual tasks by the T'ang court, and was assisted in solving these by the ghost of an earlier diplomatic messenger disguised as a demon. The scroll, which in all measures eighty feet, is full of colour and humorous incident.

100 (below). **Tosa Hirokata.** *The Tale of the Young Heavenly Prince* (detail). *(Amewakahiko no sōshi.)* Kyōto, Muromachi period. *c.* 1450. Ink and colour on paper. h. 12⅝ in. (32·2 cm.). Ostasiatische Kunstabteilung, Staatliche Museen, Berlin. This scroll contains the second part of the text and seven illustrations to the story of the human wife of a heavenly prince, who after various trials was allowed to meet her husband once a year. In various versions, this story spread throughout the Eurasian continent. The text was written by Emperor Go Hanazono personally and the illustrations are by a court painter of the Tosa school, who worked at the Painting Bureau with the rank of *E-dokoro-azakari*.

101. **Rock gardens of the Daisen-in,** Daitoku-ji, Kyōto.
Muromachi period, *c.* 1509. This layout is one of the most
famous of the so-called 'dry landscape gardens' *(kare-sanzui)*.
It was probably laid out by the Abbot Kogaku himself in front
of his living quarters in the Daisen-in. As contemporary ink
paintings show, these gardens were of modest size, employing
symbols—pebbles indicate water—to 'translate' a natural
landscape into one of highly condensed form. Such gardens
were not entered, but viewed from a veranda as if they were
paintings.

102. **The Golden Pavilion** *(Kinkaku-ji)*, Kyōto. Muromachi
period, erected 1397 (reconstructed). Shogun Askikaga
Yoshimitsu built this pavilion on the edge of a lake to serve
partly as a villa and partly as a monastery. The building was
covered with rich gold leaf. After the regent had officially
renounced his governmental responsibilities in order to
manipulate politics from behind the scenes, he lived a leisured
life indulging his aesthetic inclinations in this splendid villa,
where he even received visits from the Emperor.

154

103 (above). **Portuguese arriving in Japan.** Six-fold screen. Early Edo period. 17th century. Musée Guimet, Paris. The arrival of the Jesuits in Japan in 1542 aroused great interest in the manners and customs of the Western world. These screens called *Namban Byōbu* (screens of the southern barbarians) reflected all the excited curiosity that was felt at that time. Portuguese merchants, bearing the produce of the West, land from their ship accompanied by missionaries.

104 (below). **Hasegawa Kyūzo** (attr.). *Cherry Blossom.* Momoyama period. Late 16th century. h. 68½ in. (173 cm.). Chishaku-in, Kyōto. This painting is attributed to Hasegawa Tōhaku's son, Kyūzo, who died at the age of twenty-six. It bears obvious resemblances to the father's work, though the general treatment is perhaps more gentle. It is possible that Kyūzo assisted his father in the production of the famous folding-screen paintings in the Buddhist temples at Kyōto.

105. **Ogata Kōrin.** *Plum Blossom*. Middle Edo period. 18th century. Pair of two-fold screens. Colours on gold paper. Each screen 5 ft. 5⅜ in × 5 ft. 7¾ in. (166 × 172 cm.). Atami Museum, Shizuoka. Kōrin belonged to a family of prosperous drapers who also produced Nō costumes at Kyōto. He is generally regarded as one of Japan's greatest decorative artists. These screens show his work at its purest. He was at pains to render plant and flower forms accurately, yet arranged in a perfectly balanced composition. When the screens are joined the stylised river joins to become a single stream, opening out in the foreground to form a wide pool.

106. **Honnami Kōetsu.** *Album leaf with calligraphy*. Early 17th century. Ink and pale colours on paper. 7¼ × 6⅜ in. (18·3 × 16·2 cm.). Ostasiatische Kunstabteilung, Staatliche Museen, Berlin. Kōetsu was a potter, lacquer worker and calligrapher, but it is upon his calligraphy that his reputation rests. The album of which this page is an example is considered to be among his outstanding works. Here he writes, in his intensely personal style, a 12th-century poem by Kamo no Chomei, which was included in a famous Japanese anthology compiled in the 13th century. A literal translation would be: 'The autumn wind is blowing through all the villages/but my sleeve is wet because of the tears falling from my heart like the dew of the evening.' Only the calligraphy is Kōetsu's. The background painting of ears of rice in water are by another hand.

107 (opposite). **Atsu-ita,** male costume
for the Nō theatre. Momoyama or early
Edo period, about 1600. l. 4 ft. 8 in.
142·3 cm.). National Museum, Tokyo.
In contrast to the conservative content of
the Nō drama and its highly stylised
methods of performance, the costumes
and masks of the actors often have an
extraordinary splendour. The text
running diagonally across the garment is
a Heian poem celebrating the arrival of
spring.

108 (above). **Tea Bowl** *(chawan)*.
Painted Shino ware, Mino province.
Momoyama period, *c*. 1600. Ceramic
with opaque greyish-white glaze and
underglaze painting. Height 4⅜ in.
(10·1 cm.). Ostasiatische Kunstabteilung,
Staatliche Museen, Berlin. The few
known painted examples of Shino ware
are among the earliest examples of
Japanese underglaze decoration. The
shapes of these thick-walled tea bowls are
lively and free, for they are formed by
hand and not on the wheel. They were
especially prized in the tea cult of the
Momoyama period.

109 (below). **Nonomura Ninsei.** *Vase
with red plum blossom.* Early Edo period.
Mid-17th century. Ceramic with gold
and enamel colours. h. 11¾ in. (30 cm.).
National Museum, Tokyo. In the style
chosen for the painting of this vase,
Ninsei, one of the most famous Japanese
potters, has gone to the decorative
paintings of the Kanō school. The form
and decoration of the piece are purely
Japanese in character and no influence
from Chinese porcelain is discernible.

110. **Porcelain ewer with dragons.**
Ko-Kutani ware. Tokugawa period.
Late 18th–early 19th century. h. 8 in.
(20·3 cm.). Victoria and Albert Museum,
London. Kutani enamelled porcelain
has a highly individual style. The
colours are strong and the brushwork has
a freedom which is particularly attractive.

111 (opposite). **Suzuki Harunobu.**
Woman with a Fan at the Garden Fence. Left
leaf of a diptych. Edo period, 1766–70.
Colour woodcut. 10¾ × 8¼ in.
(27·4 × 20·9 cm.). Kunstbibliothek,
Staatliche Museen, Berlin. This diptych,
of which the left-hand panel is illustrated
here, alludes to the 'Yugao' chapter of

the *Tale of Genji*. Harunobu is famous as
the creator of elegant feminine figures,
which rank alongside actors and the later
landscapes as leading aspects of the
'floating world' of Japanese prints. At the
left side of the print is written 'Sakei', the
name of the leader of a circle of poets
who gave Harunobu many commissions.

東洲齋寫樂画

same body of sculptors was responsible for both categories of work.

THE KAMAKURA PERIOD

After Minamoto Yoritomo had driven the Taira clan from the power, he moved the seat of his new military dictatorship or shogunate far from the distracting metropolis of Heian to Kamakura to the north-east. Since political life was now centred in this city the years between 1192 and 1338 are called the Kamakura period. The legitimate Tennō monarchy continued a shadowy existence in Kyōto, while Yoritomo held the upper hand with the support of warriors from his local district. But with the extinction of the Minamoto family the shogun himself also became a puppet, and true power lay with the regent *(shikken)* of the Hōjō clan. Although two Mongol assaults were repulsed (1274 and 1281), the prestige of the Hōjō declined steadily because of the excesses and cruelty of its leaders.

For the first time Japan had two cultural centres: the old imperial city of Kyōto (Heian) and Kamakura, where new fashions were decreed by the lords of the warrior caste. The military government intentionally kept its followers away from the softening ways of Kyōto. Closer links with the China of the Sung and Yüan dynasties opened the way to a new wave of mainland influence. Nevertheless Kamakura culture presents a number of inward-looking traits. Scholarship flowered, and the famous Kanazawa Library was founded in Musashi in 1275. But Buddhism acted as the real guardian of literary traditions: its teaching of the transience of all earthly things appealed to the military lords, to whom it offered a spiritual basis for the knightly virtues of courage and fidelity. Legends of Buddhist saints, folk tales and heroic romances were composed. The newly-awakened interest in the *Manyōshō*, the poetry collection of the Nara period, was paralleled in art by restoration of the Nara temples and their sculptures, which had been damaged by fighting.

New tendencies were at work among the Buddhist sects. The priest Shinran (1173–1262) elaborated the Amida teachings, emphasising the equality of all men in the sight of the Buddha. The Amida cult flourished especially in the north and the east. Although the school's new trend stressed devotion to images less than the earlier teaching had done, some important sculpture appeared, notably **98** the colossal Amida of Kamakura, which was cast in 1252 in imitation of the giant Buddha of Nara and installed in a

112 (opposite). **Sharaku.** *The Actor Morita Kanya VIII in the Role of Uguisu no Jirōsaku.* Edo period, 1794. Colour woodcut. 14⅝ × 9¾ in. (37.3 × 24.8 cm.). Kunstbibliothek, Staatliche Museen, Berlin. This half-length portrait shows the actor playing the part of a sedan-chair bearer in the Joruri drama *Hana-ayame omoi no kanzashi* ('Iris Headdress of Remembrance'), which was performed in the Kiri-za Theatre in the fifth month of 1794. In these half-length portraits the print-maker Sharaku succeeded in capturing the personality of a theatrical performer in a few economical strokes.

103. **The Shintō Goddess Nakatsu-hime.** Heian period. 9th century. Painted wood. h. 10½ in. (26.7 cm.). Yakushi-ji, Nara. This small figure shows the Shintō goddess in Japanese court dress. Some features, the full face for example, suggest the influence of T'ang sculpture. The piece undoubtedly comes from the circle of sculptors working for the great Buddhist temples.

104. **Bokusai** (?) *Portrait of Ikkyū Sōjun.* Muromachi period, second half of the 15th century. Hanging scroll. Ink and light colour on paper. 6⅛ × 10½ in. (16·2 × 26·7 cm.). National Museum, Tokyo. This painting is probably a sketch made from life for a larger portrait of the famous Zen monk Ikkyū, and may perhaps have been executed by a pupil of Bokusai. It is consequently more intense and immediate than the usual type of portrait *(chinzō)* of Zen priests, examples of which were awarded as a kind of graduation diploma to successful students of the masters.

105. **Reliquary in the shape of a pagoda.** Kamakura
period, 13th century. Gilded copper. h. 14 in. (37 cm.).
Saidai-ji, Nara. A *shari-tō* is a miniature pagoda to contain the
shari or sacred ashes of the Buddha. Inside the pagoda is a
container of vase form, reputedly holding grains of the sacred
ashes. The veneration of the *shari* or *sarira* became a popular
cult in the late Heian and early Kamakura periods. Many such
reliquaries were made, though this is probably the finest.

vast temple hall that was later destroyed. This colossus
shows the style of Kaikei, who, with the celebrated Unkei
was the leading sculptor of the age. In the second half of
the 13th and in the 14th century Buddhist sculpture enjoyed a last great flowering in the powerful realism of
Kamakura statuary. The effort to render things as they
really are—the use of rock-crystal eyes to make faces life-
like—betrays a certain influence of Sung work. After the
14th century the vitality went out of Japanese monumental sculpture; only portraits and the masks carved for the
Nō theatre are of real interest.

A new Buddhist sect that enjoyed wide popularity
among the people was the Hokke founded by Nichiren in
1252. (The sect was named after the Hokke *sūtra*, which is
the central focus of its teachings.) With Nichiren a vehe-
ment, even fanatical element appeared in the otherwise
rather pietistic Buddhist church. Nichiren sought to influence the course of politics through petitions to the
government, but he received only exile for his pains.

Of the greatest importance for the further development
of Japanese art, and indeed for the whole civilisation of her
people is the appearance of Zen Buddhism, which penetrated in strength from Sung China at the first half of the
13th century. The attainment of mystical enlightenment
through concentrated spiritual exercises and meditation,

together with the absolute simplicity of the cult and of
monastic life, which eschewed all display, and finally the
close relationship with nature—all these features appealed
strongly to the members of the warrior caste, who made
the Zen teachings their own. The shogunate actively
fostered this school, whose tone was set more by individual human contact than by any organisational structure,
so that the sect could never threaten to become a state
within a state. In 1202 the government established the
venerable abbot Eisei in the Kennin-ji Monastery in
Kyōto, which became the centre of Zen Buddhism.

Many Japanese monks journeyed to late Sung China
where they could study Zen teachings first-hand; a little
later Chinese monks fled to Japan before the ravages of the
Mongol invasion. So it is not surprising that the buildings
of Zen monasteries depend directly on Sung prototypes,
and that their architecture should be termed 'Chinese
style' *(kara-yō)*. The Tōdai-ji in Nara was rebuilt in a south
Chinese form somewhat misleadingly called 'the Indian
style' *(tenjiku-yō)*.

The spirit of Zen is most easily seen in the monochrome
ink paintings *(suiboku-ga)*. The first approach to the Chinese monochrome technique is found in the 13th-century
Takuma school, but this new style reached its full flowering only in conjunction with far-reaching aesthetic reforms in the 14th century that affected many aspects of art.
A special category of Zen paintings is priest portraiture
(chinzō), which strove to convey the living presence of the
great spiritual masters. These works were often provided
with an inscription and presented to students as a kind of
diploma to mark an advance in spiritual progress. The
adepts thus honoured were accustomed to practise meditation before the picture as if in the presence of the master
himself. In keeping with the personal nature of this branch
of painting the interest focused largely on the realism of the
face, whilst the drapery was handled in a conventional
manner. A later example which shows the forcefulness and
immediacy that were so much prized is a portrait of the
great monk Ikkyū made by one of his students in the late *104*
15th century.

In the Kamakura period the narrative scrolls *(e-makimono)* enjoyed especial favour at court and in the monasteries. The painters of the increasingly powerful Amida
monasteries produced terrifying pictures of illness, suffer-
ing and hellish torments, directing their work to a large
public in order to awaken the hearts of the people to the
need for salvation in the Paradise of Amida. In addition,
the monastic painters excelled in broadly conceived scenes
of the lives of famous monks. The court painters were also
drawn to themes close to daily life, for which the turbu-
lence and variety of the heroic romances gave them ample
scope. Court artists also liked to illustrate poetic works and **99**
novels of the Heian period. This trend towards the objec-
tive rendering of reality reached its height in the second
half of the 13th century; in the following century it declined into a series of clichés and repetitions. Nevertheless

106. **Vase with design of chrysanthemum leaves.**
Kamakura period, 13th century. Fired clay with blackish glaze.
h. 9½ in. (24·2 cm.). National Museum, Tokyo. The pottery
jars of the Kamakura period display certain links with Sung
ware. But the vigorous drawing of the chrysanthemum leaves
and the sturdy yet graceful appearance of the vase is typically
Japanese.

107. **Mokuan.** *The Four Sleepers.* Muromachi period, 14th
century. Ink on paper. 27½ × 14⅛ in. (70 × 36 cm.). Maeda
Ikotokukai Foundation, Tokyo. Mokuan was a Japanese priest
who visited China in the 1320s to study Zen Buddhism. He
was much influenced by the style of the Southern Sung artist
Mu Ch'i. *The Four Sleepers* shows the Chinese Zen priest Fêng-
kan with his pet tiger and two disciples, fast asleep.

one court painter of the 15th century—well into the following Muromachi period—succeeded in illustrating a
100 folk tale with true poetic feeling.

105 While workers in metal preserved much of the elegance
and luxury of the late Heian tradition, Japanese potters of
the Kamakura age began to pioneer entirely new paths.
Admittedly the potter Katō Tōshirō had perfected his
technique during a stay in China before he made Seto in
Owari province the centre of native ceramics (from 1227),
but the potters active there were soon able to use Chinese
106 methods to produce a powerful style of their own.

THE MUROMACHI AND MOMOYAMA PERIODS

The Emperor Go Daigo, aided by the powerful warrior
family of the Ashikaga, and taking advantage of the general
unrest and dissatisfaction with the Hōjō regents, was finally
able to break their domination and to annihilate the clan.
However, Ashikaga Takauji, an ally of the emperor who
was disappointed by the rewards of his cooperation, decided to deprive the Tennō emperors of the fruits of victory by making himself shogun. Since he moved the capital back to the Muromachi quarter of Kyōto, the period
beginning at this time is called the Muromachi or Ashikaga era (1338–1578). This period saw a further concentration of power in the hands of the warrior clans, whose
loyalty went primarily to their feudal lords, rather than to

the shogunate. Under the politically weak Ashikaga shoguns the provincial feudal lords (*daimyō*) became increasingly autonomous finally creating independent
governments for their own lands in the early 16th century.
The *daimyō*, whose power depended on their vassals and
armies, became embroiled in struggles for power degener-
ating into a series of ruinous civil wars waged almost in-
cessantly from 1465 to 1600.

An extraordinary phenomenon in Japanese history is
the fact that the arts continued to flourish throughout this
tempestuous age. As many Chinese emperors had done
before them, the Ashikaga, who proved indifferent rulers,
threw themselves wholeheartedly into the patronage of art.
The Hana no Gosho palace at Kyōto provided the setting
for their ostentatious court. The third Ashikaga shogun,
Yoshimitsu (1358–1408) cast off his governmental responsibilities and indulged his artistic tastes in a pleasure pavilion covered with gold leaf. This building, erected in a
delightful garden setting, was later converted into the
Kinkaku-ji, the 'Temple of the Golden Pavilion'. Behind **102**
the scenes, however, Yoshimitsu still manipulated the
reins of power: in the year of his death he received a
ceremonial visit from the emperor.

As at the Heian court, in Ashikaga Kyōto the various
aspects of a cultivated and aristocratic way of life were
carefully elaborated to make up an aesthetic whole. This

108. **Sesshū.** *Landscape scroll* (detail). Muromachi period, dated 1486. Ink and pale colour on paper. h. 14 in. (37·9 cm.). Mori Collection, Yamaguchi. This famous landscape scroll was painted when the artist was sixty-seven. Although apparently conventional or even academic in treatment, this painting reflects the artist's deep understanding of nature, and shows his ability to render the delicacy and movement of the trees and rice fields even within the terms of the precise, calligraphic style.

109. **Box for writing materials.** Muromachi period, 15th century. Black lacquered wood with *maki-e*. 9 × 8⅛ in. (22·7 × 20·8 cm.). Nezu Art Museum, Tokyo. The scene on this box illustrates a poem praising the beauty of the cherry blossom at Shirakawa. Three characters from that poem are written in gold on the trunk of the tree. 'Poem pictures' like this were popular in Japan from the Heian period.

climate nourished the Nō drama, which was suffused with the Buddhist spirit of withdrawal from the world. In the Nō, all the main characters wear masks so that they are reduced to types. The great theoretician of this drama was Seami (1363–1443). In the middle of the 15th century the tea ceremony took shape in close conjunction with the art of flower arrangement. Connoisseurs developed exquisite ways of appreciating works of art: rooms had a special place for exhibiting them, the alcove of the *toko-no-ma*, where they displayed individually, one at a time.

This courtly way of life was strongly imbued by the Zen spirit. In Muromachi times the Zen monasteries became the true centres of spiritual life. Their influence spread not only among the nobility and the military, but was carried by the latter to the common people who appreciated Zen simplicity. During this period, Zen so deeply affected the structure of Japanese life and society that its influence is still clearly discernible among the Japanese people today. Poetry and poetic theory were shaped by Zen. The art of

landscape gardening, which grew up at this time alongside monochrome landscape painting, was pioneered by the monasteries of this sect. Besides the planted areas, the gardeners liked to create the so-called 'dry landscape' *(kare-sanzui)* before the abbot's quarters. Made up of **101** carefully selected picturesque stones and beds of raked pebbles, these dry landscapes may be fittingly compared with the ink paintings since they represent a kind of abstraction of nature achieved in a small area and by simple means.

The ink painting of the Muromachi period remains the art most deeply affected by Zen. Some Japanese painter-monks had studied in China itself and they brought the works of Chinese masters into Japan. Mokuan, one of the early masters, went to China in 1326, dying there three **107** years later. With swift sure strokes that look like writing, Mokuan captured the image of the half-legendary T'ang monk, Fêng-kan with his two famous attendants and his tame tiger.

In the art of Sesshū (1420–1506), monochrome ink painting achieved a maturity of expression and a characteristically Japanese form. Sesshū spent two years travelling in China, but he did not care for the work of contemporary painters, preferring the inspiration of earlier masters and even more the stimulans of the majestic landscapes themselves. He excelled not only in the free, expressive technique deriving from the Sung masters but also in a more conventional academic manner. The latter provided the model **108** for the painter family of the Kanō who were active from the beginning of the 16th century onwards. The academic artists patronised by the shoguns came mainly from this family. Their paintings on sliding doors and screens integrated the classic Sino-Japanese precision of the ink line

110. **Himeji Castle.** Himeji, Hyōgo prefecture. Momoyama period, completed 1608. Under the influence of European techniques, stone castles of this type were built in the late 16th and 17th centuries following the introduction of firearms, which made the older wooden redoubts obsolete. The form of these castles shows a mixture of European elements and Chinese city-fortification practice. The main part of the castle was the keep which has several storeys (*tenshu*).

111. **Hasegawa Tōhaku.** *Pine trees.* Momoyama period, late 16th century. One of a pair of six-fold screens, l. 5 ft. 1¾ in. × 11 ft. 4⅝ in. (156 × 346 cm.). National Museum, Tokyo. This famous pair of screens were probably painted by Tōhaku when he was in his mid-fifties. Although certain technical features show the influence of Sung China the artist has absorbed these to produce a work which is entirely his own, exploiting to the full the poetic possibilities of ink painting.

into a composition marshalling broad flat surfaces in a highly decorative manner, thus opening the way to the decorative painting of the 17th century. In contemporary lacquer work, which catered for the luxurious requirements of the courts of the shoguns and the *daimyō*, the occasional appearance of Chinese reminiscences in scenes following the Yamato-e style is unmistakable.

In the course of the bloody *daimyō* wars towards the end of the Muromachi period general Oda Nobunaga occupied Kyōto in 1568. With the assistance of his henchman Toyotomi Hideyoshi he subjected most of the feudal lords to his will. After his master's death Hideyoshi continued the work of unifying the realm, a task which could be regarded complete by 1590. The brief time from 1573 to 1615 is called the Momoyama period after the site of one of Hideyoshi's palaces near Kyōto. Culturally the period was marked by the ostentatious taste of the great war lords. Typical of the Momoyama architecture are the imposing castles of the regents and the *daimyō* clans, which were erected under European influence as fortified towers with heavy masonry.

Contact with the West had begun somewhat earlier. In 1545 the Portuguese Fernão Mendez Pinto brought the first firearms to Japan, where they were soon adopted by the Nobunaga army. In 1549, the celebrated Francis Xavier reached Japan, where he converted many people to the Christian faith, first in Kagoshima and later in Kyōto itself. Trade with the West was carried on by the shogun,

by the feudal lords in western Japan and by the great monasteries. The Europeans, the so-called southern barbarians (*namban*), brought more guns, medical knowledge and instruments for astronomy and navigation, stimulating the interest of the Japanese in the natural sciences. But these influences did not effect the broad mass of the people, whose life was rigidly circumscribed: in 1591 a law forbade anyone to change his status in any way, thus confirming the traditional social order.

The new castles of the war lords with their big reception rooms called for an art form that could hold its own in such a setting, and the Momoyama artists developed a type of decorative painting that was typically Japanese. The purely decorative qualities of painting on screens and sliding doors, exemplified by the work of the Kanō masters, were intensified. Against a bright ground of gold leaf the artists worked with strong colours applied in a flat manner. Compositions are bold and at the same time well balanced. However, a certain tendency to overloading and to dry standardisation appears in the last years of the Momoyama period. The earliest master of the style was Kanō Eitoku (1543–90), who ran a workshop employing many painters. He was followed by his adopted son Sanraku, formerly a page of the shogun, who became famous for his decoration of the Momoyama palace. More varied than the Kanō was Hasegawa Tōhaku (1539–1610), who not only mastered the elements of coloured decorative painting, as shown by the famous examples of 1592 in the Chishaku-in temple

112 (left). **Main Gate (Sammon) to the Ninna-ji Temple, Kyōto.** Early Edo period, first half of the 17th century. Founded as early as 886 under imperial patronage this Shingon Temple gradually became a large complex. Big portals of this kind mark the entrance to the sacred precinct of important Buddhist temples, with a pair of overlife-size Guardian Kings *(Ni-ō)* fiercely protecting the entrance. Although built in the 17th century, this gateway demonstrates the conservatism of the Japanese architect, for in all its major features it is identical with structures that were being built ten centuries earlier.

113 (opposite). **Main building of Katsura Rikyū in the vicinity of Kyōto.** Momoyama and early Edo periods, late 16th and 17th centuries. This villa with its splendid gardens was probably designed by Kobori Enshū. Begun at Hideyoshi's order for Prince Tomohito, it was enlarged after 1642 by Prince Toshitada. The charm of the whole derives from its conscious simplicity closely linked with the aesthetic of the tea ceremony.

which come from a memorial temple for Hideyoshi's favourite son, but also achieved distinction as a painter in monochrome ink. His screen of the *Pine Trees in Mist* ranks among the finest and most powerful ink paintings of Japan, demonstrating that the black-and-white technique could also be effective in a decorative context.

The need for sumptuous display in the Momoyama period was balanced by the moderating influence of the tea ceremony and its aesthetic; Sen no Rikyū (1521–91) is its presiding genius. His ascendency even extended to the design of Hideyoshi's Jurakudai palace, which unfortunately has not survived. Moreover, Sen no Rikyū was one of the organisers of the celebrated tea ceremony staged in Kitano in 1587.

A fine example of the villas built near the capital is the Katsura Rikyū, erected by Hideyoshi for one of the princes. Begun in the Momoyama period, the villa was completed on an enlarged plan in the early Edo period. The skilfully composed garden reflects the influence of the garden designer Kobori Enshū. The rooms of the villa are intentionally sparsely furnished so that the fine proportions and the quality of the materials can be seen to full effect. The villa fits harmoniously into an artificial landscape setting. In the Katsura villa the sophistication and conscious simplicity of the age's romantic feudalism reached its height.

THE EDO PERIOD

After the death of the mighty Hideyoshi, the no less powerful Tokugawa Ieyasu, who was the guardian of Hideyoshi's son, made himself regent. In 1603 he was confirmed as shogun and after his final victory over the Toyotomi clan there were two and a half centuries of peace in Japan—an epoch which is called the Tokugawa or Edo period

(1615–1867). Ieyasu confined the feudal system within narrow limits, exercising close supervision over the *daimyō*. The government was strongly centralised, with the legitimate Tennō emperors reduced to playing the part of ceremonial figureheads even more than before. The seat of the shogun's government was moved to Edo, the present Tokyo, which gives it name to the period. A division of the people into four classes of warriors, peasants, artisans and merchants was rigidly imposed.

The dominant class, the warriors, favoured Confucian philosophy instead of Zen; Buddhism became mainly a popular religion under the supervision of the central government. After an initial toleration Ieyasu forbade Christianity in 1612 and introduced a policy of isolation from the outside world, that was to continue for many years. Although this worked for internal stability, it crippled the development of the country by cutting it off from intellectual stimuli from abroad. Despite restrictions imposed by the shogunate, the study of Dutch science *(rangaku)* began in about 1720, and from 1750 western medicine became increasingly known to Japanese savants.

The brisk international trade which had flourished at the beginning of the Edo period was soon stifled, and the subsequent growth of large cities made it inevitable that commercial intercourse should be concentrated in the cities. While the warriors tended to sink into relative poverty, a prosperous middle-class flourished among the *nouveau-riche* Edo, led by a number of merchants families. Dissatisfaction with the shogun's government strengthened the imperial party and shortly after Commodore Perry opened the country to foreign trade in 1854, they deposed the last Tokugawa, restoring the imperial house in the person of Meiji. The wise policies of this ruler, who

reigned from 1868 to 1912, followed paths that his nationalist supporters had not anticipated. His reign saw the
beginning of the powerful political, social and cultural
revolution that made Japan a progressive and modern
state enjoying full equality with the western nations.

The art of the Edo period reflects the social changes of
the time. While craft work was mostly in the hands of
the established families supervised by the *daimyō*, the
rising bourgeoisie of the cities required new forms of art.

The official painting schools of the Kanō and Tosa
families became increasingly mannered, but in the hands
114 of a few gifted masters decorative painting enjoyed a new
flowering. The economic basis of this was provided by the
newly rich middle class. Honnami Kōetsu (1558–1637),
the first of these great masters of decoration came from a
prominent family of fencing masters. He was primarily a
calligrapher and a patron of the arts. A collection of pages
of poetry, written on paper prepared with a painted ground
design *(shikishi)* continued an old Japanese tradition, but
106 filled now with a new spirit. The ground designs, which
were often executed by Kōetsu's friend Sōtatsu, borrowed
their manner and themes from large-scale screens and
sliding panels. In this way they became attractive com-
posite works of art integrating poetry, calligraphy and
painting, which capture perfectly the aesthetic note of the
age. The recognition and appreciation of other artist's
qualities is reflected in Kōetsu's successful undertaking to
gather together a group of artists working in various styles
in the village of Takagamine near Kyōto where they could
live and work together.

The two other distinguished decorative artists of the
Edo period both come from the middle class. Sōtatsu,
Kōetsu's collaborator, belonged to a family of brocade

merchants and it is not unlikely that certain features of the
screen painting he practised with such mastery derive
from prior experience in textile design. Similarly, Ogata
Kōrin (1658–1716), who was active almost a century later, **105**
came from a family of rich cloth merchants. He squan-
dered a large inheritance and was compelled to earn his
living as a decorator for rich patrons. His screens are outstanding in the subtlety of their composition. It is not surprising in the circumstance that women's clothes and
theatre costumes of this period are rich in texture and **107**
colour, which often appear to us to be excessively sumptuous.

Apart from the mainstream of painting just described,
there flourished a more naturalistic school under the influence of Maruyama Okyo and a Chinese-oriented literary painting *(bunjin-ga)* favoured by educated dilettantes.
Finally, as early as 1789, Shiba Kōkan experimented with
European oil-painting and copper-plate engraving.

While pottery for the tea ceremony had long been free **108**
from dependence on Korean and Chinese models, creating
the underlying aesthetic of the tea cult, Chinese stimulus
lay behind the achievements of such porcelain factories as
Kutani, which was active as early as 1650, soon developing **110**
a bright surface painting that is unmistakably Japanese.
In this field Ninsei, a friend of Kōrin's brother Kenzan, **109**
combined technical brilliance with a subtle design to produce superb decorative effects.

Edo sculpture is generally stiff and cold. Of some
interest, however, is the work of certain wandering priests,
who chip-carved statues out of wood with an axe, leaving
them in a crude, half-finished state. The rustic charm of *115*
such pieces contrasts with the elegant traditional sculpture
of the period.

114 (left). **Miyamoto Niten.** *Crow on a Pine Branch.* Early Edo period, first half of the 17th century. Hanging scroll, ink on paper. 5 ft. (152 cm.). Formerly Viscount Matsudaira Collection. Niten, the son of a noble, was adopted by the *daimyō* family of Miyamoto and led a soldier's life. Renowned as a fencing master, he practiced ink painting as a hobby and the hand of the skilled fencer may be detected in the bold, sure strokes of his brush. The directness, simplicity and vigour of his painting make it an eloquent example of Zen art.

115 (right). **Enkū.** *Self-portrait.* Edo period, second half of the 17th century. Wood. h. 18½ in. (47 cm.). Senkō-ji, Gifu province. The monk Enkū (1628–95) travelled as a wandering priest throughout the Japanese islands, including Hokkaido. Although not a professional sculptor, he left simple carvings in the villages and temples he visited as thank offerings for his rustic hosts.

116 (below right). **Kitagawa Utamaro.** *Women Amusing a Child.* Middle Edo period. Wood-block print. 14¼ × 9¼ in. (36 × 23 cm.). Victoria and Albert Museum, London. This print is one of a series called 'Popular collection of Seven Eyes'. It shows women in an intimate domestic scene, a favourite subject with Utamaro.

The art of Japan achieved a last autumnal flowering in the woodcut, which was closely linked to the writing of popular stories and to the theatre. In the 16th and 17th centuries the so-called city painters *(machi-eshi)* had done screens with popular genre scenes and in the second half of the 17th century scroll pictures appeared featuring beautiful women *(bijin)*. Finally, books with black-and-white illustrations showing the varied life of the pleasure quarter of Yoshiwara in Edo gave rise to the 'pictures of the floating world' *(ukiyo-e)* of the woodcuts. The founder and perfecter of the technique is Suzuki Harunobu (1725–70), whose figures of women display an inimitable charm. Apart from courtesans, the world of the popular Kabuki theatre, which flourished as an alternative to the aristocratic Nō drama, furnished many themes for the masters of these prints. Among the many artists working in this field Sharaku stands supreme. Possibly himself an actor, Sharaku's highly expressive actor prints were all created in a period of ten months in 1794–95. The colourful life of Edo's middle class is clearly mirrored in the art of the woodcut print. Later masters, Hokusai, Hiroshige and Utamaro exercised an important influence on the French painters of the second half of the 19th century.

With the opening up of Japan, western art forms of all kinds began to modify or replace Japanese work. Some of the work produced under European influence is more 'western' than western art itself. Once more Japan has set out on an intense, perhaps over-intense process of assimilation, which is still continuing today.

Glossary
India and South-East Asia

Abhaya-mudrā. Buddhist ritual gesture of fearlessness.

Ahimsā. Jain, Hindu and Buddhist doctrine of refraining from harming others or taking life.

Āmalaka. Name of a fruit. In architecture, the crowning finial in the shape of a ribbed cushion (see plate 25).

Antarāla. Vestibule of a sanctuary.

Āranyaka. One of the Vedic commentaries that formed the basis of Brahmanism.

Ardhanari. Siva and his female energy united in a single person.

Asura. Originally Vedic demons, enemies of both gods and men, controlled by prayers and magic words.

Atman. The individual soul (Vedism and Brahmanism).

Avadāna. The edifying stories of the Buddhist tradition.

Avalokitesvara. The merciful Bodhisattva.

Avatāra. The incarnation of a god, especially associated with Vishnu.

Bhairava. 'Frightful, terrible, horrible' (see also *Siva*).

Bhakti. 'Trusting worship' or personal devotion to Vishnu or Buddha or Krishna. In Brahmanic thought one of the three pathways to salvation (see also *Jñana* and *Yoga*).

Bodhisattva (bodhi = enlightenment + sattva = essence). A being that compassionately refrains from entering *Nirvana* in order to minister to the needs of others. In Mahāyāna Buddhism the Bodhisattvas are worshipped as deities.

Brāhma. Chief god of the Hindu Trinity and absolute creator of all things. The universal self.

Brāhmana. One of the Vedic commentaries that formed the basis of Brahmanism.

Brahmanism. Evolving from Vedism, the Indian religion which stressed the pre-eminence of Siva, Indra and Vishnu, the identification of *atman* and *brahma*, and service as the principal path leading to escape from *samsāra*.

Candi. Javanese commemorative structure or shrine.

Chaitya. Buddhist sanctuary.

Chakra. In Buddhist iconography the wheel which symbolises the first sermon of the Buddha and the progression of the Law.

Dhoti. Pleated skirts such as Hindus now wear.

Garbha griha. The cella of a sanctuary.

Gopuram. The gateway of an Indian temple; the massive pyramidal tower over the gateway.

Harihara. Siva and Vishnu united in one god.

Harmikā. The small railed balcony surmounting the dome of a stūpa.

Hasta. Speaking gesture, ritualised like the *mudrā*.

Indra. King of the Vedic gods, personification of the Aryan warrior and god of the atmosphere and thunder.

Jainism. Indian religion traceable to Vardhamāna Mahāvira in the 6th century BC, based on *ahimsa* and asceticism.

Jātaka. Previous lives of the Buddha.

Jñāna. Spiritual knowledge, one of the three pathways to salvation in Brahmanic thought.

Kāla. Monster-head motif.

Kalan. Isolated towers in Khmer architecture.

Kudu. In architecture the decorative motif which evolved from a window form (see plate 26).

Mahāyāna. 'The Great Vehicle' of Buddhist thought, that is, the later branch of Buddhism which emphasised the worship of the Buddha rather than concentration on his doctrine and which is distinguished from Theravadic Buddhism by the appearance of the Bodhisattva and universal salvation.

Maheshamūrti. Brahmanic triad which unites on one body the three heads of Siva representing his three aspects, the majestic one, the feminine one, and the terrifying god.

Makara. Indian sea-monster motif.

Mandala. The magic circle, the imagined shape of the cosmos; the diagram of the Buddhist hierarchy.

Mandapa. Columned porch evolving later into a pillared hall (see plate 21).

Māra. Buddhist 'Evil One', tempter of Sākyamuni.

Matrikā. The Seven Mothers, each embodying a different female power (see figure 48).

Mithuna. Sculptural group of a loving couple.

Mudrā. Ritual gesture, which grew out of a simple gesture of the Buddha, symbolising in mime or dance mystical power or action.

Nāga. Water spirits of serpentine form, the protectors of cisterns and sacred waters.

Natarāja. See *Siva*

Nirvana. The final escape from *samsāra* into a state of perpetual enlightenment.

Pancha yatana. The arrangement of five sanctuaries. in a quincunx, i.e. one at each corner of a square and one in the centre.

Parvati. Siva's wife.

Prajñaparamita. Perfect Wisdom.

Rāgamāla. Music-painting, translation of a poetic theme into pictorial terms according to a melodic mode.

Rudra-Siva. The Rudras were pre-Vedic gods of destruction. Siva's dual nature was always that of destruction and regeneration.

Sakti. The 'female energy' of a god which completes his power.

Sākyamuni. 'Sage of the Sākya', the earthly and historical Buddha.

Samsāra. The soul's wandering through the unending cycle of life and rebirth.

Sāstra. Canonical treatise on art, a compendium of aesthetic and iconographical rules.

Sikhara. The tall, curved roof of a sanctuary.

Siva. Third member of the Hindu Trinity, repository of great destructive and procreative power. Also known as Bhairava, 'frightful, terrible, horrible'; Natarāja, 'master of the dance'; and Vīnādhāra, 'master of the arts'.

Stūpa. A reliquary based on the Vedic funerary mound; in Buddhist and Brahmanic architecture, the stūpa represented the cosmic mountain, the pivot of the world. It was designed to contain holy relics or to commemorate the sacred character of the place or an important event.

Sūrya. The sun god who, like Apollo, drives a four- or seven-horse chariot across the sky trampling upon the powers of darkness.

Tārā. Female counterpart of Avalokitesvara.

Theravada. The earlier form of Buddhism (Hinayana) from which the Mahāyāna branched off. It presents a much more dogmatically doctrinal interpretation of the way to salvation.

Torana. The monumental gateway of a stūpa (see plate 3).

Tribhanga. Attitude of triple flexion—one of the attitudes laid down in iconographical treatises as a graceful, ritual pose (see figure 13).

Upanishad. A class of philosophical writings which gave rise to Brahmanism.

Ūrnā. One of the distinctive signs of the sacred nature of the Buddha, the curl of hair on the brow.

Ushnīsha. The cranial protuberance of the Buddha; its representations in art grew out of a mistaken interpretation of the knot of hair at the crown of his head.

Vajrapāni. The Bodhisattva called the 'Bearer of Lightning'.

Vedism. The basis of Vedism is the Veda, the collection of earliest known Indian religious texts. Pantheistic and animistic, Vedism was very broad in emotional and philosphical scope. The essential expression was sacrifice, which consisted primarily in a libation of a liquor made of vegetable matter, called *soma*.

Vihāra. Buddhist monastery.

Vimāna. Sanctuary, including porch and surrounding buildings.

Vīnādhāra. See *Siva*.

Vishnu. The Preserver, second member of the Hindu trinity, mild and benevolent, offering through Krishna, one of his incarnations, and through his eternal benevolence, salvation to the devout.

Wayang. Javanese shadow theatre.

Yaksha (male), **Yakshi** (female). Nature and tree spirits. The female aspect is associated with fertility and the male with wealth and natural richness.

Yoga. Asceticism leading to absolute self-control, one of the three Brahmanic pathways to salvation.

Glossary
China, Korea and Japan

Amida Buddha. The Buddha of the Western Paradise. In 11th-century Japan his saving grace was believed to be so potent that mere repetition of his name was sufficient to ensure salvation.

Be. In early Japan, closely-knit guilds of craftsmen.

Bijin. Japanese scroll pictures of the 17th century, featuring beautiful women.

Bosatsu. Japanese word for bodhisattva.

Bunjin-ga. Chinese-oriented literary paintings of the Edo period in Japan.

Celadon. North Chinese and Korean porcelain characterised by a pale grey or bluish green glaze derived from iron.

Ch'an. Buddhist sect, known as Zen in Japan, emphasising contemplation and self-discipline and the teaching that the Buddha is inherent in all things. The followers of the Ch'an sect believed that spiritual enlightenment could be achieved directly by the unaided human mind.

Chinzō. Japanese Zen priest portraiture (see figure 105).

Chiphyon-jon. Korean scholarly academy.

Chung'in. The lower division of the Korean upper class from which came less important officials than those from the *Yangban*.

Chung-kuo. The 'Middle Kingdom', i.e. the kingdom which is at the centre of things. From the earliest times, China's conception of herself.

Daimyō. Provincial feudal lords of Japan.

Dōtaku. Prehistoric Japanese bronze bells of religious significance (see plate 87).

E-busshi. Japanese priest-painters who worked for Buddhist temples.

E-dokoro. Painting bureau of the Japanese court, founded in 886.

E-makimono. Horizontal scrolls which were illustrated by court painters in the Yamato-e style.

Haniwa. Ceramic cylinders, sometimes with human or animal heads, found around burial grounds of prehistoric Japan (see plate 88).

Hiragana. A cursive Japanese syllabic script which was developed in the 8th and 9th centuries through a refinement of rapidly written Chinese characters. Also called *Onna-de* or 'Women's Style' because it was used predominantly by women.

Hokke-shū. Fanatical Japanese Buddhist sect founded by Nichiren in 1252.

Hokkyō. 'Bridge of Doctrine', a high Japanese ecclesiastical title.

Hua-yüan. The Academy of Painting, attached to the Imperial Chinese court whose members bore official titles.

Kannon. The Japanese name for Avalokitesvara.

Kara-yō. The 'Chinese style' of architecture in which Japanese Zen monasteries were built.

Kare-sanzui. The 'dry-landscape' of a Japanese garden, created by Zen monks (see plate 101).

Katakana. Angular Japanese script abstracted from the graphic components of regular Chinese characters.

Kokubun-ji. The Japanese provincial monasteries which were founded by the Imperial decree of 741.

Kondō. The main hall of a Japanese monastery.

Lalitāsana. Buddhist pose of Indolence (see plate 60).

Li-chi. The compendium of detailed ritual prescriptions as composed by Confucius out of the prevailing Chou ideology.

Liu-i. The 'six accomplishments' of the Chou nobility; ritual music, the script, calculation, chariotry, archery, poetry.

Machi-eshi. Japanese painters of the 16th and 17th centuries who did city genre scenes.

Maitreya. The Bodhisattva who will appear as the next Buddha. In Japanese, Miroku.

Mandara. See *Mandala* p. 169.

Mikkyō. Esoteric doctrines of the Buddhist sects, *Shingon* and *Tendai*, which derived from Indian Tantrism.

Mokoshi. Mezzanines with their own roofs between the actual storeys of a pagoda (see plate 89).

Mono no aware. A sentimental sympathy with 'things'. Part of the highly aesthetic attitude of Heian Japan.

Namban. Japanese name for 'southern barbarians', i.e. Europeans.

Ni-ō. The two protectors of the faith in Japanese Buddhist art.

Nō. The classical Japanese drama originating in the 14th century and deriving from ritual temple dances. There are two main actors, no scenery, but rich costumes, and the presentation is highly stylised.

Sanggam. Korean technique of black and white slip decoration beneath the glaze.

Sesshō-kampaku. The regents and councillors of Heian Japan who were the real power behind the throne.

Shên-tao. 'Spirit path'. In China the avenue of approach to a tomb.

Shi-awase. Poetry competitions in the Chinese style held in Heian Japan.

Shih. Social class to which Confucius belonged. Called 'the proletariat of the nobility', the clan arose from the changing fortunes of the Chou dynasty and was made up of political advisors, scholars, philosophers and knights errant.

Shikishi. Japanese painted-ground designs on which were written poems.

Shikken. Japanese regents, such as of the Hōjō clan in the Kamakura period.

Shimbashira. The mast which acts as the central support of a pagoda (see plate 89).

Shinden-zukuri. Style of Japanese domestic architecture where the buildings were built composed within the context of a garden and a lake.

Shingon sect. Founded by Kūkai, the Shingon sect, with the *Tendai*, was the major centre of esoteric Buddhism in Japan.

Shintō. The indigenous religion of Japan characterised by the reverence for deified nature spirits and spirits of ancestors.

Sowon. Private, but state supported, Korean academies where would-be officials could learn Confucianism.

Suiboku-ga. Japanese monochrome ink painting of Zen inspiration.

Tantrism. A school of Mahāyāna Buddhism originating in Northern India and incorporating Hindu and Pagan elements, such as pantheistic mysticism, spells, the worship of female divinities, and teaching that the individual can obtain essential Buddhahood and earthly benefits by invoking and communicating with spirits and deities.

Taoism. Traditionally founded by Lao-tzu in the 6th century BC, Taoism teaches conformity to the Tao and retirement from the world in order to pursue a life of utter simplicity. The Tao is the unitary, first principle from which all existence and all change in the universe spring.

T'ao-t'ieh. Fantastic glowering mask, made up of animal motifs and called the 'glutton'. In prehistoric China it was believed to ward off evil.

Tendai sect. Founded by the monk Saicho, the *Tendai* was one of the two major esoteric Buddhist sects which came to Japan *c.* 800. Like the *Shingon* sect it derives from Indian Tantrism.

Tenjiku-yō. 'Indian style', actually from South China, which was used in Japanese Zen monasteries and in the rebuilding of Tōdai-ji.

Tennō. 'Exalted Heavenly Ruler', the Japanese emperor who was regarded as a direct descendant of the Sun Goddess.

Tohwa-so. Official Korean art bureau made up of professional painters from the *Chung'in* class.

Toko-no-ma. Alcove in a Japanese house where a work of art is displayed.

Ukiyo-e. 'Pictures of the Floating World', i.e. of the Edo pleasure quarters, mainly done in woodcuts.

Uta-awase. Poetry competitions in the 'Japanese' style held in Heian Japan.

Waka. A native Japanese form of lyric poetry.

Waka dokoro. A bureau set up by the Japanese emperor in 951 to preserve and collect *waka*.

Wa-yō. A Japanese style of sculpture which is best seen in the work of Jōchō and is typically Heian in its lightness and elegance.

Wên-jên. Chinese 'literati' officials who in their private lives practised poetry, calligraphy, painting and music.

Yakushi. The Buddha of healing.

Yamato-e. Literally 'Japanese painting'. The delicate native style which developed in the 9th century from the earlier Japanese style, the heavily derivative *Kara-e* ('Chinese painting').

Yang. In Chinese cosmology the bright, masculine, positive principle in nature that with its opposite *yin*, the feminine and negative principle, combine to produce all things.

Yangban. The Korean upper class was divided into two sub-classes, the higher of which, the *Yangban*, produced the most important officials and bureaucrats.

Yosegi. Technique of carving a piece of sculpture from several blocks of wood joined together.

Zōbutsu-jo. The sculpture department of a Japanese temple in which many artists were employed to make cult images.

Further Reading List

The Art and Civilisation of India

Archer, W. G. *Indian Painting*, London, 1957
Auboyer, J. *Introduction à l'Etude de l'Art de l'Inde*, Rome, 1965
Auboyer, J. *Les Arts de l'Inde*, Paris, 1967
Auboyer, J., and Zannas, E. *Khajurāho*, The Hague, 1960
Banerji, R. D. *Eastern Indian School of Medieval Sculpture*, Delhi, 1933
Barrett, D. *Sculptures from Amarāvatī in the British Museum*, London, 1954
Basham, L. *The Wonder that was India*, London, 1954
Bose, N. H. *Canons of Orissan Architecture*, Calcutta, 1932
Brown, P. *History of Indian Architecture (Buddhist and Hindu)*, Bombay, 1942
Brown, P. *Indian Painting* (3rd ed.), Calcutta, 1953
Combaz, G. *L'Inde et l'Orient Classique*, 2 vols, Paris, 1937
Coomaraswamy, A. K. *History of Indian and Indonesian Art*, London, 1927 (new edition, New York, 1965)
Coomaraswamy, A. K. *La Sculpture de Bodhgayā*, Paris, 1935
Cunningham, Gen. Sir A. *The Stūpa of Bharhut*, London, 1879
Fergusson, J., and Burgess, J. *Cave Temples of India*, London 1880
Foucher, A. *L'Art Gréco-Bouddhique du Gandhāra*, 2 vols, Paris, 1905–18
Gravely, F. H., and Ramachandran, T. N. *The Three Main Styles of Temple Architecture recognized by the Silpa-sāstras*, Madras, 1934
Gunasinghe, S. *La Technique de la Peinture Indienne d'après les Textes du Silpa*, Paris, 1957
Hackin, J., and Hackin, R. *Recherches Archéologiques à Begram, Chantier no 2 (1937)*, 2 vols, Paris, 1939
Hackin, J., and others *Nouvelles Recherches Archéologiques à Begram*, 2 vols, Paris, 1954
Jouveau-Dubreuil, G. *L'Architecture du Sud de l'Inde*, Paris, 1914
Kak, R. C. *Ancient Monuments of Kashmir*, London, 1933
Kramrisch, S. *A Survey of Painting in the Deccan*, London, 1937
Kramrisch, S. *The Hindu Temple*, 2 vols, Calcutta, 1946
Kramrisch, S. *The Art of India through the Ages*, London and New York, 1954
Mackay, E. *Early Indus Civilizations*, London, 1948
Marshall, Sir John, and Foucher, A. *The Monuments of Sāñchī*, 3 vols, Delhi, 1939
Ramachandran, T. N. *Nāgārjunakonda 1938*, Delhi, 1953
Ramachandran Rao, P. R. *The Art of Nāgārjunakonda*, Madras, 1956
Renou, L., Filliozat, J., and others *L'Inde Classique : Manuel des Etudes Indiennes*, 2 vols, Paris, 1947, and Paris-Hanoi, 1953
Rowland, B. *The Art and Architecture of India* (3rd ed.), Harmondsworth, 1967
Sivaramamurti, C. *Amarāvatī Sculptures in the Government Museum, Madras*, Madras, 1942
Sivaramamurti, C. *South Indian Bronzes*, Bombay, 1962
Stern, P., and Benisti, M. *Evolution du Style Indien d'Amarāvatī*, Paris, 1961
Vogel, J. P. *La Sculpture de Mathurā*, Paris, 1930
Wheeler, Sir Mortimer, *Mohenjo-daro and the Indus Civilization (1922–27)*, 3 vols, London 1931
Wheeler, Sir Mortimer, *The Indus Civilization*, Supplementary vol. of 'The Cambridge History of India', Cambridge, 1953
Wheeler, Sir Mortimer, *Ancient India*, London 1964
Yazdani, G., and others *Ajanta*, 3 vols, Oxford, 1931–46

Indian Art in South-East Asia

Bernet Kempers, A. J. *Ancient Indonesian Art*, Cambridge (Mass.), 1959
Coedès, G. *Les Collections Archéologiques du Musée National de Bangkok*, Paris, 1928
Coedès, G. *Pour mieux comprendre Angkor*, Paris, 1947
Finot, L., and others *Le Temple d'Angkor Vat*, 7 vols, Paris, 1929–32
Groslier, B. P. *Indochine, Carrefour des Arts*, Paris, 1962
Heinegeldern, R. *Sumatra, the Archaeology and Art*, Vienna, 1935
Krom, N. J., and Van Erp, *Beschrijving van Barabudur*, 4 vols, The Hague, 1920–31
Parmentier, H. *Les Sculptures Chames au Musée de Tourane*, Paris, 1922
Stern, P. *L'Art du Champa et son Evolution*, Toulouse, 1942
Stutterheim, W. F. *Indian Influences in Old-Balinese Art*, London, 1935
Zimmer, H. *The Art of Indian Asia*, 2 vols, New York, 1955

General Books on the Art of East Asia

Herberts, K. *Oriental Lacquer : Art and Technique*, London, 1962
Honey, W. B. *The Ceramic Art of China and other Countries of the Far East*, London, 1945
Koyama, F., and Seckel, D. *Keramik des Orients*, Würzburg, 1959
Kümmel, O. *Die Kunst Chinas, Japans and Koreas*, Wildpark, Potsdam, 1929
Seckel, D. *Buddhistische Kunst Ostasiens*, Stuttgart, 1957
Speiser, W. *Die Kunst Ostasiens*, Berlin, 1956
Swann, P. *Art of China, Korea and Japan*, London, 1963

Chinese Art

Ashton, L. *An Introduction to the Study of Chinese Sculpture*, London, 1924
Bachhofer, L. *A Short History of Chinese Art*, New York, 1946
Boerschmann, E. *Die Baukunst und religiöse Kultur der Chinesen : Pagoden*, Berlin and Leipzig, 1911–31
Boyd, A. *Chinese Architecture*, London, 1962
Cahill, J. *Chinese Painting*, Geneva, 1960

Chavannes, E. *Mission Archéologique dans la Chine Septentrionale*, 3 vols, Paris, 1909–15

Chêng Tê-k'un, *Archaeology in China*, several vols, Cambridge, from 1959

Chiang Yee, *Chinese Calligraphy* (new ed.), London, 1954

Consten, E. *Das alte China*, Stuttgart, 1958

Garner, Sir Harry *Oriental Blue and White*, London, 1954

Goepper, R. *The Essence of Chinese Painting*, London, 1963

Gray, B., and Vincent, J. B. *Buddhist Cave Paintings at Tun-huang*, London, 1959

Gulik, R. H. van *Chinese Pictorial Art*, Rome, 1958

Hobson, R. L. *Chinese Pottery and Porcelain*, London, 1915

Jenyns, S. *Later Chinese Porcelain*, London, 1959

Lee, S. E. *Chinese Landscape Painting*, Cleveland, 1954

Lin Yutang *Imperial Peking*, London, 1961

Sickman, L., and Soper, A. *The Art and Architecture of China*, 'Pelican History of Art', Harmondsworth, 1956

Sirén, O. *Chinese Sculpture from the Fifth to the Fourteenth Centuries*, 4 vols, London, 1925

Sirén, O. *A History of Early Chinese Art*, 4 vols, London, 1929–30

Sirén, O. *Kinas Konst under Tre Årtusenden*, 2 vols, Stockholm, 1942

Sirén, O. *Chinese Painting, Leading Masters and Principles*, London, 1956–58.

Speiser, W. *Meisterwerke Chinesischer Malerei*, Berlin, 1947

Sullivan, M. *Chinese Art in the Twentieth Century*, London, 1959

Sullivan, M. *Introduction to Chinese Art*, London, 1961

Watson, W. *Archaeology of China*, London, 1960

Willetts, W. *Chinese Art*, 2 vols, Harmondsworth, 1958

Yang Yu-hsun *La Calligraphie Chinoise*, Paris, 1937

Korean Art

Eckhardt, A. *A History of Korean Art*, London, 1929

Honey, W. B. *Korean Pottery*, London, 1947

McCune, Evelyn *The Arts of Korea*, Rutland, Tokyo, 1962

Japanese Art

Binyon, L., and O'Brien Sexton, J. J. *Japanese Colour Prints*, New York, 1923

Buhot, J. *Histoire des Arts du Japon*, Paris, 1949

Drexler, A. *The Architecture of Japan*, New York, 1955

Hillier, J. *Japanese Masters of the Colour Print*, London, 1955

Hosiguchi, S., and Kojiro, Y. *The Tradition of the Japanese Garden*, Tokyo, 1962

Kim Chewon and Kim Won-Yong *Korea, 2000 Jahre Kunstschaffen*, Munich, 1966

Kuno, T. *A Guide to Japanese Sculpture*, Tokyo, 1963

Paine, R. T., and Soper, A. *The Art and Architecture of Japan*, 'Pelican History of Art', Harmondsworth, 1955

Seckel, D. *Emakimono*, London, 1959

Soper, A. *The Evolution of Buddhist Architecture in Japan*, Princeton, 1942

Swann, P. *An Introduction to the Arts of Japan*, Oxford, 1958

Warner, L. *The Craft of the Japanese Sculptor*, New York, 1936

Watson, W. *Sculpture of Japan*, London, 1959

Yashiro, Y. *2,000 Years of Japanese Art*, London, 1958

Yashiro, Y. *Art Treasures of Japan*, Tokyo, 1960

Index

Acknowledgements

Photographs were provided by the following:

Colour: Jeannine Auboyer, Paris 1, 2, 23, 24, 26, 31, 32, 45, 53; R. Braun-muller, Munich 55, 69, 71; British Museum, London 57, 68; J. Allan Cash, London 66; Professor Friedrich Funke, Cologne 22; Dr. Roger Goepper, Cologne 82, 84, 97, 98, 101; Michael Holford, London 4, 5, 6, 7, 8, 9, 10, 11, 12, 13, 14, 27, 28, 33, 37, 38, 41, 42, 46, 47, 48, 49, 50, 56, 59, 61, 75, 103, 110; Holle Verlag, Baden-Baden 79, 80; Erhardt Hürsch, Zürich 72; Institut Pedagogique National, Paris 44; Prem Chand Jain, Delhi 36; Kunstbibliothek, Staatliche Museen, Berlin 111, 112; R. Lakshmi, Delhi 29, 30; J. A. Lavaud, Paris 43, 51; Kyung Mo Lee, Seoul 78, 81, 83, 85; Museum of Fine Arts, Boston 95, 99; Museum for Ostasiatische Kunst, Cologne 87; Orion Press, Tokyo 88, 89, 102; Ostasiatische Kunstabteilung, Staatliche Museen, Berlin 54, 63, 64, 70, 74, 76, 86, 100, 106, 108; Colin Penn, London 73; Percival David Foundation of Chinese Art, London 67, 77; Josephine Powell, Rome 3, 19, 20, 21, 25, 34, 35; Rapho, Paris 52; Rietberg Museum, Zürich 60, 65; M. Sakamoto, Tokyo 90, 92, 96, 104, 105; Madanjeet Singh, Delhi 15, 16, 17, 18; Shosho-in, Nara 91; Smithsonian Institution, Freer Gallery of Art, Washington 58; Wim Swaan, New York 39, 40; Tokugawa Art Museum, Nagoya 93; Tokyo National Museum 94, 107, 109; Victoria and Albert Museum, London 62

Black and White: Archeological Survey of India 2a, 2b, 25, 29, 31, 41, 42; Jeannine Auboyer, Paris 3, 9, 10, 20, 23, 26, 33, 34, 47; Benrido Co., Kyoto 101, 110, 113; E. Boudot-Lamotte, Paris 5, 7, 8, 22, 46, and 1st titlepage; British Museum, London 61, 62, 63; Cleveland Museum of Art, Ohio 83; Yves Coffin, Paris 52, 53; Dominique Darbois, Paris 66; Editions Arthaud, Paris 81; Louis Frederic/Rapho, Paris 39, 58; Girau-don, Paris 16, 17; Dr. Roger Goepper, Cologne 67, 69, 70, 71, 82, 85, 87, 90, 102, 112, 115; Musée Guimet, Paris 11, 15, 24, 36, 51, 55, 56, 59, 64; Michael Holford, London 21, 32, 34, 40, 48, 49, 50, 60, 63, 78; Holle Verlag, Baden-Baden 95; Martin Hürlimann © Conzett and Huber, Zürich 19, 27, 30; India Office Library, London 12, 43, 45; Prem Chand Jain, Delhi 6, 28, 37, 38; Kyung Mo Lee, Seoul 86, 88, 91, 92, 93; Leonard von Matt, Switzerland 54, 57; Municipal Museum, The Hague 89; Museum für Volkerkunde, Munich 72, 84; National Museum, New Delhi 2c, 2d, 4; National Palace Museum, Taiwan 73, 74, 77; William Rockhill Nelson Gallery of Art, Kansas City 75; Orion Press, Tokyo 96, 103, 108; Ostasiatische Kunstabteilung, Staatliche Museen, Berlin 94a, 94b; Penguin Books, London 114; Josephine Powell, Rome 1, 12; Marc Riboud/Magnum 79, 80; Rietberg Museum, Zürich 65, 68; Royal Academy of Art, London 13; M. Sakamoto, Tokyo 98, 105, Wim Swaan, New York 44; Tokyo National Museum 76, 104, 106, 111; Victoria and Albert Museum, London 116.

MONGOLIA

TURKESTAN

Tun-huang

KANSU

Yellow R.

Ch'ang-an

Mai-chi-shan

CHINA

TIBET

SZECHUAN

R. Y

YÜNNAN

INDIA